Cg

LINGUA FRANCA
IN THE MEDITERRANEAN

LINGUA FRANCA
IN THE MEDITERRANEAN

J.E. Wansbrough

CURZON
PRESS

First published in 1996
by Curzon Press
St John's Studios, Church Road, Richmond
Surrey, TW9 2QA

Typeset in Palatino by Excel Books, New Delhi
Printed in Great Britain by
TJ Press Limited, Padstow, Cornwall

British Library Cataloguing in Publication Data
A catalogue record for this book is available from the British Library

Library of Congress in Publication Data
A catalog record for this book has been requested

ISBN 0 7007 0309 8

Table of Contents

Preface

The subject of this study is the language of commerce and diplomacy during the period from 1500 BCE to 1500 CE. Based on texts of chancery provenance, its aim is identification of a linguistic subsystem that informed and effected the major channel of international relations. The standard procedures of contact and exchange generated a format that facilitated inter-lingual transfer of concepts and terms. *Lingua franca* refers to the several natural languages that served as vehicle in the transfer, but also to the format itself.

My interest in the subject is now some thirty-five years old, but as in most such endeavours, has been intermittent. First uttered in print in 1971, the task was envisaged as a comparative analysis of the Arabic and Italian versions of commercial treaties in the late medieval Mediterranean world. With time and sporadically renewed vigour, it came to include study of similar instruments from the Late Bronze and Iron Ages. Three thousand years is a long stretch for an historian, and encompasses far more lacunae than it does continua. It was the persistence of certain formulaic components, set out here in Chapter 2, that tempted me to try a synthesis. I thought I could discern a cumulative technology, witness to the slow but steady rationalisation of management procedures. These were located in the marketplace (information and contract) and in the archive (storage and retrieval). I saw the documentary format as primarily semiotic and designed for immediate intelligibility. Layout and sequence generated a juridical *koine* which became the context of communication, to some extent independent of verbatim translation. Of course the latter had to be achieved, but seldom at the expense of expectation. In perusal of a chancery document there were very few surprises indeed. For the several techniques involved, such as transcription, calque, translation and transposition, I have employed the term *homology,* of which the linguistic deposit became a common property of all Mediterranean vocabularies.

It is impossible to record all the occasions of support, advice, criticism and revision I have encountered in the course of my work. All were of value and none enough to deter me from seeking a wider readership. Since completion of the typescript in September 1991, several titles have come or been brought to my attention that might have had that effect but in the event did not. I refer to such as M. Liverani, *Prestige and Interest* (Padova 1990), the second volume of M.Bernal, *Black Athena* (London 1991), and the conference volume edited by N. Gale, *Bronze Age Trade in the Mediterranean* (Göteborg 1991). There are undoubtedly others, but now in deep and untroubled retirement, I am not likely to hear of them.

There ought to be some words appropriate to signing off. It is common for teachers to thank former students and colleagues for their interest in and contribution to ongoing research, and here is no exception. While in recent years time for research has dwindled, students and colleagues have proliferated, all of them at least in my experience helpful and generous. In particular I wish to thank two old friends, Michael Brett and Mark Geller, for reading and commenting upon the final version of my text, which they found arduous but apparently not without some merit. Many others in that remarkable community of scholarship, the School of Oriental and African Studies, have assisted in various ways the progress of my work and life among them. It was a good experience and I am grateful for the very long stint in an environment which these days seems threatened by so many incalculable pressures. The willingness of the School to bear the cost of publishing this last attempt to make sense of a least one historical record is a characteristically magnanimous gesture. Sed retro actis seculis / Vix licuit discipulis / Tandem nonagenarium / Quiescere post studium.

John Wansbrough

Abbreviations

AAS	Annales Archéologiques de Syrie
AfO	Archiv für Orientforschung
AHw	Akkadisches Handwörterbuch
AION	Annali dell'Istituto Orientale di Napoli
AJA	American Journal of Archaeology
AO	Acta Orientalia
AOAT	Alter Orient und Altes Testament
AS	Assyriological Studies
ASV	Archivio di Stato Venezia
BAR	British Archaeological Reports
BASOR	Bulletin of the American Schools for Oriental Research
BO	Bibliotheca Orientalis
BSOAS	Bulletin of the School of Oriental and African Studies
CAD	Chicago Assyrian Dictionary
CIA	Corpus Inscriptionum Arabicarum
CIS	Corpus Inscriptionum Semiticarum
CSCO	Corpus Scriptorum Christianorum Orientalium
CTA	Corpus des tablettes en cunéiformes alphabétiques
DCD	Development of the Canaanite Dialects
DIC	Documents from Islamic Chanceries
GLECS	Groupe Linguistique d'Etudes Chamito-Sémitiques
HUCA	Hebrew Union College Annual
IASH	Israel Academy of Sciences and Humanities
IEJ	Israel Exploration Journal
IJMES	International Journal of Middle East Studies
IJNA	International Journal of Nautical Archaeology

ILR	Israel Law Review
IOS	Israel Oriental Studies
JAH	Journal of African History
JANES	Journal of Ancient Near Eastern Studies
JAOS	Journal of the American Oriental Society
JBL	Journal of Biblical Literature
JCS	Journal of Cuneiform Studies
JEEH	Journal of European Economic History
JESHO	Journal of the Economic and Social History of the Orient
JNES	Journal of Near Eastern Studies
JNWSL	Journal of North West Semitic Languages
JRAS	Journal of the Royal Asiatic Society
JRS	Journal of Roman Studies
JSS	Journal of Semitic Studies
KAI	Kanaanäische und aramäische Inschriften
KTU	Die Keilalphabetischen Texte aus Ugarit
MM	The Mariner's Mirror
OA	Oriens Antiquus
OIP	Oriental Institute Publications
OLP	Orientalia Lovaniensia Periodica
Or.	Orientalia
PAAJR	Proceedings of the American Academy for Jewish Research
PIASH	Proceedings of the Israel Academy of Sciences and Humanities
PRU	Le Palais Royal d'Ugarit I-VI
RA	Revue d'Assyriologie et d'Archéologie orientale
RB	Revue Biblique
RDAC	Report of the Department of Antiquities Cyprus
RIH	
RLA	Reallexikon der Assyriologie
RS	Ras Shamra
RSO	Rivista degli Studi Orientali

SI	Studia Islamica
SIAS	Scandinavian Institute of Asian Studies
SIMA	Studies in Mediterranean Archaeology
SSI	Syrian Semitic Inscriptions
SVT	Supplements to Vetus Testamentum
TAPA	Transactions of the American Philological Association
UF	Ugarit-Forschungen
UGAR	Ugaritica I-VII
UT	Ugaritic Textbook
VT	Vetus Testamentum
WO	Die Welt des Orients
WZKM	Wiener Zeitschrift für die Kunde des Morgenlandes
ZDMG	Zeitschrift der Deutschen Morgenländischen Gesellschaft
ZRP	Zeitschrift für Romanische Philologie

1

Orbits

Extrapolated from mariners' charts and envoys' reports, a 16th century map of the Mediterranean would be heavily inked with the traces of movement. That network of routes and terminals exhibits the accumulated expertise of at least three millennia, possibly more were the record accessible. What can be, and to considerable extent has been, perceived is that the 16th century density was not the product of steady growth but rather, of intermittent surges generated by technological advance. For that the most obvious factor might seem to be innovation in nautical techniques, e.g. compass, rigging and hull design. While it would be perverse to ignore the relevance of such to the organization of trade, one might wish to recall that the acceleration and volume of exchange was also a product of economic, political and administrative input, of the sort that determined not merely modes of production and distribution, but also the pace and rate of communication throughout the Mediterranean. A manageable axiom might be that *diplomatic contact* was the indispensable matrix of long distance trade.

It is in support of that proposition that the following arguments are formulated. The focus is upon *chancery practice,* source and framework of state diplomacy, and the perspective diachronic: to trace its Mediterranean expression from the 16th century to what appear to be Bronze Age origins. The immediately tangible evidence of contact would be routes. That these might be described as orbital can be gleaned from the simple observation that ships and emissaries were expected to, and mostly did, return to their points of departure. The implication is merely that the voyage home was the concomitant of every outward journey, and that some sort of feedback was thus the

1

anticipated consequence of every input. For the historical record, that would produce a completed ship's log or an ambassadorial account. For the evolution of technology it would signify a helical development that compounded principal and interest generated, wherever and however that might have been provoked. A juridical example lies to hand. In the matter of Florentine consular representation in early 16th century Egypt, the factors of procuratio and collective responsibility were operative, especially as regarded the substance of safe-conduct. The Islamic principle was that of delegation by the local authority to a single person who became thereupon accountable for the conduct of the community he represented. The procedure has an early root in Muslim jurisprudence, and that it should have found its way thence into medieval European law is just possible. For that period there are, of course, diplomatic instruments expressed in the languages of all participants to any given transaction, from which the transfer of concepts might be inferred. An irony of this particular instance lay in the later repudiation by the Ottoman empire of the celebrated "Capitulations", then thought to be inimical to Islamic tradition.[1]

Now, the structure underlying this kind of conjuncture is conceivable, but difficult to document. The longterm data are retrogressively discrete and diffuse. For example, routes do not in the earliest historical period produce a thickly inked circuit diagram. Their reconstruction requires a different sort of extrapolation: from dispersed archaeological sites and random toponyms. Putative networks linking these rest upon imaginative study of the terrain and conjectural reckoning of the pace between stages. Such has been done for tracing the movement of commodities like gold, tin, ivory and lapis lazuli, and for plotting the diffusion of industries like Mycenean ceramics and Levantine shipbuilding. Actual itineraries are rare, but paucity of data has naturally not imposed silence. Quite to the contrary: the scatter of non-native material and artifact has provoked some remarkable analyses, not only of source and distribution, but also of exchange mechanisms exhibiting non-random patterns. A stunning example is the reconstruction of prehistoric trade in obsidian, based on laboratory analysis of specimen artifacts and known deposits.[2] While it is true that the resulting maps indicate "interaction zones" rather than transport routes, it seems clear from the distribution of Middle Eastern findspots and their dominant mineral types that a communication network can be mooted. The quantification of these data suggests, in turn, a mode of exchange both directional and hierarchical ("down-the-line" trade), a point of considerable significance at least for the diffusion of raw materials. Whether the movement of artifacts can be so plotted is, of course, a different problem and dependent upon other variables (e.g. imitation and local reproduction).

For the most part, however, and certainly for the historical period, the kind of analysis proposed for obsidian is *complicated* by documentary witness. The presence and movement of commodities is attested in such a bewildering variety of archival and literary sources as to make an exponential distribution array impossible. Here the directional and hierarchical factors are obscured by a mosaic of intersections, itself imposed by the mere mention in so many contexts of a single item of extraction, production, alienation, acquisition, processing and transfer. The putative vector, if it can ever be resolved, would exhibit unequivocal components only for those commodities like, say, ivory and lapis lazuli whose sources are acknowledged to be limited.[3] For anything else, a different model has got to be devised. This is always a theoretical construct, admittedly derived from analogy, but posited and pursued with the normal conviction of disciplinary training. It is largely a matter of idiom: the habitual mode of exegesis that determines the perception and allocation of data. In other words, it is from anticipated answers that questions are formulated.

It has become fashionable in recent years to experiment with *idiom juxtaposition*, from which it must seem that the traditional academic division of labour can only impede progress in what ought to be an interdisciplinary field of study. Archaeology and ancient history have benefited from the persistent attention of anthropologists (Adams, Kohl, Larsen, Yoffee) and economists (Polanyi, Silver), serving to highlight a curious and abiding dichotomy between data and theory. Difference in treatment is signalled not so much by disparity of subject as by distinction of style. If reading is thus made arduous, one can only suppose that writing is more so. The extent to which the explanatory paradigm could be in danger of emancipation from the always exiguous data was already apparent in the work of Polanyi, a hazard since obviated.[4] But the impact of mathematics and the predictive sciences upon history is not yet expended, so nicely illustrated in the concept of "transformations".[5] Recasting archaeological, archival, even literary data as formulaic and statistical quantity is still something of an innovation. If there is a stylistic loss in the algorithm or histogram, it can hardly be denied that morphogenesis is as useful in the description of socio-economic as of biological forms.

In a general but very important sense, "trade" may be taken to comprehend the processes of change as well as the procedures of exchange. As a descriptive concept it would thus be seen both to encompass and to engender all the forms at either end or during a trajectory through time and space. To characterize that process as diffusion is a prejudgement of the many transactions involved, since there is very little that ever survives the route entirely intact. An easy alternative is polygenesis, which evades the problems of contact, adjustment, and above all, improvisation. But wherever and however often duplicated, "invention" is less likely to be ex nihilo discovery than deliberate or even accidental manipulation of accessible data. Archaeological data are mostly, perhaps inevitably, read as evidence of result rather than of process. Detection of similarities or analogies could not, of course, in the absence of witness to historical contact, help in a decision for either diffusion or polygenesis. For that the explanatory paradigm is essential, which is merely to say that the question is methodological rather than empirical.

Now, the study of a technique such as *chancery language* and its dissemination from one or many centres may draw upon not only a considerable stock of analogy but also of historical contact. Like all exchange commodities, this particular artifact (and for the archaeologist it can be nothing else) must have been subject to the usual spectrum of reception mechanisms, such as need, efficiency and prestige. Catalysts and/or obstacles, whether spatial or temporal, would have to be plotted within and across linguistic/cultural borders. Assessment of these might be thought calculable in terms of *literacy*, which, however difficult to determine statistically, must be at least one arbiter of improvisation in chancery practice.[6] And there is no compelling reason why the spread of literacy should be very much different from the acquisition of expertise in some other trade or profession, say ceramics or metallurgy, that is, consonant with a standard demographic curve. The locus of *scribal technique* is admittedly crucial: the behaviour of a temple guild would hardly be that of a municipal chancery. But competence is also a functional parameter, and one would expect increased literacy to accompany any diversification of administrative activity. And of the latter, historical records exhibit an erratic but for the most part obstinate augmentation, even if its precise mapping is difficult.

The virtue of "activity analysis" is its attention to process rather than (merely) to result.[7] While that is an obvious advantage in the exegesis of notoriously discrete data, it must be conceded that its value lies primarily in acceptance of the proffered paradigm. The concession is important and will become more so at later stages of this investigation, when I shall attempt a reconstruction of technology transfer (Chapter 2). For the immediate aim, it is a matter of receptivity to the routes of *stimulus diffusion*, in other words, the paths of communication that are likely to have generated innovation. Clearly, some were more productive than others. Calculation of these requires some insight into the parameters of decision-making, i.e. the difference between necessary and sufficient causes of change. These will vary according to local circumstances, of course, but also according to stimulus provenance. Here we have to do with such behavioural factors as role, status, prestige and opportunism, for all of which the source of inspiration is as important as its practical value. Performance will always depend as much upon these as upon the ineluctable logic which might with hindsight be thought to have dictated a change of course.

One component of that logic is the computation of *transaction costs*, a gift of economists to the beleaguered predicament of archaeologists. This particular calculus cannot, however, be more than notional, involving as it does not merely risk but probability. The concepts of gain and goal-motivated behaviour have naturally to be reckoned, but only as adjunct to the overall composition of human conduct. Anyone, after all, can be seen to have acted against what with hindsight and distance must have been his "best interests". It is precisely the probabilities and costs that would have to be assigned to every alternative in the decision process that could make the historical reconstruction persuasive. It is of course to that issue that every historian aspires, but it is nonetheless important to recall that his conclusion cannot but rest upon a hypothetical construct.

The question is thus *location of orbits,* in the sense both of geographical route and channel of cultural dominance. Like their electrical paradigm, these circuits would be susceptible to variable conductors (resistance), voltage gaps (collapse), and inconsistent amperage (motivation). The model is one in which feedback, both positive and negative, is the norm, and fresh input always liable to adjustment, diminution or oblivion. A version of the imagery was employed by Braudel who, in his description of the "greater Mediterranean", wrote of the configurations of a "magnetic field" fluctuating with the ebb and flow of forces seasonal, mechanical, and spiritual.[8] Visually helpful, the metaphor cannot really be challenged, though his exegesis of much of the material from which it was elicited has been. It is, ironically, the very abundance of documentation that generates a range of defensible interpretation rather than a single "correct" version. But the advantage of a "field of force" model is its accommodation of *random and non-contiguous* elements. No amount of evidence, for example, would make readily apparent the reasons why despatch of business should take so much longer in Habsburg Spain than at Venice. Here the elusive factor is not geographical, and certainly not ethnic, but rather, the difference in pace of bureaucratic procedure between an empire and a merchant republic.[9] One can imagine, even without being able to quantify, the variety of managerial pressures respectively brought to bear upon what was essentially the same transaction. Whatever techniques may have been devised in one context will seldom be appropriate to the exigencies of another, and yet both must be calculated in any joint enterprise or encounter.

Some impression of the décalage can be inferred from the course of diplomatic relations between Venice and the Mamluk sultanate of Egypt in the late 15th and early 16th centuries. During a period of seventy years (1442-1512) six commercial treaties were concluded between the two powers. The attendant negotiations exhibit spans of time and contact quite out of proportion to the results achieved. An example is the treaty of 31 May 1507: a major Egyptian embassy was extended to seventeen months owing to the limited authority delegated to the envoy by his principal, whose intervention in matters of detail could only be effected by resort to an interim return journey. In the end the sultan refused to ratify the agreement on the grounds that his instructions had not been followed. In 1512, after five years of long-distance and acrimonious dispute, the Signoria was compelled to de novo negotiation.[10] It was, of course, not always oriental autocracy that impeded the despatch of business. The conclusion of a commercial treaty between Egypt and the republic of Florence in October 1489 was considerably complicated, and delayed, by the role of the Vatican, whose bureaucratic machinery was not merely inscrutable but geared to a view of Mediterranean politics quite different to that which obtained in Tuscany.[11] The significance of such discrepancy lies in its effect upon traffic patterns during a period for which these can with some confidence be plotted on maps. The calculation of space depends, in other words, upon temporal data. Where these are wanting, the concept of orbit becomes distorted, but not, I think, impossible.

Without a chronological dimension *cartography* would reflect a space bound by lexical convention, that is, compass points, commodities and toponyms. Its accuracy would be restricted to (approximate) direction, (assumed) relation, and (conjectural) orthography. The sum could be a confirmation, but hardly a calculus, of contact. Had one been designed and transmitted, a Bronze Age map of the Mediterranean, not yet conversant with the lucubrations of Ptolemy, Idrisi, Mercator and Ortelius, must have resembled the lenticular Babylonian tablet displaying familiar landmarks.[12] Data empirically derived tend to attract a schematic design, imposed upon rather than elicited from adventitiously available report. It is within these admittedly stringent but ineluctable limits that reconstruction of the ancient traffic patterns must be attempted. An interesting example of commodity transfer may be seen in efforts to explain the extent (!) of contact between Egypt and Mesopotamia during the Old and Middle Babylonian periods.

A conceivable distinction between the two periods ($c2000$-1600 and 1600-1200 BCE, respectively) is derived from a single control: the presence/absence of gold. Unmentioned in the earlier period, it figures as both luxury and medium of exchange in the later, documented from the Amarna correspondence.

Now, that archive is crucial but also sui generis, and hardly solid evidence for an alteration in import/export activity. To ascribe (as Edzard does) the change to a Kassite predilection (earlier and somewhere else generated) for gold does not, in terms of economic analysis, make much sense. That exegesis could be read either as Egyptian unwillingness to part with its traditional treasure until pointedly invited to do so or that there had been no capital (gold) to dispense before its mention in the so far available documentation.[13] It must be obvious that data such as these are not likely to contribute much to a map of commodity exchange, but also that it is precisely this kind of material that, with the honourable exception (e.g. Eratosthenes), tends to generate the maps of pre-Ptolemaic cartography.

And these, whatever the margin of distortion, are the only means of determining the coordinates of frequency and distribution in a standard Cartesian graph, from which just might be inferred the substance and nature of exchange. The above-mentioned instance exhibits all the shortcomings of the genre. And I think it is not wayward to speak of a "genre". For despite the utterly random character of its components, these attract a *linear configuration* in most efforts to describe change from one state to another. It can be, and has been, argued that this arrangement of spatial and temporal data is the consequence of a methodological failure, i.e. the "before-after" syndrome in which change is depicted in terms of tangible result.[14] It might also be suggested that linearity is simply the consequence of syntactic structure, i.e. the average sentence generates its own logic. An escape from this linguistic prison is conceivable by recourse to some such device as symbolic notation or diagram, but that would make, as I have already suggested, for some pretty arduous reading and probably overtax the mathematical skills of most historians. The alternative is to accept the constraints of ordinary prose and to recognise in historiography a literary mode subject to standard expectations of that art. These must certainly include the impingement of literary mimesis upon historical referent, but that is surely no more than to acknowledge the value, indeed necessity, of models for the task of reconstruction. It is of course not only linearity that characterizes the logic of sentence structure. There is the concomitant, and ineluctable, feature of causality generated by selection of either parataxis or hypotaxis. Every clause entails a commitment one way or the other. The purpose of these homespun truths is simply to recall that the elucidation of historical referent is largely a stylistic exercise.[15] Witness to Egyptian gold in Mesopotamia, in other words, exhibits no more than commodity displacement = "before-after". Exegesis of that datum involves the syntax of a more generously conceived model.

For the 16th century, the residue of Anglo-Ottoman commercial relations provides a convenient paradigm. In addition to the overland routes, themselves an extension of the Baltic trade and employed between 1578 and 1588 in order to evade the sphere of Venetian influence, the standard Mediterranean channels are attested.[16] What might be described as the "northern tier" = Barcelona, Aigues-Mortes, Gaeta, Naples, Corfu, Coron, Modon, Crete, Chios, Rhodes and Cyprus, came gradually to be replaced by a "southern tier" = Algiers, Palermo, Tunis, Malta, Tripoli and thence into the Levant.[17] The reason for that was not merely the hostility of Venice to English interlopers but also the presence of Ottoman authority from Oran to Alexandria and the Syrian ports. An admittedly adventitious factor, that political configuration could not but have an influence upon traffic patterns. These were of course calculated, even in the 16th century, only as time spent underway, from which at least transaction costs can better be reckoned than from computation of mere distance. But statistics require a baseline, and for Alexandria, Constantinople and the Levantine ports the requisite data are not to hand. For Venice however, in despite of its circumvention in this particular trade, an impression of Mediterranean dimensions is available.[18] The variation is remarkable: the journey to Alexandria could take from 89 to 17 days, the normal time being 55. To Istanbul the corresponding figures are 81, 15, and 34 days; to Damascus 102, 28, and 76. For this computation the transferred commodity was news, so that one would have to weigh letters against bales on the quayside. Nonetheless, when compared with the times taken to Western European centres such as Valladolid, Lisbon and London, these calculations suggest that the sea route was longer than overland, that Venice was more securely locked into Continental than into Levantine exchange, and that the length of the Mediterranean (2,330 miles) was not much less or more than two months. The relational factor, however, deserves scrutiny. Bulk commodities, like cotton and grain, even if the

overland route to, say, Augsburg, Nürnberg and Hamburg/
Lübeck were obvious, could hardly have reached Syria and
Egypt in that way, nor would they have been so fetched. Time,
in other words, was a product not merely of mode but also of
substance, and one cannot but suspect that this feature had
always obtained. Thus, the movement of copper ingots in the
Bronze Age Mediterranean must have involved more manpow-
er, calculation and overheads than gold, incense and ivory. For
these latter calculations there are, of course, no relevant data,
but the calculus derived from time/bulk ought to be included
in any reckoning of commodity transfer.

So plotted, "routes" can only be a theoretical construct. A
16th century map of the Mediterranean might well exhibit the
terminals and contacts, but never or seldom indicates the labour
input into each or all. For that one needs a different sort of data.
These would have to include "time" reckoned as procural,
accounting and lading, as well as its differential according to the
nature of the transaction, e.g. gift, exchange, market sale. Granted
that say, Venice and Alexandria are stable features of Mediterranean topography, their recorded variation in distance (time)
one from the other is the more important factor for historical
analysis. The spread of news, after all, will more often than not
exhibit a short circuit of the standard channels.

If the time span between topographical points is difficult
to calculate for the 16th century, it is nearly impossible for
earlier periods. Records of terrain traversed may be provided
with notation of administrative and other obstacles, but very
seldom or never with a calendrical sum of stages, e.g. the eight
day trek from Razamā to Mari. The envoy (mār śiprim) could
be traced from origin to destination in terms of diplomatic tasks
but not in terms of the time expended upon these. Concomitant
with this opacity is that of the *itinerary* itself, rarely set out: what
for example could the statement "messengers en route from
Babylon, Eśnunna, Ekallātum, Karanā, Qabara and Arrapḫa . .
to Yamḫad, Qatanum, Ḥaṣura" mean on the ground? The route
from Arrapḫa to Yamḫad, some 600 miles, is neither spelled out
nor furnished with anything approaching a time-scale.[19]

This of course is the standard disability of ancient sources,
from which one might be inclined to infer that efficiency was
negligible. While I am inclined to doubt that such was the case,
it must be admitted that the so far available record hardly serves

to answer the questions about time and space. For instance, even the Razamā-Mari span above-mentioned is complicated by appearance of the former toponym in several quite different regions, thus generating a problem roughly comparable to that involved in the precise location of (Syrian) Apum in the Mari correspondence.[20] Such confusion extends to uncertainty about the referent of apparent toponyms: city, state, region, or merely a generic epithet?

One source for ancient cartography is the commemorative stele, on which could be inscribed the record of a military campaign or territorial dimension of a particular reign. From such materials has been pieced together a fair portion of the history of Egyptian penetration of Palestine and Syria during the later Bronze Age. For many of the areas in question they are also the only source for mapping local terrain, an exercise further impeded by uncertainty as to orthographic correspondence where two or more languages are involved. An example of the kind of problem encountered may be seen in the dispute about whether Ugarit figured in the first Syrian campaign (1447 BCE) of Amenophis II: in addition to the questionable spelling in the Karnak stele, the putative route from Nii to Ugarit has been thought to have been unmanageable by a fully equipped army in the ten days allocated to the expedition. Admittedly ingenious, Astour's solution does depend upon a number of imponderables associated with the terrain itself and selection of a feasible itinerary.[21] Extrapolation of the latter from the data of a royal inscription is not likely to produce an accurate roadmap, though for certain kinds of terrain, such as the desert campaigns of the Neo-Assyrian rulers some seven centuries later (see below), the degree of plausibility is enhanced, due inter alia to the known position of landmarks (oases) and the calculable range of transport (camels).

An alternative mapping procedure, derived from the *principle of contiguity,* is implicit in the political grid of Egyptian rule in Palestine and Syria. For this operation royal inscriptions have been supplemented by evidence from the Amarna archives (c1387-62 BCE: Amenophis III and IV), and the concern to identify precise routes replaced by the postulation of spheres of administrative influence. So, for example, the division of Egyptian hegemony into now three, now two provinces, with capitals at Ṣumur, Kumidi and Gaza, or at only the two latter.[22] The extent to which "influence" may be read as "authority" requires more information than is available in the Amarna correspondence. The configuration of "provinces" encompassing the contiguous regions of Amurru, Ubi and Canaan, now nearly a datum of 14th century Syrian history, presupposes a network of communication between these regions, but in fact attested only in missives despatched to and from a foreign capital whose concern with local Syrian conditions was mostly indifferent, at best pragmatic. The variant perceptions of political expedience, i.e. "Egyptian" as contrasted with "Asiatic" (= imperial vs feudal) have been nicely set out by Liverani, especially in respect of Rib-Adda at Byblos, whose abiding concerns could only provoke boredom and occasionally annoyance in Amarna. While the nature of that triangulation is of considerable importance for the evolution of chancery practice (e.g. the transfer of epistolary formulae), the actual tracks between say, Şumur, Kumidi and Gaza are not depicted.[23] My concern in adducing these data is merely to recall that geographical borders are per definitionem ambivalent: the concept of contiguous Egyptian provinces in Syria is to some extent an adventitious construct, dependent upon the part played by an extraneous factor imposed upon otherwise unknown local circumstances.

Implicit in all this is a *geometrical paradigm,* of which the dimensions ought to correspond to topographical vectors. Instead, they reflect political, and to some extent economic, trajectories, themselves susceptible of plotting only on a graph of quantified contact, never or seldom in terms of modal propinquity. How, in other words, did the components of Egyptian Syria, or for that matter, Hittite or Assyrian Syria, communicate amongst themselves and with their metropolitan centres? Triangulation can only produce the standard reply: "peripheral Akkadian", but hardly explain or even describe the gaps in what must have been daily or at least weekly communication. The linguistic mode (to be analysed in Chapter 3) is mostly read as product not as agent of the contact. The latter is identifiable as a composite: originator + envoy + addressee, whose names (usually) and motives (often) may be discerned in the epistolary residue. Distance traversed is never calculated, time consumed only in cases of the extreme detention of envoys, say, up to three or even six years, a notice of negligible value in the computation of transaction costs. The Amarna archive attests to the fact of communication and employment of a lingua franca; upon the modality of exchange it sheds virtually no light at all.[24]

The partly contemporary evidence from Ugarit could have been more helpful. Both the time span (c. 1500-1200 BCE) and coverage of administrative detail (some 3000 as compared with 400 Amarna tablets) ought to provide some useful data for the mapping of contacts outward from the metropolis. The attempt has been made more than once: e.g. Liverani, Astour, Heltzer, and it would be unduly grudging not to acknowledge their single and collective enterprise. The historical reconstruction lacks, however, all or nearly all the data essential to a persuasive cartography of the Levant. Without the factor of time, distance can only be notional. It may also be impressionistic. The density of Astour's map exhibits not so much a network as a settlement continuum, from which one might infer more or less uninterrupted traffic, extending to c150 km north, east and south. The documentary basis for this is not a gazetteer, but a territorial demarcation imposed upon northern Syria by the Hittites c1350 BCE, that is, not a commercial route, but a political border whose course is hardly patient of reconstruction.[25] While the documentary type itself was probably a Hittite innovation, it is no substitute for an itinerary and cannot be so employed. That it was expressed in Akkadian is of course relevant to the general problem of contact and communication. The otherwise ample commercial and administrative documentation, of which about half is composed in alphabetic cuneiform, is for the fact of contact instructive, but hardly so for its pace and extent. The movement of goods, and of information, has got to be differently plotted, possibly in terms not of long distance transit but of *concatenation*.

Though in certain respects less exiguous, the somewhat later Phoenician material is no more helpful in determining the pattern of Levantine and other contacts. However one defines "Phoenician", whether as ethnic identity or as behavioural category, witness to language and artifact exhibits a fairly random distribution.[26] Spatially impressive, it provides the earliest physical record of what with time became the standard traffic pattern between Levant and Atlantic. The settlement focus is predominantly coastal but hardly contiguous, so that staging can only be conjectural. Neither logistics nor distance (time), in the light of general ignorance about early Iron Age shipping, can be calculated, though some legs (e.g. Byblos-Cyprus) are more readily conceivable than others (e.g. Tyre-Sardinia). The historical emergence of "Phoenicia", as composite of Sea Peoples in the Levant, Philistine settlement of Canaan, and maritime colonization westward, has been more than once essayed and the syndrome is not devoid of a persuasive charm.[27] Allusion to the "Iron Age" could be misleading: if the political framework for all that activity is generally conceded to be Neo-Assyrian imperialism (see below), it is worth recalling that Canaanite maritime commerce is attested from the Middle and Late Bronze Age, when the best documented agent was the north Syrian port at Ugarit. The movement of commodities as far west as Crete, as far north as Lycia, as far east as Mari, and as far south as Egypt must be related to the two shipwrecks at Cape Gelidonya and Ulu Burun containing the celebrated "oxhide" copper ingots, as well as other materials attesting to Aegean-Levantine traffic. There at least is evidence of a Levantine coastal(?) route of the sort reckoned to be a concomitant of contemporary nautical technology.[28] In other words, a putative distinction between "Canaanite" and "Phoenician" commerce would have to be not merely political but technological, and there is no evidence of an industrial revolution accompanying the political reorganization of the Levant in the early first millennium BCE.

That is, revolution in navigational techniques, hull design and locomotion. While it is true that such innovations as star-sighting, round ships and the bireme are from time to time ascribed to Phoenician genius, the chronology is difficult to fix, besides a distinct possibility that "Phoenician" is a generic reference to any Mediterranean sailor.[29] However that may be, the steadily increasing data relevant to marine enterprise at Ugarit point to shipbuilding of proportion and refinement, though here too, it would be difficult to trace a linear development in nautical design.[30] If it happens that the range of Ugaritic shipping is not attested beyond Crete (Kaphtor?), and that voyage only once, it would still be rash to infer that the much wider focus of Phoenician activity was, at least from the outset, a consequence of more sophisticated seafaring than had hitherto been available.[31] It was after all some time before the galleys of the Greek maritime diaspora made their appearance and alleged impact upon nautical distance in the Mediterranean.[32]

The standard alternative to a technological quantum leap has been the impetus generated by Assyrian imperialistic expansion from the period of Shalmaneser III (859-24 BCE), an argument compounded of political, economic and ideological ingredients.[33] The notion of territorial acquisition as a means to procural of raw, rare and other materials is likely to figure in any model of imperialism ("flag follows trade"). That emporia, maritime and other, should be left undisturbed, in fact guaranteed operational freedom in return for certain fiscal arrangements ("no man's land"), is less often adduced but more than merely plausible.[34] Reference to the Assyrian kāru established at the Egyptian border and on the Phoenician coast at Tyre, Sidon and Arwad, not to control but to exploit the ongoing trade, might be thought to exhibit a policy of calculated restraint.[35] However unusual, or unexpected, such would the more easily permit the westward extension of Phoenician trading posts and eventually "factories".

It is, however, only an alternative. What can be gleaned from the Assyrian sources is some fairly reliable information about *overland* routes between Mesopotamia and the Mediterranean. Because some of these were desert routes, they involved contact with nomadic tribes, the use of camels, and reckoning the distance (time) between watering-places.[36] From application of these factors, almost constant (e.g. a camel can bear a load of 180 kilogrammes and travel 100 kilometres = 3 days without water), one can calculate with some accuracy both direction (the oases are mostly identifiable, though some desiccation may be assumed for the last three millennia) and distance/pace, as well of course as the number of animals required (e.g. to provision an army) and hence, the nature of negotiations with their breeders/owners. For example, the celebrated passage in which establishment of the entrepot for Egypt (kār muṣur) was announced by Sargon II (722-05 BCE) can now be amplified by reference to the same ruler's settlement of "Arabs" in Palestine/Samaria as consonant with a policy of stimulating overland trade toward a Levantine outlet.[37] The role of cameldrivers, their points of embarcation, their managerial control and willingness to be impressed into that traffic, have got to be read as evidence of a political context in which transaction costs could be estimated. These would include not merely distance (time), but also the effect of relocation (along a familiar trajectory of nomadic activity) and the inducement offered (up to but not including outright conquest). From all this one has the impression of infinite adjustment to a fluid situation in which gain was the common aim. It was an exercise engaged by both agent and patient along traceable routes.

Admittedly, these data depict military expeditions, not commercial caravans. But it is unlikely that trade could have proceeded differently. As often as not, however, the crucial evidence is lacking. For example, neither of the two consignments handled by the Chaldean merchant Nādin-aḫi, though specifying the provenance of some commodities (iron and copper from the Aegean(?), alum from Egypt, iron from Lebanon) and precisely dated (5th and 6th regnal years of Nabonides = 551-50 BCE), indicates the mode and route of transit to Babylon/Uruk.[38] While a navigable stretch of the Euphrates is not implausible, it is certainly not the only possibility, for instance, the overland route from Larsa to Emar (see below). Moreover, the 100 miles (163 km) from Emar or Carchemish to the coast would be mostly or entirely overland. As it happens, the famous and approximately contemporary campaign of Nabonides to Tema', is also not quite traceable, owing to a lack of crucial toponymy, a reminder of how little of the ancient terrain can be confidently mapped.[39] And yet, some few centuries later, at the onset of Nabataean, Parthian, and eventually Roman domination of the desert traffic, the evidence of the caravan cities (e.g. Hatra, Dura, Palmyra, Bostra, Gerasa and Petra) attests to the regularization of routes that cannot have been all that different from those of the earlier period.[40]

If it can be assumed that the actual mechanics of desert travel (camel + oasis) remained more or less unchanged, its administrative organization may well have altered. There, as in the remarkable Phoenician expansion of sea routes, the underlying technology might be identified as *rationalization of management*. Its traces would be accessible in chancery records. For the early historical period these, I have already observed, tend to be if not exiguous then at least opaque. Neither the commemorative campaign inscription nor what might qualify as itinerary has so far generated perspicuous cartography.[41] The best of the latter, the Old Babylonian routier from Larsa to Emar, is far from clear;[42] and even the much analysed Old Assyrian trade from Aśśur to Kaniś has not yet yielded an unambivalent route.[43] Phoenician movement is mostly reconstructed by the simple concatenation of archaeological findspots.[44] Now, it is certainly possible that even were these records more abundant or better preserved, they would still not provide the essential information. The very concepts of orientation, proportion and topography could very likely not be extrapolated *in relational terms* from even a complete set of Bronze or Iron Age data. On the basis of what has been preserved one might anticipate that the flaws would be literary (range of genres in which toponyms happen to be collected), spatial (discrete areas of primarily local concern), and pragmatic (functional notation devoid of general dimension). Thus, in despite of the dozen or so specimens accumulated by Assyriologists and Egyptologists, the materials exhibit a *pre-cartographic* perception of the known world.[45] Production of a map presupposes not merely physical and mathematical, but also conceptual coordinates of a kind not documented in sources prior to Anaximander (*c.* 610-546 BCE).[46] That the combination of theoretical and empirical investigation of terrestrial space should be linked with the expeditions of Alexander the Great and his contemporary Pytheas of Marseille means merely that a fair portion of earlier Mediterranean and probably Asian cartographic lore was either lost or subsumed in the later formulations.[47] Irrecoverable as such, that wisdom, which in some practical form must have accompanied the Greco-Phoenician conquest of the Mediterranean, might be constructed by resort to accessible but different data.

Models of contact, exchange, and spatial analysis are plentiful. I have mentioned analyses of the ancient trade in obsidian, ivory and lapis lazuli. Owing to the limited sources of the commodities involved, these were essentially directional and diffusionary. The mechanics of dispersion have been often conjectured and tabulated, e.g. direct contact, indirect and arbitrary exchange, and central place distribution.[48] But even these, it must be acknowledged, are seldom patient of precise translation into terrain, time, motive and cost, let alone the

socio-political context of such transactions. By adding the
factors of production and consumption to that of distribution,
some impressions of context are from time to time adduced,
usually in terms of complementarity.[49] That is, exchange is
interpreted as redress of source imbalance, which in turn furnishes the salient characteristics of societies participant to the
exchange. In addition to its circularity the argument tends to be
strenuously utilitarian, though certainly not implausible. Neglected in such a model are the fashionable, the frivolous and
the fortuitous, modes of consumption not easily identified on
archaeological sites. Whilst "nebulously defined hierarchical
levels of information flow and decision-making abilities" might
seem to inspire very little confidence indeed, some such criteria
must be deemed relevant to the patterned distribution of artifacts.[50] Now, as is well- known, "patterns" are always discernible. Admittedly, some are more persuasive than others, but
without them exercises in analogy and systems of coordinates
would be impossible.[51] Since both are indispensable to the tasks
of description and explanation, a means of projecting patterns
onto a linear plane will inevitably be found. I have alluded
above to *contiguity* and to *concatenation*. As cartographic
principles the former tends to yield a settlement continuum or
unfocused interaction zone, the latter an abstract network or
grid. Not altogether useless, neither exhibits more than a first
step in spatial analysis. At least contiguity provokes a question
about borders: do these function on the ground as barriers or as
catalysts? If they were geophysical only, types might be mutually exclusive: a mountain range would be a barrier to contact,
a river catalyst to interaction.   But there are other kinds:
ecological boundaries have been thought to generate reciprocity, even complementarity, and ethnic ones to issue in an untidy
cultural mix. A *distinction* that has gained some currency is one
between "boundary" as impediment and "frontier" as symbiotic zone in which various "border mechanisms" (e.g. kinship
and fictive versions thereof, nomadism, and ports of trade)
serve to facilitate contact.[52] It need hardly be said that historical
data, however meagre, turn up far more frontiers than boundaries.

Quantifying those data is of course the problem. That
exercise has largely consisted in the stylistic allocation of arti-

facts on a typological grid of locally dominant features. Deviations from the established local type are read variously as stimulus diffusion, exchange, or as the production of resident alien craftsmen. A combination of all three might generate the notion of an "international style".[53] While that exegesis is more than merely acceptable for the imperial sweep of Roman, Byzantine and Islamic traffic in the Mediterranean, the interpretation of earlier periods suffers from uncertain chronology. And, depending upon how "exchange" is defined, from a failure to identify boundaries, frontiers and routes. To that end statistical sondages have been deployed. From a baseline of isolation (i.e. in the archaeological record) it has been thought possible to calculate cultural contact from the periodic accretion of alien materials. While there is about the proposition a mild danger of tautology, such contact can be plotted as *hierarchical nodes* in a circuit diagram. Direction must be inferred from other data, e.g. material provenance and transport technology. In an elegant contact model for Bronze Age Cyprus and the Aegean, Portugali and Knapp plot interaction in terms of quantity (of artifacts) and distance (from alleged source), intensity being in direct proportion to the former and inverse proportion to the latter. While that result could hardly surprise, the concomitant distinction (quantitative, in descending order) between destination, junction, and station provides refinement of the mechanical concatenation of archaeological findspots.[54] Moreover, the traffic is shown to be orbital (Cypriot artifacts in the Aegean, Aegean artifacts in Cyprus); that it was àlso commercial is an assumption (based upon contemporary Cypriot metallurgy). Once made, that assumption permits speculation about the extraction and marketing of copper in Cyprus. A noticeable shift in intensity from Toumba tou Skourou (west) to Enkomi (east) could be read as a Levantine extension of Aegean traffic.[55] Not identified in this model are the agents and socioeconomic context of the traffic.

While evidence of increased interaction can be (and has been) interpreted as a symptom of enhanced managerial techniques, whether as cause or effect must vary from one set of circumstances to another. Decisions about priority tend in any case to reflect criteria other than the quantitative manipulation of artifact, for example, the textual witness of archival records.

And while it is also true that at least tentative conclusions about production (e.g. bulk and standardization) can be (and have been) inferred from the analysis of artifacts, the most arresting achievement of this model is the differential staging of routes.[56] In the absence of cartographic materials (itineraries, logs and portolani) a formula for assessing direction, pace and logistics has got to be welcome. A hierarchy of nodes would of course imply both long distance and direct contact trade; for indirect exchange and central-place distribution every node must be a station or a junction. That might fit a tramping (cabotage) orbit, but not one with a payload destination. Thus, the classification of sites might be thought to presuppose a fairly sophisticated commercial policy. What, in other words, is a "destination"?

If merely the furthest point from start in an orbit, or even the terminus of a single voyage, that would reflect only the sample of sites selected for analysis. And selection, if not quite arbitrary, tends to be serendipitous, the combined result of archaeological fortune and uncertain chronology. Definition, when one is found, must relate "goal" to "motive", even if the latter were not so much a matter of policy as merely adventitious, say, exploration, adventure, exhaustion, piracy, or bad weather. After all, any schematic diagram of Phoenician movement in the Mediterranean will show Cypriot (and Levantine) artifacts far west of Crete. Dating these has generated an academic industry of considerable vitality. Nonetheless, the concept of "destination" is valuable for its implicit connotation of origin, impetus, and feedback. If "trade" may, as I have proposed, be taken to designate contact and change as well as exchange, the stages of every trajectory will involve encounter and at least momentary symbiosis. For description of those the now standard paradigms are mostly economic, linguistic, or behavioural, each of which is informed by a kind of formalist-substantivist polarity. The response to Polanyi's massive cleavage between market and administered economies is still too loud and clear to need further comment;[57] the current controversy about genetic regularity and multiple ancestry in language transmission is the subject of my third chapter; the tension between systemic and entrepreneurial models for explanation of cultural change is of immediate concern. While *identification of agent* is certainly related to "destination", as would be the social, political and economic context in which the latter is articulated, neither is likely to emerge from spatial analysis as so far conceived. But modified by hierarchical taxonomy in which every site could find an appropriate slot, that kind of analysis could eventually produce contiguity, and the central-place as junction might expand concentrically to fill the space.

In such context "agency" could be less dynamic, strategic and innovative. Location not at the centre ("nuclei of settle-ment") but at the perimeter ("foci of communication") would facilitate, indeed dictate, exchange in what was essentially a continuum. Entrepreneurial activity would be interstitial ("bro-kerage") and trade a matter of "relay" rather than terminal focus.[58] However constrained by technology and terrain, con-tact is mostly the ad hoc product of unforeseen and hence uncalculated circumstance. Accidentally exhibited in the ar-chaeological record, isolation is nonetheless a *rare* condition. Where the record is perspicuous, as in the celebrated Aśśur-Kaniś segment of Middle Bronze Age trade, all the refinements and vicissitudes of social intercourse are nicely exhibited.[59] That tableau does not of course depict the nature of every encounter nor even the precise route employed by the dramatis personae (see above), but that is the record not the event. Construction of the one beyond the often exiguous data of the other varies according to discipline. For example, the agential role of the temple in Sumerian economy of the third millennium is a postulate derived by archaeologists from the debris of building plans (e.g. the presence of storage containers in sanc-tuary precincts) and by philologists from scraps of textual evidence (e.g. allocation and ration lists in sanctuary archives). Modification of the dominant "temple economy" and of its concomitant "Sumerian temple city" is plotted in terms of a diachronic development from "temple" to "palace" manage-ment with sporadic injection of "private enterprise". While the model is admittedly plausible as reflex of the so far available record, it would seem to depend upon a dichotomy between the spheres of sacral and secular activities, for which some such notion as "church versus state" might be thought responsible.[60] But apart from the ambivalence of many such "archives" (e.g. Śuruppag/Fāra), the distinction itself would be questioned by an economist. To be effective, whether alone or in competition, the direction of economic affairs depends upon *managerial criteria* indifferent to the source of its authority. In any case, the location of sanctuaries at boundaries or along routes; the role of divine oracles and auspices in planning commercial ventures; of the oath to deities in contractual relations; of syncretism as deliberate reduction of transaction costs; of sacrifice and philanthropy as conspicuous consumption in aid of social prestige; of protection, exemption and franchise as marks of divine favour (and hence confirmation of ethically proper conduct); all these suggest that "sacral" authority is quite appropriate to commerce, and have of course been noticed by economists.[61] As such, "agency" is primarily a social phenomenon, its locus symbiotic and its role to demonstrate contact.

It is also composite. For calculation of input, neither temple nor palace can be monolithic: from the archival records, such as they are, emerges sharply the *role of kinship,* manifested in the nuclear but especially the extended family.[62] Together with the subsystems of patronage and clientship, these were the units that comprised and enabled the macrocosm of long distance trade. For later periods, from which prosopographical data are abundant, the relation of entrepreneurial activity to kinship is patent and detailed (e.g. family networks in Venice and its colonies, to which were linked not merely the North African littoral, but also Nürnberg, Braunschweig, Lübeck and the entire Hansa).[63] If it were needed, a further ingredient becomes conspicuous from the early Middle Ages: the Jewish diaspora exhibits a both real and metaphorical subsystem of contact, obligation and responsibility that alone could support the considerable volume of Mediterranean commerce.[64] Almost infinitely flexible, the network would serve a political spectrum from free enterprise to regalian imperative. If that particular case represents an ideal, it illustrates nonetheless what seems to be a social fact: that the extension of kinship (by marriage, partnership and patronage) generates a fragmentation of autonomy (by breach of lineal and topological boundaries). The immediate economic consequences include division of labour, accumulation of surplus, and exchange. In such context, neither isolation nor inertia can persist, at least not for long. It is the ineluctable circumstance of man to be in continuous motion and uninterrupted contact.

Now, if that were absolutely true, it might seem that all movement must be centrifugal and all stimulus endogenous. If, on the other hand, it were only relatively true, the image would be one of intersecting circles radiating from multiple discrete nuclei. Intersection would generate feedback which, whether positive or negative, must be exogenous and to which response would be centripetal.[65] It is of course this model of movement that accommodates more readily both the lacunar historical record and the *concept of orbit*. A premise of discrete nuclei is uncomfortably abstract and historically simplistic, but as a metaphor for Early Bronze Age demography just tolerable. The devised model, though hardly free of problems, is patient of simulation and a fair range of permutation.[66] Since all input must be variable, calculation can produce necessary but very seldom sufficient causes of change. The crucial ingredients are *feedback* and *threshold,* the liminal determinant of retention and/or innovation. While it is tempting to define retention (conservatism) as homeostasis, it may be doubted whether that condition is empirically persistent, even if theoretically possible. Perception would, admittedly, depend upon the time-scale employed or merely available (i.e. in the chronological dispersion of artifacts), but might also reflect nothing more than concession to such lexical items as "tradition" and "stability".[67] By way of illustration, a 16th century example: despite the adoption of artillery in the 14th century, the production on a massive scale of cannon in the 15th, the extensive use of this weapon in siege and fortification, the training of a unit in the use of handheld firearms, and the perceived threat of foreign invasion, the rulers of Mamluk Egypt and Syria declined to avail themselves of a well-known battlefield tactic for application of the technology.[68] The consequence was defeat and occupation of their territory by the Ottoman Turks, who had taken advantage of its deployment in mobile warfare. The standard explanation is found in the structure of Mamluk military society: its social rigidity and concomitant snobbery, entrenched attachment to (literally) "chivalry", and psychological disinclination to change. All of this has solid basis in contemporary report as well as sociological fact, but it is worth recalling that the decision taken by or in Ottoman military society was based on access to the very same technological data. In any case, the result for Mamluk Egypt and Syria could hardly be called homeostasis.

The *specific technology* being adopted, adapted, or rejected may be less than critical. The introduction of firearms, say, in other parts of Africa by both Ottomans and Europeans, could have quite unpredictable and non-military effects (e.g. ceremonial, decorative, magic).[69] More important would be the matrix of stimulus reception, not easily deduced from even an explicit array of artifact. Though some substantive difference between the Mamluk and Ottoman military regimes can be detected, their respective responses to stimulus diffusion is more reliably calibrated to a conjectural growth curve plotted between points of vitality and ankylosis. In the early 16th century, for example, the difference between Ottoman and Mamluk politics would surely have been observed by a Venetian merchant and probably by a Portuguese soldier, though neither could have predicted the outcome of their military encounter. What does seem critical in this example is *management*, that is, the practical deployment of new information. Means to that end are likely to be prior to acquisition, already in place, as it were, owing to earlier and successful experiment or good fortune. But the record is seldom perspicuous: ample documentation for both powers is available long before 1516 and does not yield evidence of the kind here sought. Only with the result to hand can the process leading to it be discerned.

Returned thus to a "before-after" syndrome (see above), one might be inclined to argue from paucity of relevant data that no conclusion is foregone. As the primary datum, "management" may be elusive but is not invisible, else its products would also have gone unnoticed. A mode of relating the one to the other can be extrapolated from the residue of Mediterranean cartography, an accumulation of expertise to which I have alluded.[70] "Accumulation" is approximately right: not merely the ancient lore (of sailors, astronomers and mathematicians) but also the accuracy, practicability and commercial production (for professional consumption) demanded of an economically viable technology are exhibited in the medieval sea-charts known as "portolani". With mysterious pedigree (i.e. circumventing both the Ptolemaic legacy and the mappaemundi) the portolan reflects empirical knowledge (scale, toponymy), abstract concepts (rhumb lines, compass points), and rudimentary symbolism (hydrographic notation). While there can be no doubt that the earliest portolan (c. 1270) must reflect contemporary navigational techniques, these would be cumulative even if undocumented in cartography. Some relation between the charts and navigation manuals (periplus) has been mooted, a link that could be ancient, e.g. the Massaliote or Scylax of Caryanda (both 6th century BCE). The possibility of input from Roman (Marinus of Tyre, c. 100 CE) and Arab (Idrisi, c. 1150 CE) geography might seem not unreasonable, though neither has been demonstrated.[71] Factors like dead reckoning, atmospheric clarity, frequent landfalls and the "basin" configuration of the Mediterranean are the legitimate data of speculation only. Their metamorphosis as instruments and tables for measurement and calculation would appear from the available record to be precipitate, if not quite miraculous. As resolution of an historical problem, that is altogether unsatisfactory, and one is inclined to situate this particular epiphany in a context of general economic rationalization.[72] If it would be unwise to dismiss the inventive properties of warfare and naval strategy (especially Roman),[73] a graph of maritime acitivity over any segment of recorded Mediterranean history would show the preponderance of commerce. Considering the late introduction of magnetic compass and sextant (13th century), it may be supposed that navigation as such was an occupational transmission (of sailors and merchants, if these were not the same) ancillary to the related but different activity of long distance trade. It would be to improved techniques in this realm that development of the chart as nautical vademecum (and as profitable enterprise) can be attributed. Its production signalled an expansion in the volume of exchange elsewhere prepared and long since underway.

One such technique, analogous to the chart and approximately a century earlier (i.e. c. 1170), is attested in the proliferation of archival data relating to business transactions. To describe that as a "diplomatic revolution" may seem extravagant, but the very abundance of official correspondence and commercial treaties between Mediterranean states from the late 12th century onwards, if not merely an accident of preservation, would suggest an enhanced and formalized contact. *Rationalization of procedure* is implicit in both juridical content and chancery format.[74] Of course the paucity of such materials before that date could be read simply as evidence of less contact, but in the light of the similar and sudden appearance of the sea-charts as well as of earlier informal witness to intensive commercial traffic, I am inclined to postulate technological refinement. The manner in which that would affect transaction costs must be crucial. Because it is informal (i.e. private and non-archival), the earlier witness above-mentioned might seem inappropriate to the task of comparison: notoriously fragmentary, the papers of the Cairo Geniza have nonetheless been interpreted to yield a profile of Mediterranean commerce that demonstrates continuous contact over a period of two centuries (c1025-1225). While its salient feature is the role of kinship in the maintenance of contact, remarkable also are the results of calculating distance/time across the network.[75] The impression is one of very little change for the millennium since the establishment of Roman naval domination, in despite of known changes in nautical design and locomotion as well as a radically altered political configuration. That these very factors could have been mutually cancelled or neutralized by yet others has of course got to be reckoned in an argument for homeostasis or even cumulative change.[76] Of those canvassed, easily the most celebrated is the political one adduced to depict a "dark age" of rupture and stagnation.

Modified beyond recognition, rebutted and eventually superseded, Pirenne's thesis on the fragmentation of Mediterranean unity provoked an industry of close cultural analysis.[77] But his own agenda was exclusively economic, extrapolated from displacement of commodities (papyrus, luxury cloth, spices, gold currency) and hence necessarily concerned with routes. However, that concern was never more than implicit and the actual conveyance of goods (or, in the event, its cessation) was not analysed. This imbalance was to some extent redressed by his critics, with references to shipbuilding, fleet formation and naval expeditions undertaken by the new rulers of the Mediterranean.[78] That the Arabs, by 711 in occupation of the southern littoral as far as the straits of Gibraltar, could neither have benefited from nor have been interested in a maritime blockade of the northern littoral must be clear to anyone familiar with colonial logistics. Apart from

the exigencies of naval warfare, communication and the movement of supplies and tribute required feasible traffic patterns.
While ports were marked on the schematic maps of Arab
geographers, precise data on routes and distances are not
available.[79] It was of course Pirenne's purpose to document
what he supposed to be the profound difference between the
Merovingian and Carolingian economies, and a catastrophe
model (the Arab invasion) must have seemed appropriate.
That particular problem has been redefined or differently
solved, and there remains the question of why the voyage
between Marseilles and Alexandria took as long in the 12th
century as it had in the 2nd. The only answer can be that
nautical technology, whatever else it may have achieved in the
way of bulk haulage, safety and comfort, had not been able to
reduce the time under sail. Alternative land routes, documented for both Europe and Africa, and inland waterways, for
Europe, may have in some circumstances required less.[80] But
time underway is only a portion of that component in calculating total transaction cost. As I have now often intimated, one
would look for savings and thus increased efficiency of *administrative input.*

If that quest seems unavoidable, or at least to be recommended, it could also turn out to be merely tautological, i.e.
lower costs generate greater activity which exhibits lower costs.
On the other hand, activity analysis (see above) must include
risk and the possibility of nil return, as well as serious miscal-
culation, at any rate in the short term. Over a longer period, loss
(e.g. shipwreck, piracy, war, bankruptcy, disease, death) can be
sustained and is of course calculable. And it is the longer period
that generates the curve from isolation to concatenation to
contiguity. It also introduces a third dimension (time) into
spatial analysis. In this context time is not the correlate of
distance hitherto noticed, but rather, a sequence of repetition,
experiment and innovation. Whether perceived as linear or
cyclical, it must be *historical time that permits spatial lacunae
to be filled* or at least bridged. The space so treated is not only
topological (mapping), but also technological (invention) and
iconographic (design). Without the third dimension neither
scale reduction nor magnetic compass nor lateen sail are conceivable. Time itself may also be perceived as orbital, perhaps

more accurately as helical: the operative constant is reaction (feedback). Its apparent opposite, inertia, is, like isolation, only hypothetical, if admittedly useful in the construction of a model. The image thus envisaged, indeed predicated, is of ineluctable contact (see above), for which the apposite caption would as often be "sooner or later" as "before and after". That is not of course to say the Arab invasion of the Mediterranean or the feudalization of the Carolingian empire were inevitable. As historical constructs, it happens that the former ensued and the latter not quite, but the demonstration of both propositions depends upon data that could be (and have been) read in a variety of ways. That is standard practice, naturally, and only the provocatively creative instances, like Pirenne's thesis, are memorable. A less interesting case, but nonetheless relevant to my concern, is a dispute about Mediterranean cultural unity in the 16th century.[81] In contrast to Braudel's "field of force" paradigm (see above), Hess selected confessional emblemata to postulate a stark polarity fixed at what he called "the forgotten (Ibero-African) frontier". Its crystallization as barrier (!) is exhibited in a self-conscious and xenophobic quest for Gleichschaltung, i.e. the expulsion from Christian Spain of Jews and Muslims in 1492 and of Moriscos in 1614. So perceived, the familiar data could be interpreted to reveal longstanding dichotomies in the Ottoman and Habsburg assimilation of technology (military and nautical), in their respective imperialist aspirations (terrestrial versus oceanic), and in their resolution of internal religious tensions (pluralism versus uniformity); disparities in their capacity to fund the logistics of warfare (e.g. the treaty of 1580) and to organize resources for economic competition (e.g. the reception of English overtures in 1579); and the gradual development of a mutually complacent view of the other. Much of this is, correctly, derived from the perusal of different materials (Ottoman and Arabic contrasted with the European archives deployed by Braudel), but also, more importantly, from a quite different paradigm. Such concepts of space as ecological, meteorological, and socio-economic imply a view of time as refractor rather than magnifier, events as symptoms rather than causes. Braudel did not, of course, overlook the "frontier", in his view not a barrier but an emphatically symbiotic zone.[82] The notion of Islam as an entity radically different from Christendom is anyway a concomitant of that view of it as having been imported readymade from Arabia into the Mediterranean. That such could hardly have been so is now more or less common knowledge.[83] And the orbital movement of Sephardic Jews from the Iberian peninsula to Tuscany to the Ottoman Balkan provinces and back through North Africa to Morocco in the course of the 16th century might suggest something very close to a cultural continuum.[84] The context is not much different from that depicted in the documents of the Cairo Geniza four centuries earlier. Polarization is, after all, not quite alien to the image of a magnetic field.

Projecting this image onto a map of the Bronze Age Mediterranean might be thought to risk overtaxing the third dimension of spatial analysis. The frailty of such structures as have been erected to that end lies along the margins of chronological tolerance. Would, for example, the change from lodestone to compass or from square to lateen rigging have been evolutionary or abrupt? Do the rhumblines on portolani exhibit traditional dead reckoning or mathematical innovation? There would anyway be an incalculable time-lag between invention, diffusion and application that must make a *calendar of technology* very conjectural indeed. A *map of technology* must be equally tentative. Both widespread and stratigraphically abundant, *ceramic residue* constitutes the classical artifact. Its taxonomy, spatial and temporal, is as sophisticated as any available. Typological components like shape, colour, decoration and use can be correlated with one another but not always with a socio-economic framework that would exhibit distribution, consumption and hierarchy. The distinction between formal order (autonomous) and informal order (contextual) is here crucial, but need not inhibit postulation of some kind of link. It is the artifactual environment (even as preserved) that generated technological experiment and modification. If never quite perspicuous, the relation between object and subject must have existed.[85] With that rudimentary but enduring conviction the edifice of causality may be conceived and historical time constructed. The advantage of pottery for such an enterprise is that it is both tangible and trivial. Not the relation itself, but its residue, it is also (mostly) not produced for posterity, but for practical purposes (carrying, cooking, storage). Thus neutral, and extrinsic to historical time, the sherd might be thought the ideal raw material for a specimen chronicle of technology. A pottery sequence is both temporal (continuous) and spatial (contiguous), irrespective of context (society) and agency (motive). Disjuncture arises, or may be perceived, on a single site as result of catastrophe, between sites owing to deliberate modification or lapse of tradition, but may also be concealed by evolution of an "international style" (see above). The historicization of such material is difficult but not impossible. Unlike obsidian and metallic ore, whose witness to technological process is only indirect, the ceramic artifact incorporates a signature. If that is, admittedly, merely a stylistic imprint, it is also formulaic and traceable. Thus, as it is possible to depict the history of art without reference to artists, the development of ceramic design can be traced without notice of individual potters. The additional factor of reproducibility (emulation) generates a theoretically infinite network that is anonymous and directly related to the artifact. In the circumstances here invoked, that is not merely welcome but about as much as one could expect.

Now, if the relevance of all this to elaboration of *chancery practice* is not quite obvious, it would be well to stress that the merits of the model are precisely the elements of anonymity and reproducibility. Contact is a datum and communication its purpose. Modality is a variable, but cannot be idiosyncratic to the point of losing contact. And since communication is by definition reciprocal, the orbit is assured. Here, the earliest technology in question is visible language, or *writing*.[86] Though productive of much curiosity and conjecture, the question of origin is not, and is not likely to be, answered. One is inclined to settle for polygenesis or a polite but unpersuasive nod towards stimulus diffusion. Like any code, language is culture-bound and it is reasonable to suppose that any device for depicting it would also be. A taxonomy of such must include pictograph (iconic), logograph (semantic) and ideograph (mnemonic), even if all the putative precursors of script cannot be neatly allocated. The latter range from potter's mark (insignia) to seal (emblem) to symbol (design) to calculi (numeration), and share with script both representational and spatial features. But evolution from the one to the other is neither logical nor straightforward, nor for that matter diachronically attested. The crucial quality of script is its emancipation from locally fixed values, whether iconic, semantic or mnemonic, such that a single or compound sign might evoke concepts beyond or other than its graphic content. Some way to that end can be achieved by simple spatial arrangement, like isolation (cartouche), juxtaposition (ligature) or segmentation (column, row, palindrome), but most is accomplished by linguistic re-interpretation, e.g. paronomastic (polysemy), parasemantic (polyphony), and affixing determinatives (semantic) or complements (phonetic). The extent to which these several procedures exhibit conscious manipulation or are merely self-generated (e.g. what concept or word does not evoke unurged at least its opposite?) would, if it could be known, affect a history of writing. But even without the diachronic location of these events it is possible to detect a process of sign production independent of any specific cultural code. The end result is of course the alphabet, which by investing a minimal series with universal values combines extreme economy of input with virtually infinite application.

The process has been felicitously described as transition from pleremic (informed) to kenemic (empty) code, somehow provoked by the *recognition of redundancy*.[87] Now, that recognition is usually acknowledged as quite remarkable, if not indeed miraculous, and to signal a revolution in the assembly, storage and utterance of perceptual data.[88] But redundancy is the standard concomitant of any accumulation and, save in moments of extreme ankylosis or archaism, more than likely to be not merely noticed but eliminated, or at least reduced. Linguistic history furnishes ample evidence of that tendency, salient especially in circumstances of borrowing and language shift. And it is precisely those circumstances, characterized by intensive contact, linguistic interference and bilingualism, which might also be thought conducive to the perception and elimination of features in a writing system borrowed or adapted for a language other than that for which it has been originally designed.[89] While the evolution from Sumerian of Akkadian cuneiform is not the tidiest example of such adaptation (e.g. retention of logographs in a perfectly adequate syllabary), the emergence from the latter of the Ugaritic alphabet exhibits nicely the perception of redundancy.[90] And that was a product of chancery practice, in which a specific problem of technology was solved in a more or less recoverable context. Its subsequent development is coterminous with the history of Mediterranean lingua franca and of communication organized on a scale up to that point unknown. Much of that history has been written as diffusion of the alphabet, its penetration of areas occupied by other writing systems, and its gradual modification appropriate to the requirements of other languages. Considerable attention is devoted to the nature of writing materials and instruments, to the perpetuation of scribal tradition and training, and to the probable expansion of literacy that ought to have facilitated or resulted from that technological "revolution". Like firearms and sea-charts, the alphabet seems to appear suddenly, to spread easily, and to diminish the cost of movement, exchange and territorial expansion. Thus perceived it is in mild danger of interpretation as a cause rather than as a symptom of attendant circumstances.

That impression might be dispelled by reference to a more inclusive principle of rationalization. I have mentioned as one such principle the perception of redundancy; another would be the phonological matrix recently asserted to underly the sequence of both Ugaritic and Phoenician alphabets.[91] Even if not absolutely convincing (articulatory phonetics without access to informants must seem risky), perception of a *non-random mnemonic principle* in the transmission of a writing system might be thought to comprehend more than the system itself. That this was lost during subsequent diffusion of the alphabet matters less than the fact that other systems of notation were displaced or superseded. While the context of that process is not exactly recoverable, it is only conceivable within an established network of communication. For this particular example of technological insight could not otherwise have been expressed or documented. It is of course only by analogy to later and more abundant evidence of chancery practice that the imagery of research and development can be postulated. The residue of *experiment* at centres such as Byblos (cuneiform, pseudo-hieroglyph, and linear alphabetic) and Ugarit (eight languages exhibiting five scripts) may, however, be interpreted as witness to the same proceess.[92]

As it happens, Byblos and Ugarit are also primary nodes in the network of contacts that can be extrapolated from the very artifacts attesting to chancery experiment. In a tangible and very practical way these toponyms symbolize the source of both innovation and diffusion. The quantitative analysis of both, increasingly conspicuous in modern scholarship, is a by-product of remarkable gains in the field of Semitic epigraphy.[93] The emergence of event from inscription is an exegetical exercise not easily forsworn, in despite of well-known perils. Those of linear typology have been recently and elegantly stressed.[94] That morphological evolution should exhibit predictable uniformity might be demanded by a botanist, but is a dangerous hypothesis for an epigrapher. The occasion happens to be the now (since 1980) celebrated Akkadian-Aramaic bilingual from Tell Fekheriye, but the admonition may be allowed a wider range, that is, the transmission history of the Phoenician alphabet. Like ceramics, writing systems are peculiarly susceptible to morphological taxonomy, but, rather like structuralism, this does not provide a chronological, biographical or historical datum. What it can do is generate a *stylistic analysis* internal to the class of artifact, whose diffusion might well have suffered both spatial and temporal hiatus. Neither contact nor orbit is thereby demolished, but that is because the technology in question is merely part of a more extensive syndrome. The value of Byblos and Ugarit lies also in their position as epicentres of an artifactual symbiosis based on a spectrum of non-linguistic materials. The ease with which these latter can be arranged to document an hypothesis of intensive cultural contact is well-known and now standard practice.[95] As with epigraphic data, putative contact and especially its intensity require a denser chronology than is in fact available. An obvious alternative to temporal certainty is recourse to a spatial concept intended to provoke an impression of contiguity. Here too the analysis is quantitative and its underlying premise an upward curve of frequency and distribution: *spatial density fills temporal lacunae.* And from a catalogue of toponyms however assembled production of a map must seem logical.[96] While toponyms themselves do not yield a graphic typology, phonetic correspondences can help to identify a place-name, its linguistic context and, occasionally, its location. Lingering disputes about Kaphtor and Alašiya exhibit most of the familiar problems of data allocation.[97] Introduction of a new method, such as clay analysis by neutron activation, may refine speculation without increasing confidence in the textual evidence.[98] Artifact and inscription may be found obstinately divergent, as in the examples of Cypro-Minoan script on "Mycenean" pottery and "oriental" tablets excavated in Ugarit.[99] Whether as evidence of exchange or of resident aliens, this kind of material strengthens the impression of contiguity. That this particular variety of the script appears not to be identical to that attested elsewhere might be thought to confirm the hypothesis of chancery experiment at Ugarit. Identification of the agents responsible is hardly straightforward, but perhaps less important anyway than the indisputable presence of such activity.

For the historian of the Mediterranean Bronze Age the manipulation of temporal and spatial lacunae is thus crucial. Even if not perceived as such, their complementarity easily becomes a methodological premise, since identical gaps in both records would be intolerable. A standard bridging device is the "international style", which seems to reflect both continuity and contiguity. Now, the alphabet might be so defined, and its diffusion (so far unquestioned) a guarantee of cultural contact.[100] But the substrata upon which this uniformity was gradually imposed exhibit discrete modes of notation (e.g. ideographic and syllabic) that must be regarded as *communicative closures*. When one recalls the remarkable diffusion of Akkadian cuneiform, it is difficult to assert that a syllabary is confined to the language for which it was devised. Nothing intrinsic, in other words, to the Cretan and Cypriot linear scripts could account for their failure to spread more widely. As is well-known, logograms are similarly and easily transferable, fixed only by insertion of phonetic or semantic signals. It is of course interpretation of these signals, initially available only as graphotactic phenomena, that is crucial to the task of reading a new language, even when it is written in a familiar script. These days the Paradebeispiel is the Semitic language dimly perceived in the Sumerograms of Ebla. If its identity is still a matter of dispute, the lessons to be learned in the process of decoding are indispensable to recognition of the technological transfer.[101] What seems to emerge from this particular example is a genius for adaptation in despite of apparently insuperable obstacles, both linguistic and technical. That it should have been adaptation, rather than invention (de novo), must indicate a context definable in terms of cultural preponderance. That becomes a sociological problem of which the political and economic dimensions tend often to be extrapolated from the linguistic data under scrutiny. The circularity involved has not gone unnoticed, and one is compelled to postulate an environment conducive to unidirectional diffusion, e.g. the "Kish civilization" of northern Babylonia.

For the Mediterranean the comparable postulates are the alphabet and "Phoenicia". Neither has been conventionally allocated to the Bronze Age, though recent studies exhibit a distinct tendency to push back both the invention and its diffusion. While assessment, or reassessment, of Byblos and Ugarit have contributed to this tendency, the historical context of these and other centres of cultural radiation is not appreciably clarified. Clear only is the evidence of *scribal experiment*. The extent to which it may be described as actually cumulative and evolutionary, endogenous or exogenous, facilitated or impeded by patronage or its absence, is still a matter of conjecture. One may be permitted to speculate that both the patronage and leisure essential to experiment would only be available in a political system characterized by wealth and stability. The source of either might be agricultural, industrial, commercial or a combination of these, and consolidated by some visible and autonomous socio-economic structure. Visibility and autonomy would probably be territorial. With that hypothesis is provoked yet again the perennial problem of unmapped space. And again, it is only the witness of the technology itself, in this case script, that documents its diffusion.

For the 7th century CE some of these lacunae can be filled. Deployment of Arabic in the Mediterranean required acceptance, or imposition, of innovation in both language and script. The pace at which this was achieved varied according to the substratum ecountered, but can be calculated from chancery materials of a kind not available for the Bronze or Iron Age. Moreover, the political system that sponsored this diffusion is not merely visible but identifiable, even if not accompanied by the socio-economic detail so often assumed. Territorial distinctions did of course affect the pace, but probably no more than did the substrate linguistic phenomena. These were Aramaic, Greek and Latin, at least at the level eventually replaced by chancery Arabic, and each had a history of function as *lingua franca*. It was that slot that Arabic was to fill, a matter of crucial significance for the ensuing transfer of technology. The process was thus not only technical and linguistic, but also formulaic and semiotic, a transfer of content, form and design. The modalities are the subject of my second chapter; here my concern is with conveyance through space and time.

The diachronic study of literary Arabic belongs to the history of Islam. It is this convenient synchrony that furnishes in one perspicuous arc most of the data pertinent to identification of agent, motive and goal. In Egypt, for example, it enables tracing an evolution of chancery instruments from Greek to Greek-Arabic bilingual (or other permutations) to Arabic within a context for which demographic and administrative parameters can be more or less safely reconstructed. The evidence for Palestine and Syria is of different character but equally abundant, while west of Egypt data masses for Tunisia and the Iberian peninsula permit inclusion of the entire North African littoral in a time-scale that accommodates an orderly replacement of technologies. Lest this outline appear unduly tidy, I would adduce the centripetal imagery earlier and in another context proposed for the Islamic concept of Arabic as *lingua sacra*.[102] Here it is a matter not of theological doctrine but of the role of a central authority in the process of acculturation. Imposition of a uniform legal code, fiscal system and linguistic register requires dissemination from a central place recognised as source of judgement and style. Its perimeter expands ideally with the extension of power. It is in this way that the history of Islamic chanceries, as instruments of that power, can be written. It would be an exercise both formal and reductive, with the advantage that the Arabic data so deployed would approximate to the kind of linguistic materials available for earlier periods of Mediterranean history. And, moreover, with the social context that is missing from the early materials. Seen from the point of view of chancery practice, the possibility of historical construction is real. The product would be intelligible but incomplete. Absent would be evidence of the language at every level other than the prescriptions of chancery rhetoric, that is, the informal registers of colloquial and trade jargon. As it happens, there is sufficient linguistic interference in chancery documents preserved, if not in their models, to diminish the danger of oversimplification. Interference of a substrate or diglossic type can be detected in peripheral Akkadian, and possibly in Ugaritic and Phoenician. It is, moreover, accessible in both Greek and Latin, as in Aramaic, so that a continuum of interference phenomena can be assembled for a study of languages in contact.

To conceive of any Mediterranean language unaffected by contact is difficult, if not indeed impossible. Evidence for the pre-Islamic history of Arabic, contained in an Aramaic format, would seem to confirm this. Script, orthography and, to some extent, lexicon attest to an underlying structure of some flexibility. It may be, of course, that this impression is a consequence of some instability in the format itself (i.e. Aramaic writing), but the witness of other inscriptional materials (Lihyān, Safā, Thamūd) might be thought to corroborate a relatively fluid profile. The elements in those three languages, as well as in Nabataean, of what eventually emerged as Islamic Arabic are not easily fixed into the conventional categories of a prototype, but do exhibit at least a condition of social and linguistic contact. The future of Arabic as lingua franca would be affected by its composite early history, as has been documented in the development of its non-Islamic (Jewish and Christian) varieties.[103] Of all these data, it is the Nabataean that illustrate most plausibly the introduction of Arabic into the Mediterranean. The *channel* was provided by the machinery of Roman imperialism developed during the period from Pompey (64 BCE) to Trajan (106 CE) which coincided with the efflorescence of Petra.[104] The later insinuation of Arab statecraft into the imperial structure itself, under Septimius Severus and Philip, exhibits a policy of dealing with the eastern frontier that crystallized as strategy at the new capital in Constantinople after 325. Three years later, the linguistic process would be nicely symbolized in the Nabataean Arabic inscription of Namārah. Much discussed and often interpreted, that document is witness not merely to a scribal technique, but also, in its latest reading, to direct affiliation of the Arabs to Rome.[105] It is, however, only symbolic: "Nabataean" is attested later (Hijr c. 356 CE) and "Arabic" earlier ('Avdat c. 125 CE; Rawwāfah c.160 CE), the latter in such guise as to confirm the mixture but defy reconstruction of the motives.[106] If the prestige of Petra was acknowledged its *script* was itself the ancient legacy of international usage, and its application to Arabic attested only after Roman annexation of the Nabataean realm. There would be thus at least three factors to facilitate adoption of Aramaic script by writers/speakers of Arabic. Amongst these it might be thought Rome was preeminent.

By that time the Aramaic chancery tradition could count a millennium at least of practical and widespread application, of which the western reach was Egypt.[107] The several imperial contexts of its diffusion, usually illustrated by the Achaemenid (539-331 BCE), exhibit some local variation and, in succeeding centuries, evolution, noticeable in the Nabataean and Palmyrene scripts.[108] Development of a specifically North Arabian ductus from either of these or from Syriac, as is conventionally postulated, is not quite perspicuous.[109] Despite the Islamic tradition on this point, gaps both spatial and temporal in the inscriptional evidence make very arduous a construction of the graphic evolution. When, in the late 7th century, chancery documents become available (Egypt) these would appear to confirm an impression of scribal experiment. Such also is a legitimate inference from approximately contemporary materials in Judaea (Khirbet al-Mird) and the Negev (Nessana, Sde Boqer, Ruḥaibah), though Jerusalem (Dome of the Rock) exhibits an accomplished lapidary style.[110] Time-lag between the developments of chancery cursive and monumental display inscriptions might well account for such discrepancy, but it must be remarked that the Negev materials cannot be attributed to either tradition. On the other hand, the East Roman (Byzantine) context may be interpreted as catalyst to a continuum of graphic experiment addressed to the eminently cultural pursuits of communication and commemoration, and the Negev, whether Nabataean, Roman or Greek, certainly belonged to that context.

For the Mediterranean, the Aramaic tradition, like the earlier Akkadian, can only furnish a paradigm. The archival residue of Amarna, Elephantine, Memphis and Hermapolis reflect the western perimeter of chancery networks whose epicentres lay further east. Orbital contact is assured. For the pre-Phoenician Mediterranean none of the known cultural systems provides much documentation extending beyond its own borders. This absence does not of course belie the fact of contact, so amply expressed in other forms. Nor is it likely to be a matter of archaeological chance, unless that should include the (admittedly distinct) possibility of perished, hence unrecoverable writing materials. From their long period of symbiosis, one could suppose that a Phoenician chancery tradition must reflect some features of the Aramaic one, or if instead Canaanite, then from Ugarit some components of the Akkadian. Now, the only Phoenician letter so far extant would appear to belong to the latter tradition, which is not quite surprising.[111] But because of its singularity, as well as of its provenance (Saqqarah) and date (6th century BCE), it is also inadequate even for speculation. For Greek epistolography, the tradition is rooted in the ancient schools of rhetoric, nurtured by the Attic-Asian controversy, and issuing in the hybrid products of Ptolemaic chanceries.[112] Its scholastic extension in Latin, both archaistic and innovative, offers a rough analogy to the adaptation of Sumerian models in Babylonian and Assyrian chanceries.[113] Both phenomena exhibit transmission of a cultural commodity that might have been lost outside an institutional framework of proven stability. Greek tradition acknowledges a debt to Phoenicians, but not in the fields of rhetoric and chancery practice.[114] These were regarded as native, and generated the paradigm which superseded those of the Levant and from which all medieval Mediterranean diplomatic derived. The underlying technology was Roman statecraft.

An attractive symmetry could be achieved by postulating for the Iron Age expansion of Greek commerce the similar function of Euboean, Corinthian or Attic statecraft. An hypothesis of endogenous growth can with ingenuity be extrapolated from the literary tradition (Homer, Hesiod) and the archaeological record (e.g. Euboea-Ischia, Corinth-Apulia), but must sooner or later confront the Phoenician data, which are at least contemporaneous.[115] The two sets of data also share considerable space, from the Aegean to the Iberian peninsula, and disentanglement has proved difficult. "Phoenician" (phoinix/ phoinikes), itself a Greek coinage, has several referents, amongst them a people who probably called themselves "Canaanites".[116] For all their denigration in the Homeric lexicon, these served somehow as catalyst in the Greek colonial enterprise and, as reflex of earlier Bronze Age commerce, might be thought to deserve organizational priority. But the literary record is Greek, not Phoenician, and for the latter one is compelled to infer a socio-political context from scrappy archaeological witness. The difference in documentation is, however, merely typological. The Greek literary record is late, conflated and confusing; the Phoenician archaeological one is abundant, but fragmentary and opaque.[117] For the historian dependent upon these ambivalent materials, the question of perception is crucial: literary evidence may be the more congenial, but addressed as it mostly is to posterity, can also be deceptive. One is thus, and I have several times alluded to the dilemma, dealing with distinct genres whose properties only with great risk allow combination. The safest conclusion to be drawn from Greek literature is that the Greeks produced literature. The schools of rhetoric are its most eloquent testimony. It would be difficult to extrapolate a comparable tradition from the extant Phoenician inscriptions. For that, as for other matters "Phoenician", the proximate reference is to the Canaanite culture at Ugarit. There both literary and chancery traditions can be shown to have flourished, but also to have been truncated by the changes conventionally adduced to mark the beginnings of "Phoenicia". The inscriptions themselves are mostly exiguous, with some notable exceptions [e.g. Aḥiram, Yeḥawmilk (Byblos), Kilamuwa (Zenjirli), Azitiwada (Karatepe), Tabnit, Eshmunazar (Sidon), Yatanba'al (Lapethos)] in the Levant, reduced to brief sanctuary dedications and signatures in the West, where the modest corpus is augmented by Punic and neo-Punic materials of a similar sort.[118] Some of the longer pieces have been investigated for traces of poetic and/or rhetorical structure (e.g. parallelism, alliteration, stereotype imagery, formulaic syntax, etc.), with the resulting impression that if the sample could be enlarged such components of stylistic aspiration as are found in most literatures would not be wanting in Phoenician.[119] But that is still a considerable distance from the circumstances of Archaic and Classical Greek, whose archaeological record in the Mediterranean is not more extensive than the Phoenician. When, of course, due account is taken of the entire "Canaanite" corpus, a kind of parity (of practice and product if not of theory) might be achieved.

As is their name, so also is the "history" of the Phoenicians a Greek construct. The account, beginning with Homer, is tortuous, anecdotal and episodic. It is also arbitrarily empirical, with virtually no reference to what might qualify as a native source, save the putative Sanchunyaton adduced for polemical purposes by Philo of Byblos (d.164 CE) or the so-called "annals of Tyre" employed for different reasons by Josephus (d.100 CE).[120] Extraction of a usable narrative from the scattered data of the Greco-Hebrew tradition is impossible: there is nothing or little from which one could deduce the technological and administrative bases of a major commercial and colonial undertaking. Neither the joint trading expedition from Eziongeber (c940 BCE) nor the foundation of Carthage (814 BCE) is recounted in a way that might help to clarify basic problems of agency and logistics. Nor do the several notices of eastern imperial intervention (Assyrian, Babylonian, Persian) in the affairs of Phoenicia furnish data directly translatable into categories of economic *organization.* From indications of economic *activity,* on the other hand, such as the Assyrian establishment of a Levantine kārum or the Babylonian distribution of western commodities, might be gained some impression of an in situ infrastructure to be tapped.[121] Its history, however, has to be gleaned from Canaanite materials of the Late Bronze Age.[122]

The décalage is disturbing, and has generated in addition to the Canaanite one, an Aegean model (Minoan, Mycenean, or even Philistine). Evidence of contact is of course not wanting and a postulate of maritime transport hardly reckless. Certainly misleading is the imagery of sudden expansion ("take-off"), dictated apparently by the chronology of archaeological sites in the western Mediterranean. Implicit in the Aegean model are motives of territorial expansion and conquest, but these could not explain "Phoenician" movement prior to Carthaginian operations against Greece and Rome some centuries later. A different concept might be sought in exploration and colonization, which would be tentative, gradual and cumulative. Given the lack of administrative context, it would also have to be ad hoc and freelance, the product of uncoordinated adventure. While this is not an impossible scenario, historical analogies from later periods (e.g. Italian republics, Catalan and Elizabethan merchant companies) illustrate metropolitan initiative and post facto investment. More significant than either, however, was the background of accumulated report and cartographic experiment, efforts that envisaged utopian projects and pinpointed uncharted terrain.[123] For an Iron Age of Discovery only Herodotus and the Homeric Odyssey could be adduced, and that at least conveys the elements of both adventure and orbit.

A *further analogy* would be the 9th century Vikings, raiders with an appropriate technology (longship) and some experience of commerce in the Baltic, Black and Caspian seas.[124] For these, however, commodities can be identified (furs and slaves) and destinations must seem deliberate: in the East Constantinople and Baghdad, in the West Lindisfarne, London and Rouen. That they were not only raiders may be inferred from the movement of silver coinage from east to west across northern Europe, exhibiting a trade network into which Viking mobility was neatly inserted. Norman colonization was a secondary development that issued in the conquest and settlement of territories as far flung as Iceland, England and Sicily. Now, insinuation into an established system is admittedly different from creating one, and it has been suggested that Phoenician expansion westward was the result of attraction to an Atlantic trade in metals (silver and tin).[125] The proposition is reasonable, although evidence for the distribution of these items in the central and eastern Mediterranean is meagre. Entirely absent from the syndrome is witness to the process of exchange: the commodities carried west by Phoenician traders. Such artifacts as have been found attest rather to colonial enterprise: establishment of communities, symbiosis, possibly participation in local economies, in short, to a Levantine/Aegean presence in the west. A conventional distinction between Greek agricultural settlements and Phoenician industrial "factories" cannot really be sustained: Phoenician residue on the Iberian coast from Almuñecar to Malaga is located precisely at the mouths of rivers whose rich alluvial soil still supports flourishing agriculture. The Viking-Norman model is thus just feasible: comprehensive direction of the enterprise is not visible.

The significance of a putative Atlantic industry for the extension of a Levantine/Aegean system will be readily conceded. Even without interstitial detail, the concept of structural expansion commends itself to historical interpretation. Where short-term, often impromptu, tactics cannot be discerned, recourse to long-term strategies and/or systemic development is an intellectual comfort. Some such paradigm as a "field of force" model is clearly welcome (see above). A plausible juncture for perception of the Mediterranean as an *integrated spatial system* would be the Roman conquest of Corinth and Carthage (146 BCE). At the threshold of empire, space was convergent: an expanding centre of order and symmetry contrasted with a receding periphery of chaos and savagery. In Latin imperial literature both Phoenician and Greek were relegated to the position of deservedly eliminated adversary.[126] Integration was achieved by the imposition of conventional uniformities: currency, metrology, cartography, a legal code and, as far as practicable, language. By such means labour, wealth and transaction costs could be regionally and comparatively calculated. The allocation of resources, division of labour and distribution of commodities (e.g. cereals and building materials) became possible on a scale of which the primary aim was *structural balance*.[127] The mechanics of empire are visually accessible in the several projects of cadastral mapping (Corpus Agrimensorum), of principally fiscal intention but also a contribution to political and intellectual control.[128] Even more significant in this latter respect was the production of imperial cartography: maps (Agrippa and Octavian) and itineraries (Antonine) to demonstrate a familiar network of physical control.[129] Time and distance could be measured for the movement of material and men, and these data hardly altered for well over a millennium.[130] A converse interpolation of them into the millennium preceding Roman hegemony ought probably to be resisted. Mediterranean topography is only apparently a constant: its employable dimensions must vary with technology. Byzantine and Islamic appropriation of the imperial legacy may have been territorially incomplete but was otherwise neatly derivative.

Amongst the many examples of technological continuity would be the design and locomotion of ships, the construction and layout of harbours, drydocks and storage facilities, the extraction of surpluses from an essentially agrarian economy, the dual role of the state as entrepreneur and principal consumer, its functions as patron of urban development and prosecutor of warfare, as custodian of routes and records. Management of space was largely a *regalian prerogative*. There were exceptions: climatic and demographic fluctuation followed independent curves, though compensation for troughs could become an affair of state. Somewhat different were the items of modified technology, like credit transactions, marine insurance, and the commenda (joint-venture), of private inspiration but capable of implementation only in the context of regalian space. Merchant

law (i.e. the 8th century Nomos Rhodion Nautikos) and chancery procedure were similarly areas in which innovation constituted return on capital originally invested by the state. In the
eastern empire even guilds owed their vitality to managerial
concern for industrial standards (i.e. the 10th century Ep-
archikon Biblion). Now, it can be (and has been) argued that the
primary feature of an imperial system is accommodation of a
redistributive economy, and that proper commercial exchange
is only generated by political fragmentation. A corollary would
be that imperial economy is essentially colonial and based upon
ecological complementarity, both natural and induced (e.g. the
planned allocation of industrial processing for specific natural
resources). If it is true that Roman trade seldom transgressed
its political perimeter (an exception was India), the same can
hardly be said of the Byzantine and Islamic empires. Each had
inherited the administrative technology of Rome but neither its
monopoly of space. The shortfall was made up by elaboration
of diplomacy: formal correspondence, embassies, and commercial treaties that regulated matters of supply, tariff, contraband
and exterritorial jurisdiction. To the bureaucratic burden of
chancery practice was added an intercultural and polyglot
dimension in which acknowledgement of borders was explicit.
That this was not quite a return to ancient Near Eastern tradition
is because a *framework* for Mediterranean communication was
now in place.

Alteration of its components has assumed symbolic value
with the epithet "Middle Ages".[131] Reconstitution lay in the
plane of "histoire événementielle", visible chiefly in political
and linguistic data. Concomitant shift in the socio-economic
infrastructure is less easily discerned, but may be inferred from
the kind of documentation increasingly available for the period
beginning with the 8th century. The material is *archival*, the
records of daily business and, unlike the chronicle, ode or
rhetorical treatise, neither pedagogical nor addressed to posterity. The genre is ancient: from the Early Bronze Age ledger,
exhibiting what is possibly the origin of notation, to the dispositive formulations of the medieval chancery, the crucial feature
was introduction of juridical expression and effect. The utterance of law could be merely programmatic or genuinely regu-
lative; reference and retrieval required a storage facility, secure
but accessible. The institutional history of the archive must

draw upon both law and architecture: there are private as well as public ones, but the concept of repository common to both is essentially acknowledgement of the written record as paradigm for the conduct of business and diplomacy.[132] Since the quantity (and quality) of such documentation varies considerably across time and space, the trajectory of international law is not so easily traced. Between the truculent recriminations of the Amarna correspondence and the petitions of Venetian merchants in Alexandria there is a world of difference, derived from recognition of a conventional code of responsibility and obligation that might on occasion be breached but was at least known and accepted as standard behaviour. Now, whether this *koine* emerged from, or itself dictated, the lexicon of international relations is one of those many and vexing sociological problems to which solutions, as I have regularly conceded, tend to reflect preconceptions if not prejudice. Such elements of the code as the laws governing shipwreck and salvage, security of person and property, and collective jurisdiction seem to reflect a general principle that need not be read as the product of diffusion. And yet, the territorial contiguity achieved by Rome might be thought to have contributed to the conceptual fabric of a koine, whatever its ultimate sources.

Like the Mosaic tablets, the Decemviral code was from the outset inscribed. Even in the light of cuneiform analogies (Bilalama, Lipit Ishtar, Hammurabi), Roman assertion of that mode is of some significance for linking social order with the scriptorium. Subsequent articulation of Ius Gentium and Ius Naturale would extend the imagery to lend imperial accommodation to any legal contingency, however remote from the original Ius Civile. It was the juridical facet of territorial conquest and guaranteed at least formal symmetry. That the process should be attended not only by an abundant literature of jurisprudence (responsa), but also by a variety of chancery expressions (instrumenta) designed to fix the terms of political and economic intercourse must seem both logical and tidy. It was when Roman law could properly be termed a legacy that these began to proliferate, response to a circumstance in which Ius Gentium was no longer an internal affair.

Acknowledgement of the legacy was general but discrete. As in the case of Babylonian law, similarity of format and identical phraseology weigh in favour of diffusion from one or several archetypes, though terms like "justice" and "equity" might seem to exhibit an abstract concept of Ius Naturale.[133] But whatever its origin, and appeal to authority, Roman law was consigned to writing, and thus generated the vocabulary of chancery usage. I am thus inclined to interpret the medieval koine as *specifically juridical* and as the motive for a spatial organization that can be located and dated. The administrative input had to be, and was, prodigious. In the history of the Mediterranean it was also sui generis, for all its dependence upon Greek philosophy and Carthaginian technology. Elusive are the quantification of men and material involved, the tolerable margin of error in calculating time and distance, the perception of change. Conventional analysis posits Actium (31 BCE) as point of no return in the historical progression, a reading of the record that identifies strategy with opportunity. But Romans were neither Phoenicians nor Vikings; they did not merely occupy, but created the space for their operations. In the event, subsequent and piecemeal fission did not annul the achievement.

Roman commerce was essentially, if not exclusively, mercantilist. State ownership of mineral resources and long distance transport, a standing army and an alienable labour force, supply led price fluctuation, and a timocratic political system would seem to indicate an economic structure of regalian design. On the other hand, taxation was not restrictive nor were payments for municipal office (summa honoraria) excessive, which suggests ample interstitial space for entrepreneurial initiative and private accumulation of wealth.[134] Because labour was so cheap, industrial and transport costs can appear almost negligible, a likely distortion owing to the paucity of records. Trace of what could be read as market forces are visible in state encouragement of population growth (by means of alimenta) to stimulate new productivity or, not quite so clearly perhaps, in contracts for the building and manning of ships. Explicit in the material analysed by Duncan-Jones is increased consumption (ratio of dedicated municipal monuments of private wealth); unfortunately only implicit is the similarly increased opportunity for reinvestment, which however must be inferred from the growth curve of the early Principate. It must also seem that a result, indeed aim, of Roman administrative rationalization (provincial nomenclature and hierarchy, allocation of privilege and responsibility) was the emergence of *contract* as the means to status. Advancement, both projected and achieved, could be calculated, by individuals as well as by the state. When they arose, occasions could be seized; if they did not, they could be staged. A fair catalogue of opportunity can be seen in the letters of the philanthropic senator Pliny, whose career in property speculation and moneylending enabled him to amass and bequeath a sizeable fortune.[135] Contractual arrangements lent legitimacy to a spectrum of conduct that enabled economic expansion on a scale that benefited both individual and polity. If that was not quite new (Athenians and Carthaginians, after all, had "constitutions"), the Roman version represents a quantitative exploitation of resource and opportunity hitherto unmobilized.

The juridical basis of that mobilization will be described in chapter 2. Its economic components, or "market ingredients", are of course discretely attested from the earliest period of literacy/numeracy. But from evidence of accounting procedures one could as easily construct a redistributive system as one could a market economy. Arrangements for storage and transport, allocations of land (e.g. tenancy) and labour (e.g. contractual slavery), subventions (e.g. credit or franchise), and formation of price (equivalency) represent the mechanics of any economic system, regardless of agency or motive. It is with the appearance of such items as fluctuating interest rates, currency and coinage, negotiable shares, suretyship and distraint, and the alternatives: sale, lease and rental for land and labour, that one is justified in suspecting the operation of something other than politically or socially determined production and consumption. The very evidence of long distance (!) transport of industrial surpluses (e.g. copper, tin, textiles, glass, faience) might be read as the investment of venture capital and the assumption of risk. Even if these do not identify agent, the profit motive is clear, as is also the unavoidable hostage to fortune. Now, with the abundant references to "marketplace", cost calculation and damage limitation, the ancient, classical and medieval economies can hardly be described as the product of political regulation or of a collective concern for social equilibrium. Inclination to do so has to some extent been dictated by the provenance of archival materials (e.g. temple and palace) from which the direction of a state enterprise may be inferred. The growing perception, however, of individual initiative and, more important, of commercial transactions patient of explanation by "market" formulae has brought considerable refinement to the conventional picture.[136]

The investment essential to production of an industrial surplus (i.e. plant and training) might alone suggest a prospect of remuneration; freight overland (or water) would be an additional cost recoverable only by foreknowledge (or empirical conjecture) of sale value at destination. For Roman management of Mediterranean production and distribution, the necessary data would have been anyway available, already calculated for logistic and fiscal purposes. In other words, it was the *established linkage* that provided incentive. While statistics are hard won and often unreliable, analysis of Roman movement in cereals has suggested to one historian that its bulk (i.e. approximately two-thirds, after deducting the fiscal portion = tribute) was available for sale, to individual buyers or, for that matter, to the state.[137]

Location of the *marketplace* has, after all, not proved so difficult.[138] Its mechanics and, perhaps especially, its radial effect can also be calculated. The primary function is information storage: supply and demand, price, brokerage and freight costs, but also forecast were amongst the data on a communication circuit that might include extensive areas of potential resource and custom. The attendant imagery is relay and orbit, of which a network would in due course constitute a spatial continuum.[139] Its temporal dimension, if not constant, is at least uniform, derived from the earliest records (e.g. Pliny) up to the 16th century (Marino Sanudo) and based on an average speed of 4.5 knots (favourable wind) to 1.5 (unfavourable).[140] The higher rate was more often achieved travelling east, but depended upon the precise route (e.g. open sea, coasting, island hopping) as well as the ship (size, load, rigging). In any case, the return journey could be reckoned as a standard cost factor, and eventually (12th century) such hazards as shipwreck, piracy and war insured against, effectively reducing the cost.[141] It was precisely such administrative devices that (more than) compensated for a nearly stagnant nautical technology (see above). Of these the most significant was the marketplace itself. As a focus of communication, it comprehended and largely stimulated development of all the procedures helpful to efficient contact, exchange and planning. Whether its origins are sought in cult centres (congregations) or toll collection points (vectigalia), the confluence of traffic and fact of assembly generated the data to be processed. The formation of supply: labour, commodities, services and other expertise was cumulative and continuously modified, as were report and rumour. A combination of informal gossip and formal registration would change shape and proportion according to distribution of membership and frequency of contact. Fairs (nundinae) could be calendrical or commemorative, markets weekly or daily or permanently in place.[142] Local authority would vary from region to region and in response to political change.

Now, as ad hoc assembly the marketplace is attested at least two millennia before the onset of imperial Rome.[143] If its earliest designations did not also include a general concept of economic behaviour, the historical problem is one of tracing lexical extension by way of metaphor.[144] Etymology is of limited value in such exercises: for Akkadian bābu (gate), bābtu (precinct), sūqu (street), maḫāzu (cult centre), and kāru (quay) "meanings" are less important than referents. Reification of maḫiru (transaction: cf. Latin merx) has an analogy in Arabic matjar (commerce emporium) and qayṣariyya (a calque of Greek: regalian warehouse). With the possible exception of kāru, West Semitic cognates of the Akkadian terms exhibit comparable extension, e.g. Ugaritic maḫādu (harbour) and Arabic sūq (market). It is, however, East Semitic kāru (Sumerian KAR) that from the first displays most of the characteristics of "market", e.g. mooring place, harbour, trading station, merchant community, and commodity unit price, all of which generate a semantic proximity to maḫīru (Sumerian KI.LAM).[145] The kāru(m) could fix dates, keep accounts, and control the movement of commodities. Its corporate nature is evident in references to assembly, settlement of disputes, rendering of verdicts, dealing with correspondence, debts and credits, admission and exclusion of merchants, the levy of dues, taxes and interest. The image is of a commercial system already sophisticated to an extent that makes difficult an historical reconstruction of its constituent parts.[146] For Mesopotamia at least, tracing the formalization of ad hoc arrangements for market transactions is a matter of transfer rather than development. Like the Classical agora, the kāru(m) was an urban phenomenon of which locus and sanction, indeed perception (e.g. "temple" vs "palace", see above) might vary from place to place and time to time. Its machinery was undoubtedly durable, prey only to excessive political intervention.

Diffusion westward may be illusory: the mechanisms of marketplace hardly require a single origin. But a steadily expanding network of (especially Syrian) archaeological sites together with attestations of Akkadian as lingua franca must confirm an impression of extensive and intensive contact. Its chronology is notoriously patchy, as is its linkage (see above). Such nodes on the Bronze Age map as Mari, Kaniś and Hattusa, Ebla, Alalakh, Ugarit and Byblos are in a sense historical enclaves, as is, for all that has been written, Alaśiya. Iron Age documentation generates a denser grid, at least as far west as Egypt and the Aegean. A fair proportion of that witness is to military contact, which would influence but hardly eliminate commerce. The appearance in Assyrian sources of Aramaeans (1112 BCE: Tiglath-Pileser I) and of Arabs (853 BCE: Shalmaneser III), initially as adversaries, eventually as clients, indicates not merely extension of Mesopotamian statecraft, but also the proliferation of routes, adoption of a new technology (camel transport), and reformulation of the political map of Syria. While commercial records are admittedly exiguous, the Assyrian foundation of Levantine kāru must reflect transfer or adaptation of established procedures.[147] From the later campaigns of Chaldean and Achaemenid rulers, attested by recent excavations in northwest Arabia and Aramaic inscriptional evidence, further diffusion might be inferred via Dumah, Tema' and Dedan.[148] At least the latter two sites reveal traces of an "urban" marketplace. The gradual appearance of Aramaic as lingua franca, sharing for a time that function with Akkadian, was of course not an exclusively Mesopotamian legacy, and its Syrian origins might well represent another commercial tradition. The specifically Arabian residue (Lihyānite, Minaean, Thamūdic) at these sites (including Jebel Ghunaym) may be read as the incorporation of new elements in a pattern of exchange, or at least movement, between Mesopotamia and Egypt.[149] The chronology is uncertain but probably prior to Nabataean mobilization of caravan routes.

A millennium earlier at Ugarit, evidence of a marketplace points, not surprisingly, to the harbour.[150] A single attestation (RS 20.123 v.21') of the lexical equivalence kāru: maḫādu is hardly an historical phenomenon, though occurrence of the latter as toponym and gentilic in the context of mercantile behaviour would seem to support a reference to "market". Admittedly opaque is the nature of transaction there: despite documentation of officeholders, buyers and sellers, a fair range of commodities including real estate, of weights, measures and prices, and of contracts and witnesses thereto, the machinery of negotiation is not perspicuous. Reference to foreign parts and alien gentilics, arrangements for extradition and indemnity of strangers, shipbuilding and maritime law, suggests a system both flexible and sophisticated. It must also have generated prosperity, for the remains of Ugarit are culturally and architecturally impressive. Some evidence of corporate entities, joint ventures, third party funding, and fiscal perception and/or exemption must exhibit a context characterized by mobility and opportunity. Regulation of all these factors is mostly ascribed to state supervision, a paradigm easily accessible in histories of the Bronze Age. But alternative exegeses have begun to appear, and it may, I think, be safely said that the terminology of Ugaritic commercial documents does not require a regalian interpretation.[151] Nor does their substance: of the commodities traded only metals (gold, silver, copper, tin, bronze) appear not to be of local provenance, and hence indicative of wider contacts.[152] Even a rudimentary notion of balance of payments would of course involve export and thus production of surpluses. It is in the juridical documents that the concept of international relations, and of central authority, emerges with some clarity. Combined with references to construction and maintenance of a fleet (a distinction between military and merchant is not clear), these might seem to indicate matters of state, at least of subvention and of jurisdiction.[153] Despite mention of such officeholders as mlk ("king"), šakinu ("governor"), and šībūtu ("elders"), a particular form of government is not readily apparent. Prosopographical data are meagre and recurrent figures too few to flesh out a managerial structure. A "kingdom" is of course possible, but only with the qualifications appropriate to Canaanite usage.[154] Something along the lines of a merchant oligarchy is also possible as in late medieval Venice or Lübeck. But however plausible the analogy, and it has some merit, the distance thence to a description of Greek and Phoenician expansion is considerable.

Lack of continuity may be, as I have suggested, nothing more than a product of the historical residue: neither epic poetry nor commemorative inscription nor archaeological site can generate the imagery contained in archival documents.[155] As it happens, those segments of history before the modern period that have been constructed from archives exhibit a random density pattern. While the lacunae can be, and have been, filled from other kinds of source material, the agenda of economic and juridical history are not so susceptible of treatment by these. It would of course be irresponsible to infer from the lack of typical documentation the absence of such activity, but perhaps not so to guess that verbal arrangements might suffice for simple, local and short-term transactions. Since, however, the converse produces a tautology (written records are evidence of complex, long-distance and long-term transactions which require writing), an argument from silence is hardly compelling. Nonetheless, I have mentioned one conspicuous surge in the volume of commercial records for the 12th century Mediterranean, at a time when that signalled an expansion, not merely the beginning, of international trade.[156] A similar, if not quite identical, phenomenon may be observed in northern Europe approximately a century later. The organizational impulse that drew the several strands of North Sea and Baltic commerce into a concentration at and around Lübeck has been attributed to the extended use of written records.[157] The Hansa was first and foremost an alliance of economic interests, based on an exchange of commodities that reflected to a large extent ecological complementarity (e.g. grain, wax and furs from the East, wine, salt and textiles from the West). But it was also a confederation of municipalities, based on similar civic structures and approximately equivalent technologies. The emergent framework of cooperation, which extended from London and Bruges to Reval and Novgorod, was a compound of commodity staple, colonial foundation and efficient communication. While the *archive component* must seem indispensable, it would have been as necessary to the municipality itself as to the commerce it conducted. The local administrative rationale it exhibits could thus generate a network of similar entities whose very existence would perpetuate the technology upon which it depended. An advantage of the Hanseatic model is its perspicuity: the evidence of Cologne in London, the foundation of Lübeck, and the eastward expansion of the Teutonic Order are documented in a way not available for what must have been a similar but earlier development in the Mediterranean. There, a confederation of complementary interests was not achieved, nor, indeed, central direction of a commercial enterprise. Instead, fragmentation of the Roman legacy resulted in several territorial zones intermittently at war and always competing for political and ideological control of an area not marked by sharp ecological distinctions. It was the imperial legacy itself that generated contact, traffic and exchange.[158] Transport was an Italian monopoly, also competitive but to some degree regularized with the Crusades and with Byzantine concessions. The archival deposit dates from the 11th century (the Golden Bull of 1082) but reflects a long Byzantine chancery tradition.[159] For the Crusader states Genoa, Pisa and Venice controlled not only the carrying-trade, but acquired commodity concessions and property rights (church and market) in every port (including Jerusalem) they helped to capture. In Alexandria and along the North African littoral they had to compete for the favour of Muslim rulers who managed to exploit that situation but not to free themselves from dependence upon Italian expertise. Save for certain raw materials (e.g. spices, resins, aromatics and pearls from the East; copper, silver, tin and coral from the West), the bulk of exchange consisted in manufactures (e.g. textiles, soap and paper) exhibiting a differential in industrial techniques that had less to do with the source of materials than with economic organization.[160] The role of the state as entrepreneur tends to be overstressed, owing to the very archival residue that illustrates the extent of administrative technology: official collections have a higher survival rate than private ones. It is thus that an archaeological accident generates an impression of state regulation that may seldom have extended beyond fiscal interest. That alone would of course have been sufficient to ensure record of the activity as such, but hardly its motive and mechanism. These were common to all the Italian participants, whose enterprise lacked however the coordination and dirigisme of the Hansa (concordia domi foris pax). Neither set of circumstances would be able to survive the massive political shifts of the 16th century.

Now, urban geographers dealing with such themes as centre, periphery and settlement pattern naturally include networks and occasionally even "orbits".[161] While employment of the latter term for *polynuclear framework* does not quite correspond to my use of it for cultural feedback, there is a shared notion of interaction and interdependence: the nucleus functions only in a larger context.[162] Gottmann traces to Athenian dispute in the 4th century BCE a distinction between the enclosed community: isolated, self-sufficient, secure and, above all, stable; and one exposed to contact, access and, above all, opportunity. For that time and place, contact was largely maritime and opportunity conquest or colonization, culminating in concepts of sovereignty, jurisdiction and, where necessary, alliance. That it was not always thus can be shown by reference to Assyrian imperialism in the first half of that millennium (see above), and that it would not always be so by the example of Rome after Actium. There is nonetheless in the rejection of Platonic isolationism a paradigm for acknowledgement of the "orbital polis". That was probably a state of mind before it became a factor in city planning, i.e. disregard for security and an eye for opportunity. On the ground, it would constitute the city-state or what came to be called a maritime republic. Spatial organization was less a matter of fixing boundaries than of acquiring spheres of influence. For some there would be no choice: neither of Gottmann's Aegean examples, Bronze Age Thera and Iron Age Delos, is conceivable except as embedded in a network of similar constituents. Boundaries were here anyway fixed.[163] For coastal settlements incorporation of the hinterland might be an option, but mostly at the risk of reduced autonomy in the area of political decisions. In the event of integration into an imperial framework, freedom of action would be entirely lost, but a degree of security and probably prosperity guaranteed. For the post-Roman Mediter-

ranean evidence of urban autonomy is late but impressive.
Between 1133 and 1508 there are eleven instances of Christian
and Muslim commercial ports in treaty relationship: Pisa-
Bougie (1133), Pisa-Valencia (1149), Genoa-Valencia (1149),
Pisa-Tunis (1157), Genoa-Majorca (1181), Pisa-Majorca (1184),
Pisa-Ceuta (1201), Genoa-Granada (1278), Venice-Tripoli/Jer-
ba (1356), Venice-Granada/Malaga (1400) and Venice-Bādis
(1508).[164] If these may be taken to represent fragmentation of the
Umayyad Caliphate in Spain and quasi-imperial powers (Al-
moravid and Almohad) in North Africa, Levantine politics
appear to have been less flexible: manifestations of urban
autonomy in Tyre, Tripoli, Aleppo and Damascus during the
11th and 12th centuries are not expressed as agencies of independent negotiation with foreign powers.[165] The imperial tradition based on Egypt proved impenetrable, even during the
period of the Crusades.[166] During the subsequent Ayyubid
restoration and Mamluk hegemony trading concessions emanated only from Cairo or a viceroy in Damascus with the
attendant bureaucracy and delays characteristic of imperial
machinery.[167]

Evolution of the polynuclear framework towards the territorial integrity of empire admits of several explanations, of
which the most simple is probably political. The dividend
would be an illusion at least of increased control from the centre
over the periphery, and the cost an enhanced administrative
input necessary to sustain this. Against that must be weighed
such economic factors as procural of materials and monopoly of
markets, both of which could, depending on distance and time,
constitute a saving. But these are variables and notoriously
unstable. It is questionable whether extension of political
power generates economic profit. A case much analysed but
unresolved is that of Arabian trade at the dawn of Islamic
history.[168] Traditional exegesis makes commercial prosperity in
the Ḥijāz the dominant cause of social dislocation provoking
remedies of the sort proclaimed by the new religion. Admittedly, that is an unadorned rendering but captures most of the
argument by postulating a causal sequence from putative injus-
tice to promised relief. That this all too familiar nexus should
satisfy neither the economist nor the historian of religion is
hardly surprising. The interest of the case lies in its contrast

with Nabataean trade, to which I have above alluded. That enterprise prospered and survived by means of clientship then absorption into the Roman territorial network, where in due course its character was effaced. The Ḥijāzī version generated its own network which eventually absorbed a major segment of its Roman model. Reasons for that development were not exclusively economic nor certainly religious. Quest for a prime factor has anyway been for some time unfashionable and was surely always unrealistic. For the Ḥijāzī complex one has begun either at Mekka, the historiographical (!) origin of Islam and as ancient sanctuary appropriate context for the initiating theophany, or from an imperial (Byzantine-Sassānid) perimeter encompassing a network of trade routes that intersect the Arabian peninsula. In electing the former one is soon ensnared by the very sources being interrogated: Islamic versions of pre-Islamic events. In electing the latter one is soon embarrassed by the absence of explicit links between the perimeter and its putative epicentre (Mekka). Evasions of both dilemmas are abundantly documented and mostly involve extension/relocation of either the centre or the perimeter. Thus, the most recent exegesis proposes either placing Mekka in northwest Arabia or attributing to it a calculated strategy for attaining rank as "port of trade" in the imperial network.[169] While certainly imaginative and fairly documented, these solutions exhibit a kind of desperation, understandable to anyone familiar with this field of study. Now, in the interests of orbital patterns and spatial analysis, it might be suggested that the emergence of Mekka was the explosive result of *technological stockpiling.* Such devices as the bilateral contract (īlāf), amphictyony (ḥums), calendrical adjustment (nasī'), writing (kitāba), and sanctuary custody (sidāna) were inaugurated, distributed and accumulated to exceed a threshold of informal containment. Mobilization of these resources, all attested in local data, post facto and admittedly invested with a sacral dimension characteristic of Islamic materials, would trigger an independent network, also local but bound sooner or later to make contact with other systems of communication. These might well be vestiges of earlier (or still?) prosperous trade routes, now renewed by fresh input. That would make the process one of basically quantitative increase, generated by the pressure of spatial constraint. But there are other possibilities. To the Mekkan syndrome was added a colonial dimension, of which the components are enshrined in that remarkable document known as the "Constitution of Medina".[170] Provisions for partnership and alliance are developed round such concepts as clientship (jiwār), security (amān), treaty (ṣulḥ), arbiter (maradd), jurisdiction (dīn), contract (dhimma) and solidarity (umma). The collective force of these was primarily territorial and political, but presupposed an economic infrastructure that enabled payment of maintenance (nafaqa), bloodwit (ma'qula) and ransom (fidya). Sources of income were initially commercial (tijāra) and fiscal (fay'/khums/'ushr), augmented in due course by territorial acquisition, e.g. Yathrib, Khaybar and Fadak, and the means of industrial production.

All this is admittedly hypothetical and requires, first, extrapolation from the evangelical imagery in which it has been transmitted and, second, assent to a tableau of Ḥijāzī society in which noone was stationary, at least for long. The patterns of movement are largely the product of tribal structures, not only in the standard transhumant mode, but in constantly forming and re-forming alliances of kinship, common and vested interests in land and connecting routes, ecological reciprocity, political alignment, temporary allegiance by service (e.g. as tax collectors, transport consortia, mercenary brigades), and more permanently in the hierarchies of family, clan and confederation.[171] One impressively analysed instance is the territorial spread and socio-economic network of B. Sulaym: the sum of toponyms, eponyms and interstitial links provides a tight grid of Ḥijāzī space.[172] If it is difficult to imagine that this was not always so, it is also possible to read it as a sociological feature of the terrain and conditioned as much by physical geography as by the perennial human condition. On the other hand, mobility and motion of that compass could persist forever without coalescing in the polity known to history as Islam. To explain that remarkable phenomenon, one might be inclined to seek a version of the "multiplier effect": a measure of systemic dislocation that generates growth.[173] As is well-known, that particular model was extrapolated from the distribution of artifacts for a period innocent of literary witness. Its application to Arabia in the 6th and 7th centuries, when such was abundant if not always perspicuous, may appear contrived but can be justified by reference to spatial and behavioural constants, e.g. landscape as symbiotic zone, livelihood as competition, contact as imperative. Equilibrium (a theoretical baseline only) would be disturbed by intersecting networks of communication, extension of territorial rights, accumulation of surpluses, and modified lines of kinship (to name but a few). Interference is a component of the system, which is why the baseline (equilibrium) is hypothetical. The gradual or, for that matter, sudden acquisition of a new dimension, responsibility or commitment would require adjustment of the existing structure which could result in collapse (catastrophe) but as readily in growth (anastrophe).[174] "Growth" is perhaps not quite correct, since the model is predicated on *discontinuity*, i.e. transformation effected by the function of variables (authority/anarchy or centrality/marginality) themselves a product of interaction. That these should in perspective be depicted as charisma, cohesion, or a conscious mission is of course inevitable, and belongs properly to the reflexive exegesis of most documentation.

A perception of space as *demanding* at least traverse and, if possible, occupation is hardly wayward. If that is itself the motive, identification of agent and mode is almost secondary, but of obvious historical interest. The conquest of space is seldom permanent acquisition, especially as a political statement, but can and does persist as literally (!) local tradition, of which one dimension might be designated as cumulative technology. That very little is ever irretrievably lost can be captured in a kind of metabolic image, in which waste (oblivion) includes only inessentials. I acknowledge the circularity inherent in that proposition (i.e. waste becomes inessential), but would recall the accumulation of dead reckoning, rhumb lines and mathematics that produced the 13th century portolan (see above), a spatial conquest in the event never relinquished. Now, the orbit is cumulative in two dimensions and helical in its third, which allows for accumulation (stacking) over time. Here, the image is one of *continuity*, and not quite adequate to explanation of the historical record, which is the product of selectivity, a varying span of attention and, above all, caducity.[175] Models are the standard substitute for patchy documentation and of proven heuristic value in the construction of sequence and narrative syntax.

Interaction models are conventionally based on a pre-sumed "difference of potential", a factor that can only be hypothetical and is mostly post hoc. In terms of centre and periphery, a further (traditional and often tacit) assumption identifies the former as source of action and point of control, the role of the latter being responsive or merely passive. The Ḥijāzī phenomenon would seem to controvert this view, as does the evidence of ancient Chinese and Roman history.[176] The fact that Arabia and Central Asia could be (to some extent) occupied as well as traversed might distinguish those regions from the Mediterranean, where basins enclosed, however partially, and a fair number of insular clusters correspond to the staging posts of overland movement. *Direction would be less important than movement itself*, enabled by the sum of contiguous points. Whatever the pace, and as I have several times suggested, that varies according to commodity, its point of generation can be calculated by source, target and local technology. The conjuncture of these is "peripheral" only in the sense that target must be different from source and hence (possibly) a "centre" of some other (distant) aggregate. The image is one of overlapping and telescoped systems, in which "centre" is movable and more likely to be not the origin but the aim of movement. Centrality is anyway a geometric and abstract concept; in cartography and on the ground it must become topological.[177] Its application to the locus of policy formulation can be a misnomer if it must also retain a semantic opposition to "periphery". It is probably true, as Strassoldo suggests, that the dyad is best restricted to polit-ical forms. Economic and technological systems are seldom contained within so obvious a framework.

Earlier conjunctures are more difficult to fix, in both time and space. For transport, innovations in nautical design like skeletal construction and the fore-and-aft rig may seem late or post-Roman in the Mediterranean, but are in fact widely dis-persed.[178] A distinction between Phoenician and Greek ship-building techniques can be maintained, but not actually traced back beyond the early Iron Age.[179] Admittedly, that might be far enough, especially if neither of those seafaring nations can be attested in the western Mediterranean before mid-eighth century BCE. Both the prevailing wind (westerly) and the colonial character of archaeological sites would seem to favour a lateen rig and the beamier Phoenician galley, of which neither can be supplied with a Bronze Age pedigree. But the considerable evidence of earlier marine movement in the Aegean and Levant has got to be calculated in a reckoning of cumulative technology: while this will hardly support an argument for continuity (!), it is sufficient to show a distinct development of local types.[180] These were still clear at Salamis (480 BCE) and were probably not effaced until well into the Hellenistic period. Greco-Roman refinement of the older skin construction with multiple mortise and tenon joints provided as much strength as the later skeletal principle, and allowed for the increased beam and bulk attested in bills of lading and numerous salvaged shipwrecks. The technique itself, however, is earlier: its exploitation to produce larger hulls would reflect the requirements of expanded commerce.[181] In other words, a time-lag in the historical record may be read as independent of progress in marine technology. It was not a single factor but rather the conjuncture of several that might generate activity on an increased scale or even of a different kind. Bulk haulage would, for example, become a major cost with Roman incorporation of the Egyptian grain market after Actium (31 BCE).[182]

Since the mortised carvel design is now attested fourteen centuries earlier, it would hardly be unreasonable to seek evidence of some practical application, even on a conjectural timescale. Transport of such commodities as grain and timber certainly, copper and oil possibly, would require substantial hulls. Of some sixty (published) tablets from Ugarit having to do with long distance trade, and hence freight arrangements, only a dozen or so specify ships by type, number or cost.[183] From these we learn the designations anyt, ṭkt and br (UT 319, cf. UT 2057, UT 2085), the terms for "crew" (UT 83: ṣbu) and "shipwright" (UT 170: ḥrś anyt), that vessels could be bought or leased (UT 2008, UT 2106, UT 2123), that there was contractual exemption from the lex naufragi (UT 2059), and that fleets could be outfitted and commissioned (UT 2061, UT 2062). Construction is elusive: a consignment of parts (spr npṣ any) is inventoried in one text (RS 20.008) and may well include "rudder" (mṭṭ) "anchor" (mślḥ), "sail" (mṣpt), "hatch" (ḥrk), "mast" (trn), "hawser" (ḫbl) and "gangway" (kpt̠), some of which are else-where attested together with as yet unidentified metal components (RS 19.26, 28, 46, 71, 107, 112, 115). Of size and mode of construction there is no evidence beyond the salvage of Gelidonya and Ulu Burun, as well as conjectural extrapolation from the weight of stone anchors found at Ugarit.[184] From the latter data one has calculated a length of 20 metres and a capacity of 200 tonnes for a thousand pound anchor, of which there are several, but also smaller ones, from 200 to 500 pounds. As it happens, that length is midpoint between the Gelidonya hull (9 metres) and that of a conjectural Phoenician trireme (36 metres).[185] From the anchor finds alone one might suppose that most of the fleet was less than 20 metres, and indeed, the often cited shipment of barley (SE.BAR) from Mukiš to Ura might well have filled two ships (200 kur = 450 tonnes).[186] Of other bulky cargos there is meagre record: timber (UT 1010, 1127), and oil (I.GIS) apparently to Cyprus (RS 20.168), but a weightier one like copper (UT 2056, 2101: t̠lt̠; RS 19.007: erû), apparently from Cyprus, would have required a substantial carrier.[187] From such terms as mt̠t̠ (rudder/oar?), trn (mast) and just possible mṣpt (sail?), one could infer that locomotion was a mixed exercise.[188]

Admittedly opaque, circumstantial evidence nonetheless suggests a level of maritime vitality consonant with the situation of seaboard and island communities not inclined to isolated existence. Although scrappy, that same evidence indicates mastery of the requisite technology some time before systematic expansion westward beyond the Aegean. Here, "systematic" must refer to the still controversial chronology of Greek and Phoenician movement west of Crete (see above). The scatter of Mycenean artifacts in Sicily, Malta, Ischia and the Italian mainland could indicate a longer period of preparation or at least experiment.[189] Though it is impossible to insist upon identity of producer and carrier, contact between Ugarit and Crete is attested only once (RS 16.238).[190] And the linkage might anyway be another: evidence of an intrusive material culture (bastions, tombs, and cult objects) has been found in the south of the Iberian peninsula and is datable to the second half of the third millennium BCE.[191] Similarities with Cycladic and Anatolian sites may suggest a nautical route, even the southern littoral by passing Italy and Sicily. From the Iberian material, which seems primarily colonial and for which there is no contemporary witness to maritime technology (Egyptian rivercraft must appear unlikely candidates), it is difficult to infer the notions of commodity and orbit. For the remarkable spread of Mycenean ware, especially in the eastern Mediterranean, neither is a problem, even if identification of the carrying-trade is. The often postulated contemporaneity of Mycenae with Ugarit rests upon a range of assumed synchronisms, not least of which was the terminal role of the Sea Peoples, emblem of a massive Völkerwanderung, of which causes and components may have been quite disparate. That much of it was seaborne, however, could have contributed to the development and diffusion of technology.[192] One notable consequence was "Phoenicia".

But that phenomenon was a by-product, not a target. Despite its basically destructive character, warfare can be remarkably inventive of goods and techniques ultimately applied to the management of peace. Examples are the catamaran and the (deck) cabin, devised to increase troop capacity and to provide protection for the ship's captain, respectively.[193] For these Hellenistic/Roman innovations diffusion would not signal difference of potential so much as fashion and proven utility. It was a matter of *experiment:* perfectly illustrated by the Arab occupation of ancient shipyards in Egypt and Syria.[194] There the local craft traditions were preserved or perpetuated, as is clear from the Arabic nautical lexicon. Modification, when it took place, was generated by Mediterranean technology, not by the fact of new political leadership: ṭarīda, for example, is a generic term for "vessel" and in Arabic at least might refer to any type from a galley to a cog.[195] Its use in Latin and the Romance vernaculars seems hardly more restrictive. Arab ship design in the Mediterranean conforms to that tradition, not to earlier Indian Ocean models.[196] Admittedly, Roman influence upon the latter, especially for the India trade, generated some uniformity of hull construction, but the traditional design of sewn planks persisted until the arrival of the Portuguese in the 16th century and even after. Rigging would be adapted to the route and, though it has not been conclusively demonstrated, the lateen was probably designed for the Red Sea and East Africa trade.

In the study of development a rigorous distinction between internally generated and externally provoked change is difficult if not impossible. A requisite technological level may be a necessary but not sufficient cause, and some other liminal, related only by contiguity (temporal or spatial), may have been the decisive factor in a new genesis. The key work is probably "conjuncture" (see above), analysis of which tends to be a *narrative of success.* But there is evidence, too, of failure, where technological achievement is not diffused. It may be simplistic to describe this difference in terms of "open" and "closed" systems, especially if the distinction does not help to identify the thresholds respectively cleared and unattained. I have adduced one such apparent contrast, in the difference between Ottoman and Mamluk reception of firearms.[197] Another was circumscription of the Cretan linear scripts contrasted with widespread diffusion of Akkadian cuneiform.[198] Since all share a combination of phonetic and ideographic, or at least logographic features, their transfer potential cannot have been too different.[199] Moreover, similarities in the notational (ledger) employment of Linear A and of Proto-Elamite cuneiform (Susa) might suggest a common approach to bookkeeping independent of the actual signs applied to the same writing material (clay).[200] To define a system as intrinsically and structurally "closed" is undoubtedly mistaken: the fragments of Cypro-Minoan found at Ugarit,[201] the linear hieroglyphic at Byblos,[202] and the not altogether dissimilar script at Deir 'Allā[203] might be thought to evoke a degree of permeability in systems generated by what was after all a common impulse. With the postulate of a genetic relation between Egyptian writing and the "proto-canaanite" inscriptions of Sinai no east Mediterranean system has been neglected.[204] All of this is merely to recall the scatter of experiment contemporary with the Levantine spread of Akkadian. Reconstruction of contact is of course frustrated by spatial lacunae and a notoriously conjectural chronology, down to and including the "Phoenician" alphabet.[205] Interpretation of the latter as final nexus has determined alignment of all putative precursors and a sequence that makes a syllabary logically prior to an alphabet. The alternative would be a random dispersion of local technologies with attendant starts, stops and reversals.

But choice of model ought not to be arbitrary. Some fit of script to the language for which it was originally devised must be discernible, as in the felicitous "agglutinating" for Sumerian ideograms.[206] And any successful transfer of technology ought to be mildly reflationary, producing a dividend visible at least to the technicians concerned. Thus observed, any syllabary, e.g. Linear A/B or Akkadian, might have been more than adequate to the morphology of a west Semitic language. So much cannot be said for the alphabetic principle, at any rate not in the Phoenician version as preserved. The elimination of vowel signs could be explained by appeal neither to redundancy nor efficiency, for the latter was only gradually and partially restored by the introduction of matres lectionis. What does seem clear is that the alphabet is easier to *write* than the many graphic systems with which it may for a time have competed. Essentially a notational shorthand, it is also easier to *learn,* as is, for example, Arabic than Ethiopic. Required in the case of Phoenician is ability to *extrapolate* sound from sign, a secondary learning procedure necessary even for a native speaker. In terms of cost, that additional input would have to be calculated against the effort of acquiring a complete syllabary, or worse, a set of ideograms demanding constant contextual exegesis. Shorthand based on a primarily CV syllable structure would reduce by a factor of four the number of signs to be learned, an advantage possibly greater than the correspondingly enhanced investment in grammar. The exercise is one of abstraction, not unlike the conversion of terrain to a set of cartographic symbols. Whatever else may be achieved, the graphic system is "opened" and capable of transfer, at least to languages of similar morphology.

For the *cuneiform* alphabet at Ugarit, where a perception of redundancy seems obvious, the concept of notational shorthand is still the operative factor.[207] The mode of writing was not altered: clay and stylus were retained but the number of impressions considerably reduced. As a chancery device for recording transactions quickly and easily, the innovation was very likely preceded by a period of experiment: some evidence is attested in efforts at syllabic Canaanite and alphabetic Akkadian. If the chronology is uncertain (1500 BCE?), the context is appropriate. Besides the environment of archive and scriptorium, the abundance of texts (*c*3000) demonstrates a degree of chancery activity that corresponds nicely with the maritime technology mentioned above. Identity of time and place must indicate an organisational impulse of some strength. Its transmission tapers to a point (12th century BCE) as close as could be to the earliest attestations of Phoenician linear.[208] That statement is not meant to imply an epigraphic genealogy, but rather, a southward shift of the generating centre. Plotting the field of energy input seems to me as important, if not more so, than accommodating the several lateral congeners (e.g. Serābīt al-Khādem, 'Izbet Ṣarṭah) of Phoenician script. Attempts to deduce the cuneiform alphabet from the latter sequence are not persuasive.[209] Nor is the chronology of Proto-Canaanite sufficiently assured to claim its priority to Ugarit.

Description of the alphabet as an "open" system is merely to acknowledge its historical diffusion. No intrinsic structural feature could have guaranteed its adaptation for Greek, Etruscan and Iberian. Persistence of the Cypriot syllabary down to the 3rd century BCE would suggest some tenacity in the face of what is most conveniently described as a wave-theory of dissemination.[210] The propelling factor was increased proximity generated by development in other technologies. Besides locomotion these included metallurgy (requiring assembly of raw materials from various sources) and ceramics (initiating experiment in design and finish), but above all bureaucracy (methods for information storage and retrieval), of which the primary expressions were fiscal and juridical. These provided the economic and political bases for exercise of authority. Whatever its source (monarchy, oligarchy or some variant) its application to the realia of everyday existence was only possible within the framework of routine administrative structures, themselves the product of written records. The Canaanite materials preserved at Ugarit demonstrate not merely a talent but also a capacity for organisation considerably in excess of that available for Phoenician commerce. Gottmann's paradigm (see above) of the "orbital polis" is indeed best illustrated not by Thera or Delos, but by Ugarit, where administrative input is both tangible and measurable. It happens also to be the earliest Mediterranean example.

It would not, I think, be mistaken to speculate that traverse of the entire Mediterranean was achieved in approximately that period, almost certainly not earlier than 1500 BCE. While archaeological finds in the West do not prove the participation of Levantine shipping, the wrecks at Gelidonya and Ulu Burun and the documentary evidence from Ugarit demonstrate the necessary technology. This is not only nautical but also organisational. However, the orbital image is not assured: neither momentum nor trajectory is perspicuous. The data so far assembled in this chapter could, if differently arranged, produce instead a helical image, compounded of movement through space *and* time. Viewed from above (diachronically) a spiral might resemble an orbit, but the illusion is a product of historical exegesis (see above). While not quite a disqualification, that view fails to identify a centrifugal force other than the technology itself. Or rather, "technologies": I have several times alluded to accumulation as the factor of propulsion, and that is merely to restate Renfrew's "multiplier effect" and anastrophe model. Unclear are the mechanics of networking and motive for the return journey. Even if the former is merely the density generated by accumulation, frequency of initiative, and habit induced by a string of successes, one might still wish to identify a tangible additive. The standard recourse is to *surplus* production and its ensuing disposal. That could of course as well be local consumption as removal to a distant place for exchange or sale. In the case of the latter one would suppose that surplus had been deliberately produced to precisely that end or something very like it. The copper ingots salvaged at Gelidonya and Ulu Burun would be an example. But whether the voyages were planned long distance transfers or cabotage is not clear, nor can it be from the further finds at the latter site: amphorae and other ceramics, glass ingots, ivory, gold, silver and bronze artifacts, faience beads and tin ingots permit a variety of readings, including (not at all impossible) a consignment of tribute or pirate plunder.[211] The latter might be thought to negate, or at least neutralise, the notion of planned surplus production, but would nonetheless illustrate commodities underway. A trace of habitual route is indicated by the two sites, but that for the time being must be regarded as fortuitous.

Quantification of such materials is anyway quite impossible, and without it relation to total production must be hypothetical. If the source of copper is likely to have been Cyprus, that of tin is less easily fixed. The transfer of raw materials points to distribution of industrial sites, indeed, but these may have catered only for local consumption. Manufactures, on the other hand, suggest a different motive which could as well be economic (trade) as political (tribute). There is in all this exegesis an unfortunate, if not unexpected, note of tautology and a reminder that a prime cause is elusive if not altogether non-existent. Familiarity with the eventual issue of these processes becomes a substitute for failure to discern their beginnings. The shipment of copper, for example, was still a feature of commercial treaties in the 16th century (not perhaps so much for production of alloys as for minting specie).[212] Provision for maritime loans, attested in Athens of the 4th century BCE, has a probable antecedent a millennium earlier at Ugarit, was incorporated in the Nomos Rhodion Nautikos (see above), and in the late Middle Ages (if not earlier : faenus nauticum) generated a form of marine insurance.[213] Over a period of time constants appear to exhibit genealogical traits that undoubtedly conceal disparate origins, different intentions and any number of false starts. In the related matters of credit, investment, and insurance an argument for linear development might be defensible in terms of social diffusion: from certainly opaque and mostly humble origins in Athens the emergence in 15th century Venice of a merchant class whose wealth and status depended precisely upon such transactions would seem to illustrate an almost logical sequence of entrepreneurial vigour. In order to develop, the technology required a multiplication of agents whose common interest sooner or later generated solidarity and social visibility.[214] The political implications, for Venice at least (i.e. composition of the Senate) though the phenomenon was not isolated, make it clear that the process was not simply additive. On the other hand, an unswerving lineal descent from, say, Athens (or even Ugarit) to Venice could not accommodate such lateral injections as from time to time impinged from the Islamic banking system. Modes of payment like the ṣakk (cheque) and suftaja (draft) were not of course Muslim innovations, but owed their wide dissemination in the medieval Mediterranean to Arabic speaking merchants.[215] More sophisticated financial procedures like the ḥawāla (credit transfer) and qirāḍ (limited liability investment) may well exhibit innovation, especially the latter, as putative precursor of the Italian commenda.[216] But like the alleged Islamic origins of procuratio, to which I alluded at the beginning of this chapter, the possibility of interference in the evolution of commenda would seem to require an *inter-national* context where imperial unity had been dissolved into regional autonomies.[217] That such was so is a matter of record: transactions involving different

currencies (themselves clear political statements) would provoke a mechanism for credit transfer (bill of exchange), or
different practices (the inevitable persistence of local traditions), a concept of territorial jurisdiction and the resulting
need for devices to ensure *exterritorial* status. These, nicely
encapsulated in the term safeconduct, include all the basic
components of what was eventually recognised as international
law.

Now, these several strands do not make a plait. Indeed,
the major catalyst in most of the technological developments I
have adduced was fragmentation: a condition of dispersed
energies, insights and materials. Their eventual composition as
identifiable techniques is most satisfactorily related to an inclusive *framework* of some kind, however hypothetical. This
might be territorial or social, economic or political, possibly all
of these at one time or other. But the likelihood of a unitary
framework that would accommodate, if not explain, all such
process is probably unrealistic. Even that vast construct called
the Roman Empire might not qualify: the complexity of Diocletian's tax reform, as Moses Finley reminds, was a result of
necessary local variations.[218] In fact, it is precisely that acknowledgement that makes his immediately preceding cleavage between "ancient Near East" and "classical antiquity" difficult to
accept, and especially as it appears to turn upon the respective
absence and presence of private ownership and enterprise.[219] It
is, after all, frontiers that generate symbiosis and innovation,
and these were/are in constant flux despite political decisions
to fix them. A feature common to the aforementioned technologies is *reduction of scale,* for which cartography itself provides
the appropriate image. Management of *space* is facilitated by
mapping, by plotting itineraries and calculating time underway. Space is also reduced by recourse to writing and concomitant dispensability of personal contact. Of that technique the
credit transaction and banking are but facets, and these, like
archival storage and information retrieval, can also reduce *time*
to at least provisional control. If these common denominators
seem simplistic, I should like nonetheless to insist upon their
effect in the organisation of experience and hence of activity by
its reduction to manageable tasks. The critical factor, then, is
scale.

Even if that were conceded to have been the collective result of technological development, questions about agency and incentive could still be posed. In what circumstances might such enterprise have been undertaken and prospered? Certainly not those, again according to Finley, that obtained in Classical Antiquity, a series of juridically defined consumer societies content to balance the books and utterly uninterested in such notions as efficiency and productivity.[220] That view, as is well-known, has generated just enough dispute to be called usefully provocative, and it may well be that the relevant political structures, say imperial Athens or Rome, did not encourage, or even make room for, entrepreneurial activity such as is attested for the city-states of northern Italy and the Baltic or Elisabethan England. But his "Ancient Economy" is a kind of torso: chronologically for selection of the period 100 BCE-500 CE and spatially for omission of the Semitic Levant. An additional disability, unfortunate but hardly the author's deed, is absence of the archival material that would illustrate such activity. Admittedly, Phoenician commerce is not better served (see above), but that is precisely why inclusion of the earlier period (1500-1000 BCE) and the archival residue of Ugarit might be thought of some practical value. Whatever the local character of the Roman Republic, the Principate incorporated, and thus inherited, a considerable legacy of commercial technology and business acumen. Assessment of its application can only be relative to data from earlier and later periods, and I have already commented on those figures pertinent to maritime routes: direction, distance and time. But in the matter of scale, these data are merely the most obvious.

And also deceptive, in that they supply only a forward (!) baseline for a millennium or so and no possibility of retrojective extrapolation. If regularity, e.g. the Ostia-Alexandria traverse, does generate a statistic (median = 57 days), it also evokes, and for the first time, an image of systematic application.[221] To interpret that image as evidence of a monolithic bureaucracy is tempting even in the light of known obstacles like variant fiscal procedures and demarcated currency zones.[222] Urban phenomena are the most persuasive: imperial cities planned, financed and governed on the model of Rome, of which emulation was a matter of prestige as well as of politics.[223] The debt to, say Athens, Carthage and Alexandria, can be sensed but not so easily measured, which is simply to concede that earlier patterns of contact were effaced by or comprehended in an inclusive orbit. Though its primary character was political and military, supporting an army and civil service in territorial occupation was an expense that quickly and far exceeded the immediate resources produced by plunder. The mechanism had to be an economic policy of some sort, by which a calculable surplus could be generated and distributed. An imaginative if also controversial model of such policy is available in the graphs and histograms of Keith Hopkins relating costs to taxes and the latter to trade surplus.[224] The key factor was taxation in money and acquisition of this through commercial profit in order to meet the tax demand. Novel was neither tax nor profit, of course, but the framework in which they interacted. Fiscal legislation was imperial, that is enacted at Rome, and affected territories from Britain to Arabia. Even without quantification, the fact of such regional heterogeneity centrally supervised and inventoried might be thought to transcend the local limits of subsistence economy. The higher consumption level of urban centres was hardly new, at least for the Mediterranean, but their linkage and multiplication must have generated an exponential increase in demand. That this should be met by commercial expansion rather than further conquest and/or plunder was undoubtedly a political, not an economic, decision. But once taken (Trajan in Parthia?), the obvious strategy would be productivity in excess of consumption. The preceding 1500 years indicate that this sector had never been limited to local transactions, and it was precisely these techniques that could be exploited. Hopkins' data on shipwrecks (art. cit. Fig.1) are mildly suggestive of enhanced movement, but fortuitously (!) skewed in favour of the western Mediterranean and probably reflect naval warfare rather than commerce. It is for the Levant that commercial sophistication is documented, though undoubtedly accessible also in the Punic colonies. Money supply (art. cit. Figs.2-4) could be read as a trade index, but also as a political gesture, e.g. commemorative coinage or as funding urban development. Whichever it might be, it is the distribution of hoards (Britain, Gaul, Germany, Balkans, Syria) that attests an imperial pattern of monetisation, even allowing for regional enclosures (Egypt?).[225] If that pattern happens to reflect

predominantly garrison settlement, it would still signal transactions of the sort that issue in commerce and eventually in the
transfer of specie. In an economic system virtually innocent of
credit arrangements the latter was inevitable.[226] Save for occasional reference to Egyptian grain, the tax-trade model does not
identify commodities. From literary sources one knows of
timber, marble, and other building materials, foodstuffs, wine
and olive oil, hides and textiles, artifacts: ceramic, amber, ivory
and glass, but seldom in a context from which quantity, equivalence or conversion could be inferred. An experiment with the
ubiquitous ceramic oil lamp led Duncan-Jones to the conclusion
that some models of this item were traded (as well as locally
produced and consumed), but within limited and spatially
discrete zones.[227] The example was selected for its trademarks
(signatures) but is for that very reason unrepresentative. Mostly, movement has got to be extrapolated from known source
concentrations (e.g. African cereals, Spanish silver, Cypriot
copper, etc.), logical consumption centres (e.g. urban need of
foodstuffs), or other marks of origin (e.g. ethnicity of slaves).

The fiscal argument is thus attractive but hardly conclu-
sive. It was the bureaucracy itself, devised to regulate the
activities of a population of some 55 millions (early Principate),
that enabled, indeed compelled juxtaposition of hitherto discrete phenomena. The impetus was *clerical* (bookkeeping)
and I think would not presuppose a concept of "economics"
that transcended Xenophon's notion of "estate management"
(oikonomikos).[228] Value added may be discerned in the perception of scale, that is, assimilation to a homely and manageable
model. I have several times alluded to features of imperial
administration: its acquisitive span of control and concomitant
consumption of time. More is achieved but less efficiently.
Since so difficult to measure, that is to some degree impressionistic, but suggests nonetheless the contradictory products of
expansion.[229] An appropriate term for the process is *koine,*
which evokes envelopment, uniformity and inevitably dilution:
concern for quantity regardless of cost. Theories underlying
and decisions issuing from this concern are not so easy to
identify, at least as intelligible propositions. Studies of modern
imperialism are nearly unanimous in pronouncing its manifestations as in the event economically unviable. Roman discus-
sions of "empire" as such appear not to have been preserved, or

perhaps not even voiced.[230] In Book II of the Politics, Aristotle's
survey of "constitutions" (= structures) includes the following
observation (1273b):

> "The government of the Carthaginians is oligarchical,
> but they successfully escape the evils of oligarchy by
> enriching one portion of the people after another by
> sending them to their colonies. This is their panacea and
> the means by which they give stability to the state."

An economic solution to what was essentially a political problem was hardly novel, as significant numbers of Greeks (e.g.
Corinthian, Euboean, Phocaean) had for some centuries before
Aristotle pursued that practice. The disposal of surplus, whether of population or produce, may be read as commerce, or
colonialism, or perhaps both. From artifactual traces throughout the Mediterranean, Boardman has extrapolated precisely
that combination of motives for migratory Greeks in the Archaic
period, but discerned nothing that could be defined as imperialist policy.[231] Notice, fairly frequent (apud Herodotus), of
Greek mercenaries in Egyptian and Persian service would
hardly qualify. Even the comparatively dense settlement pattern as far west as the Rhone (Marseilles, but not really further)
cannot be interpreted as a metropolitan network: linkage is local
and much conditioned by assimilation. But that is an archaeologist's history, based on ceramic design, some metalwork, and
burial practices. The traveller and recorder Herodotus would
have most of the known world peopled by or somehow in
contact with Greeks. But these were not constituents of empire,
a structure he knew well from observing the Persians.

The latter were heirs to a very effective and highly articu-
late imperialist tradition, compounded of military vigour, economic exploitation and sophisticated propaganda. Of its Neo-
Assyrian segment Liverani has provided an almost racy anato-
my based on centre-periphery imagery (see above), collocation
of space, time, personnel, and material, all subsumed in cosmological symmetry.[232] Essential to operation of this ideology is the
dyad culture: savagery and a version of the now familiar
"mission civilisatrice" through which a delinquent periphery
can be redeemed by an omniscient, cosmic and central power.
This is illustrated by a selection from the Akkadian vocabulary
of royal inscriptions, of which one item: nakru ("strange" hence
"foreign") is a nice equivalent of the Greek barbaroi. The

assurance of superiority can of course be sustained without resort to political or military gestures. But it was the Persian model (dynamic) rather than the Egyptian (static) that served the territorial conquests of Alexander. In the Mediterranean, however, the koine was already in place, had been for five centuries, and is difficult to depict without reference to Canaanite agency.[233] Even with that reference linkage between Ugarit, Byblos, Tyre, Memphis, Motya, Carthage, Tharros, Toscanos and Cadiz (as well as to Kition and Knossos) exhibits no trace of colonial strategy or serious metropolitan direction. But in filling the space it provided trajectories for later centres (sic!) of political and cultural diffusion, like Alexandria and Rome and, for a time, Carthage itself. Like the overlapping Greek one, the pattern is archaeologist's history, an eccentric and (it must be said) simplistic variety of the genre. Trapping both ends of a given trajectory, and thus achieving an orbit, will have been a piecemeal process, for which some evidence is available in the western sea: Reggio and Milazzo from Messina, Cumae from Ischia, Ampurias from Marseilles (Greek examples), Malta from Carthage, and Ibiza from Cadiz (Phoenician). From such uncertain collocation emerges neither motive nor agent: Aristotle's "Carthaginian panacea" (above) is a late but fairly shrewd exegesis. The fundamental pressure may have been demographic, as has been claimed for colonization from Euboea and Attica. Or population increase may have been the result of fresh economic opportunity, itself the product of new technology (agriculture).[234]

The patterns suggested, admittedly conjectural, would with recurrence expand to fill once explored space at a rate determined primarily by *emulation*. Once achieved the feat becomes progressively less arduous. That can be inferred from an artifactual array by measuring frequency and distribution: repetition generates density. Documentary witness is more explicit in providing a time scale for the process. An example: at the beginning of the 15th century Tuscans were not amongst the merchant communities represented at Byzantium or in Mamluk Egypt. The presence had traditionally been Pisan, a result of service as troop transport during the Crusades but surrendered during the late 14th century owing to conflicts on the Italian mainland and increased attention to North African commerce. In occupation since 1406 of the harbour at the mouth of the Arno and the port of Livorno further south, the Republic of Florence discerned the benefit of direct participation in the Levant trade. In due course and as gratitude for particular service (1439: a venue for ecclesiastic Council) the ancient Pisan privileges were conferred upon Florentine merchants in Constantinople.[235] Rather different was their démarche in Alexandria, where petitions were made with express reference to Venetian practice and drawn from Venetian-Egyptian documents. The process was lengthy (1422-1507) and the source of the paradigm not quite clear: openly negotiated in Venice or with their consul in Alexandria, or privately acquired by a Florentine agent.[236] The circulation (possibly clandestine) of such commercial privileges, even at the risk of increased competition for the trade, enabled the system itself to prosper and the loops to multiply. The orbital imagery is in this case enhanced by the new role of Medici Florence in the personal affairs of the Ottoman court, successors to the Byzantine regime responsible for the Tuscans' admission to eastern trade in the first place.[237] Opportunity was virtually unlimited.

The significance of all this is the emergence of a self-perpetuating infrastructure which operates irrespective of particular policies or participants. If that is merely what is expected of any bureaucracy, its components would nonetheless before coalescence have had separate histories. That these should accommodate, even generate, identical or at least similar expectations, is the spatial problem to which this chapter is devoted. Hardly solved, it has been repeatedly circumscribed in an attempt to stress the cumulative features of contact. These signal episodic but persistent acquisition of techniques, mastery of which must result in the conquest of space. To take the last mentioned example: Florentine insertion into the Levant trade involved not only industrial processing of goods and equipping a merchant fleet, but also acquiring a new vernacular and a dedicated chancery format. The mixture of Venetian dialect and Middle Arabic for Alexandria, with some Turkish (and probably Greek) for Constantinople after 1453, a technical lexicon derived from Islamic law and administration, instruments of negotiation reflecting oriental chancery practice: all these by that time an established tradition but quite new to an outsider. In the event Florence did not manage ever to rival Venice and Genoa in the east.[238] Into western commerce, however, Florentine input could be reckoned by the development (Genoese origin?) and dispersion of double-entry bookkeeping. But related techniques, like the sea loan and marine insurance, were also extended to the Levant, largely by Florentine agency in the form of resident bankers, as well as production of manuals (tarifa/pratica della mercatura) for calculating weights, measures and excise.[239] An infrastructure that enabled movement of commodities was as significant as the industry that produced them: its diffusion from London to Alexandria and from Barcelona to Reval was primarily an achievement of Tuscans.

I grant that a remark like the preceding is itself too diffuse to convey the intimacy of contact. The stages of transmission, and all but its general context, are obliterated by inclusion of too much space. To some extent the imagery evoked by *koine,* like discrete and only approximately dated deposits of artifact, generates a sense of inevitability: "sooner or later" differences were bound to dissolve. In the following chapters I shall attempt a closer examination of that process, by attention to the documentary substance of the koine, respectively its format and its linguistic content.

2

Chancery Practice

Along the many paths which composed the movement of emissary, merchant and commodity the salient feature was personal contact. Whether merely informal or extravagantly ceremonial, if it were to prosper the encounter had to be stabilised. Even where evidence is meagre or indeed unavailable, the very fact of recurrence might be thought to entail some regularity. As observed by the historian the lacunae, so frequent and so exasperating, are after all gaps in a continuum, for restoration of which standard recourse is to analogy. That can be found amongst the data of the now richly endowed discipline known as *diplomatic,* an array of techniques devised precisely to formalise and facilitate communication. Once perceived it is the uniformity of these that enables the historian to transcend the barriers of time and space, to fill the gaps in the record. It may of course be objected that more often than not contact was ad hoc and informal, hardly patient of reconstruction by way of stereotype. While admittedly so, that circumstance is to some extent mitigated by traces of initial and interim stages in the drafting of chancery documents that could just indicate, if not accurately illustrate, the pre-formal shape of such expression. As nearly always, the real problem is in depicting not the product but the process, since it is there that crucial decisions about form as well as substance were taken.

We may begin with an example from the 16th century. The entry of Elizabethan commercial agents into the interstices of Habsburg-Ottoman competition for Mediterranean trade was a complex and polyglot affair, initially conducted in English, Latin and Turkish, settling eventually into Italian.[1] Reason for the choice must have been the role of Venice, hostile but nonetheless pivot for the Baltic Hansa link with Levant trade and source of chancery paradigms for diplomatic relations between Europe and the Middle East.[2] Italian had already penetrated the traditional Arabic format, at least for merchants' petitions and administrators' directives, and figured significantly in negotiations for the Ottoman take-over of Egyptian trade.[3] There was thus a precedent for the use of Italian, coupled with the incentive provided by extension of Ottoman hegemony from the Levant to Oran and the fact that it was by leave of the Turks alone that the English entered the Mediterranean.

The language itself was remarkable: in origin Venetian dialect, swollen by rambling and pendant syntax, with heavy and often crucial lexical input from Middle Arabic, it could only have been understood on the Italian mainland by merchants with experience of the Levant.[4] Now, a mixture of vernacular with technical jargon was not unusual at the lower administrative levels of Mediterranean chanceries: the Arabic versions are of approximately the same register as the Italian.[5] This can undoubtedly be traced to certain drafting procedures, easily conceivable but also attested in the contemporary chancery guide produced by the Egyptian Qalqashandī:[6]

> And that was probably because the Franks and Muslims were neighbours at that time in Syria; agreement would be reached between the two parties clause by clause, and a scribe from each of the two sides would phrase it hurriedly in vulgar inelegant terms down to the last clauses of the treaty (hudna). Then the Muslim scribe would compose according to the contents of the rough draft (musawwada) corresponding to what the Frank scribe had written. But if the Muslim scribe deviated from it for the sake of order, elegance or clarity, this might seem to invalidate what the Frank had originally agreed to. He would thus disapprove, supposing in his ignorance of Arabic that it was not what had been agreed, so the Muslim had to retain what was in the rough draft.

The circumstances of the Crusader States, to which this passage refers, could be thought unusual and the field tactics here depicted anomalous. But that would be to ignore the informal nature of most contact and the need to improvise. From the extant specimens of commercial treaties negotiated between Muslim and Christian powers during the 14th and 15th centuries, it may be seen just how durable chancery format was. Even when punctuated with the indispensable formulae of bureaucratic utterance, the textual counterpoint of petitio and dispositio often exhibits a rendering of Italian into Arabic that can only be described as rough and ready.[7] Translation was at the best of times an acknowledged hurdle, as in the celebrated correspondence between Fatimid Cairo and Norman Palermo.[8] While the 12th century Norman chancery is traditionally presented as a special case, a longer view of Mediterranean usage might serve to modify that impression. For the entire region and throughout the medieval period, both the employment of two or more languages and the issue of multiple versions are attested.[9] But by 1500 that was, and had been for some three millennia, standard practice for international diplomacy, a fact that makes of *chancery records* a model of linguistic calque and conceptual transfer.

These records also provide a history of themselves. The compendious work of Qalqashandī, referred to above, may be read as the apogee of an ancient rhetorical tradition. Though too bulky to be called either manual or vademecum, it is notionally and functionally exactly that, being the sum of instruction necessary for an efficient director of chancery.[10] Completed in 1412, it thus comprehends some eight centuries of Muslim bureaucratic convention culminating in the elaborate and very cosmopolitan arrangements of the Mamluk sultans in Egypt and Syria. A sketch of the earlier periods and centres is included, drawn from a range of similar compositions, some of which are no longer extant.[11] While the competent officeholder is expected to know some history (as well as grammar, rhetoric, law and geography), treatment is not historical, but formulaic and practical, with an abundance of documentary specimens. From what is essentially a typological format (cartulary) a sense of modification and development may be extrapolated, mostly in the area of juridical sophistication. Not only paraph (signature) variants, but other marks of authenticity, validation, scrutiny and registration proliferate, investing the chancery product with a *semiotic* value extrinsic to its immediate message. Also extrinsic but nonetheless part of the information conveyed are the order of components in the address, the titulature, and the formulae of salutation and valediction, all of which were hierarchical.[12] Refinement of these ingredients manifests an upward curve of diplomatic nicety as well as of bureaucratic complexity. Not merely the recipients but also the originators of chancery instruments were increasingly differentiated: the outside world was reflected in the mechanics of production. Ideally, script type and paper size were also allocated according to rank (of both originator and recipient): irrespective of content the product itself was identified as symbol of a socio-political structure.[13]

Now, the impression of development in Qalqashandī lies partly in his depiction of burgeoning bureaucracy, but also in passing reference to simpler procedures in the time of the Prophet and the early caliphs.[14] One might suppose that for Qalqashandī contemporary circumstances could be explained as a linear sequence from Arabian (scil. Ḥijāzī) origins. Indeed, save for exiguous mention of pre-Islamic writers (Aristotle, Ptolemy, Orosius),[15] his description of chancery practice is stringently local. Even the long and meticulous treatment of script and its origins is emphatically North Arabian, with inclusion of (if not deference to) the celebrated conversation of Abū Dharr Ghifārī with the Prophet about divine revelation (tawqīf) of the 28/9 Arabic consonants.[16] Other scripts are of course adduced (e.g. Himyaric, Hebrew, Greek, Latin, Syriac) and their acquisition recommended as useful ancillary to the management of correspondence beyond the borders of Islam. But that world is dimly perceived: Muslims, whatever their language, employed the Arabic script. The chancery tradition was thus self-contained, an indigenous growth of undoubted vitality.

An orientation of that sort could corroborate a view of polygenetic origin and parallel development as sufficient explanation of cultural analogy. Indeed, isomorphism may provoke either this response or what appears to be its logical alternative, namely, the argument for diffusion. These need not be, and in fact seldom are, quite mutually exclusive: crucial are the units of comparison. Qalqashandī's excursus on writing might comfortably have dispensed with an observation on its origins, but such is so characteristic of Islamic literature that to omit would be remarkable. And the descriptive categories, revelation (tawqīf) or convention (iṣṭilāḥ), are standard in discussion of linguistic phenomena and generally found more or less evenly balanced.[17] As I have already indicated, writing was probably invented several times, with and without stimulus diffusion.[18] Contact becomes evident only in cases of specific structures. Without these, it might be guessed that once in place writing would itself generate certain common structures hardly distinguishable from one context to another. With some of these Goody has dealt at length in a monograph arguing the formative effect of writing upon social organization.[19] Assessment tends to cluster round the now standard contexts: temple, palace, and an ill-defined category of private transaction (sometimes identified with "commerce", but also meant to include property, penal and family law). As is well-known, the earliest evidence (tokens, seals, lists) exhibits concern with accounts and records, a functional vector that could (and did) easily generate a preoccupation with "lists" (onomasticon, pantheon, genealogy), "recipes" (medicine, divination), and "codes" (ritual, law). Whatever the original motive, much of this was "published" (e.g. display inscriptions) and thus made of private lucubration a public domain. Whether specifically clergy or merely clerk, the agency required for or at least accompanying this process assumed the role of specialist (literate and eventually lettered), introducing or perhaps only extending a visible allocation of labour. In fact, specialization is the social concomitant of an inverse effect of writing: the generalized accession to and application of utterance originating in a specific (local) context. For this effect Goody employs the term "decon-textualization" which, though felicitous, could invoke a notion of "abstract" or even "ephemeral".[20] Intended, however, is the "non-syntactic" use of language, a procedure that makes of symbols, formulae, sums and lists a genre of expression hardly available in oral discourse.[21] These fragments, essentially semiotic, become more or less infinitely transferable and thus facilitate contact, borrowing and embedding in alien contexts.[22] But again, recognition of them would depend upon their specificity, not merely upon the fact that they are written.

And yet, that fact, in addition to producing the historical record itself, generated imagery crucial to the expression of authority and hierarchy in every social context. Even if originally bureaucratic, a sacerdotal value was early on explicit in mastery of the art: a ritually acquired technique characterized by selective recruitment and intense training. This process is embedded in the lexicon of Middle Eastern monotheism: divine revelation as "scripture", law as "canon", commentary as "scholium".[23] Nowhere is this imagery more skilfully elaborated than in the formulation of Islam, which illustrates perfectly the adaptation of concepts rendered transferable by the act of writing.[24] As is authority, so are its custody and transmission sacred transactions, due in part to the divine source but also to the arcane technology employed for its expression. Indeed, the latter never ceased to fascinate: the "textuality" of monotheist religions has been so richly stressed that there is a mild danger of overlooking the social and economic context of the written word. Much, if not most, of that is reflected in the Listenwissenschaft to which I have alluded.[25] These remarkable compilations constitute a sizeable portion of the earliest notation (Uruk: the other major category being "economic", that is, numerical records and tabulation) and include such items as officeholders and professions, toponyms, animals, plants, raw materials and manufactures, and other lexical groups (e.g. "practical vocabulary"). These may exhibit a (bureaucratic) sense of tidiness or a pedagogical impulse (use in a scriptorium) or both. In either case they would exemplify non-syntactic language and the establishment of categories peculiar to writing. Between this "decontextualization" and the "deculturalization" of script involved in transfer from one language to another, there may be a kind of analogy. For the latter I referred to a perception of redundancy.[26] It could be argued that the same factor generated the telegraphic structure characteristic of lists, in which syntactical information is tabular rather than linear. Where the information conveyed was "nuclear" (substantives, infinitives, numerals), layout become crucial, that is, spatial configuration provided the only key to intelligibility. Remarkably, however, it is the introduction of "redundant" elements (determinatives, complements, inflexion) that distinguished subsequent stages of writing and brought it closer to the reproduction of speech.[27] Their eventual coalescence required recognition that sound, rather than merely meaning, could be visually represented. A history of that process, at least cast in terms of intention, is elusive: while some bureaucratic standardization (multiple entry tablets, subscript summaries) is evident, the assimilation of originally separate graphemes owing to adoption of a redesigned stylus might well have precipitated a need for phonetic and other complements.[28] As and when devised, these would of course be language-bound; their emancipation from a specific culture could only be effected by the kind of experiment that would, I have suggested, take place in a *polyglot chancery*.[29]

Now, the very existence of such must imply a sophisticated social order in which the underlying technology would be expressed in two forms: scriptorium and archive. And the earliest evidence would have to attest the existence of both. That they were at least bilingual (Sumerian and Akkadian) is clear, not merely from accounts of scribal training but also from references to the office of "interpreter" (eme-bala/targuman-num).[30] The fact of language contact is thus established from the very beginning, a noteworthy co-incidence for the history respectively of writing, language, and education. A detailed scribal curriculum has not been fully ascertained, but it seems clear that copying lexical lists would not be the most efficient method of acquiring grammar. Hymns, proverbs and other formulaic compositions in which syntax could be progressively and regularly varied have been mooted as teaching materials.[31] Information is abundant but dispersed, densest for Egypt and Mesopotamia, centres of ancient and more or less continuous traditions of bureaucracy and forensic expression. It is these to which Qalqashandī's work is unconscious heir. The pedigree is both implicit and indirect, partly owing to the ab initio character of Islamic historiography and partly to the intermediate role of Levantine schools of rhetoric. It is there, particularly in north Syria and Judaea, anyway an appropriate junction for the two ancient rhetorical traditions, that archaeological and literary residue attest to consolidation of a familiar chancery practice.[32]

Materials for a proper scribal syllabus are admittedly lacking: one is compelled instead to extrapolate from traces of scribal activity (annotation, gloss, and the occasional colophon) the professional existence of scribes and (less certainly) their academic formation.[33] Their social position (profession, guild, even class?) appears to have fluctuated: from office as effective royal chamberlain (grand vizir) and the "skilled scribe" of Ezra

(7:6) to Jeremiah's invective against futile scribal activity (8:8).[34] But such random, and probably biassed, notice has got to be weighed against the bulk of surviving documentation, itself witness to a technology upon which the propagation of authority depended. That could be either religious or secular, but for the ancient, classical and medieval Middle East it was both. There might, indeed, seem to be a kind of circularity in this assertion, since it is mostly from written records that notions of authority can be derived. But the artifacts as well, whether plinth, architrave or ostrakon, tend to be liberally embellished with that same expression of power: sovereign, proprietary, or talismanic. Of political structure and process writing was the primary mode. To be effective, even private transactions had to conform to chancery procedure, royal or ecclesiastic. Deeds, wills, sales, every kind of contractual instrument, required public validation. To that end, seal, stamp and signature were invested with juridical value, witnesses sought, oaths taken, and copies preserved. These steps, probably more or less simultaneous, were also cumulative, and produced the major form of chancery expression: the *archive*.[35]

Since the symmetry and efficiency of administration depend upon procedural rules, it is essential that these be accessible as precedent, reference and authority. Bureaucracy requires both the custody and retrievability of earlier transactions in a way that transcends the capacity of memory and vagary of custom.[36] It is thus hardly surprising that administrative records are mostly found in clusters, whatever the occasion for that circumstance may have been. Even if not immediately perspicuous, records (and that would include petitions and edicts as well as correspondence) tend to be intelligible only by dint of mutuality. Where it can be perceived, an archival array is the primary exegetical aid to analysis of administrative and institutional history. But such is seldom evident in the earliest materials, which have been recovered from dumps, caches, building rubble and mummies. If their discovery owes much to archaeological chance, their actual assembly might reveal some internal coherence (e.g. Edfu, Elephantine, Amarna, Kanis). But even so celebrated a find as the Cairo Geniza exhibits merely a long accumulation based on principles quite alien to archival collections. The rarity of these, down at least to the medieval period, is well-known and may perhaps be attributed to causes other than the fortunes of war and politics. Though it is difficult to fix an exact or even approximate term for the validity of archival documents (circumstances would vary according to genre: e.g. deeds of title, testaments, appointments, fiscal votes, penal laws, international correspondence and treaties), there is enough evidence to suggest some notion of revolving capacity, derived from such procedures as deletion, expiry, transfer, abstraction and resume. Retrieval devices, like the docket, register and calendar, as well as publication and display inscriptions, will undoubtedly have affected the bulk of "original" utterances whose long term retention for reference was thought to be necessary. Supersession may be the reason for widespread re-use of costly writing materials (palimpsest), and space restriction the obvious motive for dumping.[37]

Even if the most valuable, the collections themselves are not the only witness to their existence. In addition to the chancery manual (see above), literary references (e.g. Ezra, Esther, Eumenes of Kardia, Cato, Tacitus, Cassiodorus, Agathias), tomb inscriptions (Mekhet-Re', Rekhmire', Teji), and architecture (the Athenian Metroon and Roman Tabularium) attest to abundant and often sophisticated mechanisms for the recording and storage of data.[38] A fair precursor to Qalqashandī's instructions was the late Roman (c. 400 CE) Notitia Dignitatum, a listing by function of chancery and other personnel for an imperial enterprise grander and certainly more ambitious than any hitherto achieved.[39] If the components of the Roman design were by that time familiar and proven, its scale will nonetheless have generated concepts of communication and hence, a technology qualitatively as well as quantitatively different from those of its historical predecessors. This difference may be located, I suspect, precisely in the character of its bureaucracy, that is, a confluence of normative filing procedures and imposition of juridical uniformity. Neither could have been attempted, of course, without the encompassing territorial framework.

By Roman standards its predecessors were provincial, or at least become so in retrospect. For each, or most, of these a local modality of organized administration is attested. With the palace, the temple and the marketplace, the archive (wherever located and in whatever form) was the tangible instrument of authentication in a civil service both literate and numerate. If the ability to write and reckon generated the first archive (memorandum, file, dossier), its existence would in turn dictate the format of further records. The process is necessarily cumulative and largely self-perpetuating, since evolving business generates new data. The segment of time therein commemorated might, as I have suggested, be a constraint of space, but more likely a function of juridical utility. In other words, *contractual time* is a dimension of chancery practice that, though variable according to class of document, will determine the effective life of the archive. Preservation beyond that point, of course, enables its history to be written.

Remarkably, it is one of the most recent archaeological triumphs that has disclosed an archive in practical plan and full function. At Ebla documents and shelving were found in situ, the furniture of bureaucracy more or less intact.[40] Areas of tablet production, storage, consultation and transit between these operations can be distinguished, as well as a variable format for commodity and type of transaction. For these are largely economic archives, recording the manufacture and shipment of textiles but also consignments of cereals, livestock and precious metals. On the other hand, discovery within the same filing system of lexical lists (bilingual and monolingual), correspondence and international protocols must indicate a principle of storage other than thematic, characteristic perhaps of a scriptorium rather than of an archive proper. That distinction may anyway be too rigorous for such assemblies of data, where the term "library" with its mildly antiquarian overtone might be thought more appropriate. This problem of nomenclature is even more acute at Nineveh, where quite heterogeneous collections appear to have concentrated in royal residences, but where also the provenance of individual items is anything but clear.[41] At some sites, e.g. Ugarit, separate archives have been conjecturally located by trigonometry;[42] at others, e.g. Mari and Pylos, redrawn by postulating links (physical and hierarchical) between concentrated findspots.[43] Indeed, owing to the surely uncalculated permanence of clay tablets and their approximately contemporary witness to development of a new technology, it is the cuneiform legacy that happens best to illustrate the origins of bureaucracy.[44] The identification of "archives" (rather loosely employed to indicate anything from ledger to dossier, "current" or "deposit") by findspot, by receptacle (box, basket, jar), by internal coherence or cross-reference, is hazardous but in practice nearly valid.[45] The size of an "archive" is disputed, as is a distinction between "private" and "official" (or "public"?), matters that turn upon an inevitable overlap between personal property and public function.[46] That lack of clear demarcation would also affect the longevity of an archive, itself the consequence of a personal decision about usefulness.

Rather more critical are its implications for juridical validity, that is, procedures for registration, witness and deposit. Unless private transactions required judicial or notarial processing, one would not expect to find their record in "official" archives. Since it is unlikely that clerks, scribes and senators always and only represented themselves in lawsuits and business, their status as signatories must be differently interpreted and the eventual destination of such instruments read as concern to establish an autonomous corpus of law and precedent. It must seem that mechanisms analogous to later Athenian anagraphē (registration) and leukoma (publication) were acknowledged and operative.[47] It might also seem that the very notion of juridical validity involved recognition of authority beyond the compass of parties to a transaction and separate custody of its record. The locus of both was the *chancery*.

The etymological concept is "enclosure" (cancelli), perhaps including "relegation" (transfer=cancel), to which, curiously, there appears to be analogy in the cuneiform tradition (Mari).[48] Though of some metaphorical interest, the gesture of cancellation is no doubt secondary to the notion of custody, easily detected in such locutions as bīt ṭuppi (é. dub.ba), ginzayyā', scrinium, or to that of registration as in dīwān, bureau and exchequer. Crucial to both is the allocation of space and the articulation of rules for its use. Only at Ebla and Pylos is architectural residue fairly explicit in respect of the former. Nowhere, prior to the Byzantine and Islamic periods, is there explicit evidence in respect of the latter. Since, however, the chancery product is so abundant for its earlier stages, traces of the chancery process must be discernible. Thus stated, that assumption will seem reasonable enough, though it is unlikely to generate much more than conjecture. But like the varied circumstances of "contact" (Chapter 1) the modes of written communication are only finitely diverse: such activities as drafting, authentication and despatch are almost bound to exhibit some uniformity of the sort known to chancery practice as convention and protocol. Whether these represent stipulation or merely scribal comfort is not always clear, since either can easily become formulaic.

In all this there is an inevitable mixture of invention (discovery), imitation (borrowing), and improvisation (calque). For the chancery at Ugarit a fair amount of analysis is available.[49] The material for analysis is also substantial: of approximately 3000 tablets and fragments so far recovered, some 1350 are inscribed in the alphabetic cuneiform invented at Ugarit (exhibiting three languages) and the rest in the syllabic cuneiform adopted from Akkadian (exhibiting five languages). Beyond that, random traces of the Egyptian, Cypro-Minoan and Luwian scripts/languages are attested, all on incoming artifacts and documents, hence not necessarily productive in Ugaritic chancery practice. With the possible exception of Luwian, extant only in hieroglyphic stamp seals,[50] at least seven languages are likely to have been understood in the chancery at Ugarit: Sumerian, Akkadian, Ugaritic, Hurrian, Hittite, Egyptian and Cypro-Minoan. While Sumerian is so far attested only in a few school tablets,[51] Akkadian, Ugaritic and Hurrian are preserved in both syllabic and alphabetic cuneiform, a fact that must suggest a curriculum of scribal training but also, equally important, some degree of *experiment*. Because the market at Ugarit was a cosmopolitan emporium, its chancery had to, and did, cater for a polyglot correspondence. The mechanics of that exercise are of some interest: what was taught, learned and practised (by whom, to whom, and for whom)? The effects of multilingual competence/performance upon most linguistic expression, including that of the native speaker, has become a major area of socio - and psycholinguistic research.[52] Absence of informants makes investigation not only more arduous but different, owing to the scattered and hence largely unrepeatable phenomena of interference. Extrapolation of morphology, and especially phonology, from exclusively orthographic witness must be a dubious (as well as dangerous) procedure. That is due in part to the ubiquitous lapsus calami, but also to scribal idiosyncracy and to a feature (in this context) of Akkadian cuneiform that makes syllable representation (CV/VC/CVC) unstable and often misleading.[53]

There is, moreover, another consideration: whether writing might not be more profitably analysed as a *semiotic* rather than a linguistic system.[54] Perception that is ocular rather than aural would reflect, and generate, a different set of expectations. The underlying organization of experience, at least for "dead" langu-ages and extinct cultures, could hardly be with confidence reconstructed, but the signs themselves, together with their combinations and permutations, are of course not quite mute. Standard treatment of the alphabet is, as I have earlier mentioned, based on such notions as redundancy, kenosis and, above all, shared phonetic values.[55] But non-alphabetic writing involves another kind of technology transfer. First, the normally collateral processes of writing and reading do not depend upon a common linguistic link, that is, signs, where recognised, can be read in any language.[56] Second, semantic and even syntactic links are as often visual as they are phonetic.[57] The latter is nicely documented in the quite uneconomic proliferation of signs in at least some syllabaries, e.g. Akkadian. Format is anyway a visual datum, and it is there that evolution of chancery practice can be observed and assessed. Communication in this register is never exclusively, perhaps not even primarily, a matter of message, but rather, a statement of authority, design and intention, with a variable set of subsidiary ploys such as salutation, concern for welfare, request, complaint, and simply maintaining contact. Even when explicit, these latter are conveyed within a framework which is hierarchical, didactic and, above all, visible. From the arrangement of letterhead, cipher/paraph, and choice of formulae emerge the nature of the transaction and the respective standing of participants. To be effective such communications must be seen, not merely heard, though certain of the earliest "messenger formulae" may exhibit an originally oral delivery. This very item could indeed be an index of stylistic evolution.[58]

An impression of the range in experiment at Ugarit is found in documents containing alphabetic Akkadian and Ugaritic in syllabary. That inversion of the conventional medium for the two languages might well be attributed to exercises, even games, in the scriptorium. Neither set has been properly interpreted, but the alphabetic Akkadian is thought to be fragments of a ritual text.[59] As might be expected, the rendering of vowels is erratic and exhibits a curious fluctuation between the matres lectionis w/y and the glottal stops a/i/u. The meagre conventions for Ugaritic scriptio plena could hardly obtain in writing another language, nor, apparently, did the etymological constraint on alef.[60] In the only published example of Ugaritic in syllabic cuneiform,[61] meaning is also elusive but a striking feature is the almost exclusive use of the CV syllable, which results in stressing (and exaggerating?) the vocalic weight of Ugaritic, especially desinential. Now, that phenomenon is familiar enough from the isolated glosses in Amarna and Ugarit Akkadian texts, and has generated considerable discussion on the incidence of case inflexion in Bronze Age West Semitic (Canaanite). The problem, long since recognised, lies in the vocalic quality of cuneiform CV: whether phonetic or merely orthographic.[62] Discovery of the celebrated bilingual abecedary, in which 20 of the 30 Ugaritic signs are provided with Akkadian syllabic equivalents, has confirmed an impression of arbitrary (vowel) values.[63] Whether the same can be said of all the instances of Canaanite glossing in Akkadian is admittedly uncertain but hardly impossible. From the Amarna data, for example, one could not argue for retention of the classical Akkadian case system.[64] The anarchy in desinential vowels there exhibited must reflect ignorance or indifference, of which there is some trace in Babylonian of the Kassite period.[65] That such should proliferate in peripheral Akkadian might seem not unreasonable, the product either of grammatical error or of phonetic deletion (short vowels in final position). While the latter ought to generate VC or CVC, it is the preponderance of CVCV that is characteristic of the material from which witness to West Semitic case inflexion tends to be extrapolated. Thus, the putative diptosy in Akkadian texts from Ugarit is inferred from a statistic that, in my view, is deceptive.[66] Reduction of final vowels from three (u/a/i) to two (u/a) in three syntactic slots (nominative/accusative/genitive) would itself generate an increased frequency of 50%; from two (a/i) to one (a) in two slots (accusative/genitive) an increase of 100%, that is, if consistently applied. But no sample exhibits such consistency: from PRU VI 25 proper names in genitive position show final vowels /u/ (6 times), /a/ (5 times) and /i/ (14 times).[67] From the after all expected preponderance of /i/ it would be unwise to infer knowledge of the Akkadian tradition, since much of the variation occurs within a single text. While diptosy is admittedly characteristic of the dual and external plural masculine in West Semitic, its extension to external plural feminine and the internal plural forms is a phenomenon peculiar to Arabic, considerably distant in space and time from Ugarit and Amarna. For the latter corpus a fluctuation i/a/θ for the toponym Mitanni could be read as "optional inflexion", but more likely as evidence that the final syllable indicated consonant only.[68]

For Ugarit the near absence of bilingual texts makes arduous a close analysis of technology transfer. Besides the abecedary (PRU II 189) only two sets of documents come close to providing the kind of data essential to reconstruction of the process. The first of these constitute the so-called "Ugaritic Pantheon".[69] Comparison of the Akkadian component, a god list in distinctly non-Mesopotamian sequence (UGAR V 18), with a canonical inventory of Ugaritic deities (CTA 29) in alphabetic cuneiform has provoked an impression that the former is a version of the latter. That the scriptorium at Ugarit should produce a classical (syllabic) rendering of a local (alphabetic) text for information, practice or even amusement is not surprising. Of interest are the *modes of rendering*: transcription (knr : kinarum), translation (ym: tâmtum), and transposition (ršp: nergal).[70] The two latter will have been instructive enough, the first probably not at all and may seem to suggest that the scribe was of local origin and formation. However interpreted, the exercise offers a paradigm of linguistic contact from which general and pragmatic deductions may be inferred. As set out above, the three modes exhibit an ascending order of competence. The rendering of Resheph by Nergal demonstrates a grasp of cultural equivalence not achieved by the translation of "sea" nor the transcription of "lyre". For Akkadian tâmtum (ti'amtum) as deity (feminine!) a kind of documentation exists, but it is late (Neo-Babylonian?) and not so easily equated with the Ugaritic mythology for ym (parallel thm/thmt).[71] for Akkadian kinnārum (sic!), attested at Mari but only as a musical instrument, the match is even less perspicuous, but lexically possible.[72] One might thus characterise ršp : nergal as rhetorical adaptation (Bildung), ym : tâmtum as mimetic adoption (Nachahmung), and knr : kinarum as compromise (Anpassung) or, from the point of view of Akkadian, interference. This scale of transfer, with some refinement, may help to classify the modes, or at least the results, of language contact.

The second set of documents is more appropriate to the chancery itself. Here, the alphabetic fragment (CTA 64) of an Ugaritic-Hittite treaty probably composed in Hattusa (PRU IV 17.227) could be (and has been) interpreted to demonstrate transfer from Akkadian to Ugaritic.[73] Though eminently plausible, this hypothesis is complicated by the fragmentary condition of the alphabetic version and the assumption of a need in the chancery for an Ugaritic translation of an Akkadian document. That *assumption* has been widely exploited to account for all the Ugaritic versions of international diplomacy found at Ras Shamra, and deserves some further scrutiny. In this particular case, the Ugaritic fragment contains only a part, i.e. the tribute (or gift?) list appended to the treaty, so that its syntactic value does not exceed that of the "Pantheon" mentioned above. The yield is thus mostly lexical and formulaic (e.g. mlk rb : šarru rabū = LUGAL GAL). In the 37 lines of which something at least is preserved, there is a fair degree of "interference" : e.g. uṯryn : tartenu, tpnr : tuppalanuru, ḫbrtnr : ḫuburtanuru, sk1 : SUKKAL, being Hittite, Hurrian (?) and Sumerian terms of rank/office in Hattusa and thus not very useful additions to the Ugaritic lexicon. These appear in the tribute list itself (lines 17-37), where also some fluctuation is evident in the rendering of textile colours: e.g. pḫm : ZA.GÌN and iqnu : ZA.GÌN ḫasmānu as "reddish" and "bluish" respectively. Even if not necessarily accurate, the Ugaritic is clearer than the Sumero-Akkadian.[74] The same may be said of ks : GAL as "cup/bowl". In the narrative preamble (lines 1-6) the Akkadian formula rikilta. . . rakāsu is neaty translated by Ugaritic mṣmt . . .st ("made a treaty"), but slightly disfigured by retention of the East Semitic word order, an element that may seem to confirm the notion of an Akkadian original.[75] That (probably unconscious) mimesis would generate interference in Ugaritic, a plausible result of working from a Vorlage. Of treaty terminology proper there is not enough in the Ugaritic fragment to verify a postulate of consistent and professional translation by competently bilingual scribes. The general impression is one of improvisation, constrained only by the degree of repetition in the "tribute list."

Now, while the number of Sumerograms in the Akkadian version of this treaty is not unusually great, it is precisely these that permit lexical creativity. Like mlk : LUGAL, pḥm : ZA.GÌN and ks: GAL (above), ktn : GADA ("linen/garment") reflects a local choice, transposition rather than translation.[76] Of these only one can be said to represent a West Semitic convention, i.e. mlk = "king", not much earlier than this particular occurrence and marginally confounded by Akkadian māliku = "advisor".[77] The other, especially pḥm ("carbuncle"), are of course not simply conjectural, but at least optional. The underlying process cannot be very different from the *glossing* technique found elsewhere in peripheral Akkadian. Though occasionally quite idiosyncratic, the Canaanite lexical elements in Amarna and Ugarit exhibit for the most past standard semantic approximation.[78] Their purpose is less perspicuous. In the four quadrilingual vocabularies found at Ras Shamra the Ugaritic column follows the Hurrian and can only have served as aide-mémoire in learning Sumerian and Akkadian signs.[79] The fact, however, that the Ugaritic entries are expressed in syllabic cuneiform would suggest some mastery at least of the script by the compiler(s). Another possibility is that at the time of compilation there was no other device for recording Ugaritic or Hurrian. But a reliable chronology of the tablets has not been, and may never be, established, a lack that makes problematic not merely the character of "Canaanite glossing" but also the origins of the Ugaritic alphabet. Strictly read, glossing involves juxtaposition of two lexical items, one presumably more familiar than the other, but generally, both sustained translation and occasional recourse to a second language in any stretch of text might be said to constitute glossing. While clarity ought to be the aim, that could hardly be so of Canaanite items in the Amarna letters addressed to Egypt. If it were, those items must represent a sub-system of shared vocabulary more familiar than their Akkadian equivalents. The same must a fortiori obtain within Canaan and might even be extended to Anatolia. From the point of view of chancery Akkadian that sub-system is of course intrusive, but may exhibit the traces of a *lingua franca* of rather greater circulation than is shown in the documentary residue.

While the number of such Canaanisms is considerable, the majority consists of personal and geographical names.[80] Not

more than 200 occur as common lexical/grammatical elements
of discourse, hardly seven per cent of the extant Ugaritic lexicon
(*ca* 3000 including loanwards, Semitic and non-Semitic). Admittedly derived from an arbitrary sample (the product of
fortuitous preservation), this statistic is nonetheless instructive. West Semitic interference in the classical chancery lingua
franca exhibits not only substantives (the simplest mode of
borrowing), but also prepositions, adverbs, pronouns and finite
verbs that mix/combine root and inflexion between the two
languages.[81] Since neither Akkadian nor Canaanite could be
defined as hermetically sealed entities, it might be more appropriate to write "dialect bundles" imperfectly concealed by
graphic conventions.[82] Such would severely modify the notion
of "interference" but help to explain the ratio of lexical and
inflexional substitution, especially of semantically insignificant
prepositions and pronominal afformatives. These might be
read as glosses but must have been written as unconscious
reflexes of speech. The written record shows a Mischsprache,
due largely to the incidence of logograms that could be read in
either language.[83] The underlying spoken form(s) were, I suspect, internally more consistent.

Graphic conventions operate in other ways. The now extensive corpus of legal instruments produced by the medieval
Jewish communities in Sicily exhibit a combination of traditional
orthography, Arabic chancery formulae and juridical terminology
in the local vernacular.[84] There, Hebrew script, standard format
and bureaucratic nomenclature generated a linguistic register
that could only with obstinacy be construed as reflecting speech.
The several ingredients have been truly "decontextualized"
(see above), to reform as specimen of a bizarre but presumably
effective jargon. Lexical loans, e.g. gālūniyya: capitoli can-
onicorum or rufū' 1 -rūs: capitatio, and calques like sigill
maftūḥ : litterae patentes are not unusual and combine with
such formulae as lammā kān bi-ta'rīkh ("upon this date") and
dhālika ṣaḥīḥ thābit ("herewith authenticated") with signatures
of witnesses appended.[85] Most of the Judaeo-Arabic texts are
affidavits and thus represent a stage in notarial procedure. That
it was the initial, or at least an early, stage could be inferred from
their archival findspot in Palermo: the Corte Pretoriana, indicating
insertion into the Catholic notariat, which would be expected
for the 15th century. Several of the texts are in fact accompanied

by renderings in Sicilian vernacular, a matter of some exegetical interest since the Judaeo-Arabic itself, consisting of proper names, technical terms and numbers, is to an average extent of seventy-five per cent in that vernacular.[86] Assuming that there were/are similar renderings for all the texts, the conclusion must be that only the script, with a few Arabic locutions, constituted a confessional emblem and hence a barrier to general communication. For the Syracusan affidavit of 1187, referred to above, it may be recalled that during the Norman period Arabic was still a chancery language, and that for the even earlier court record (also Syracusan) of 1020, Arabic would have been the only chancery language.[87] In the former case, the findspot in the episcopal archive at Cefalu suggests an aide-mémoire, and in the latter, being a folio from the Cairo Geniza, a copy of one preserved in community records. In all this material, the script is a cultural code, easily and simply breached by oral articulation, but which for archival storage and retrieval had to be transcribed. In this script the only "logographic" elements are Hebrew abbreviations (pious formulae and the like), a few technical term (e.g. ketubbā : "deed of marriage"), and numbers (an alphabetic convention), all or some of which required translation. Extrapolation of an underlying lingua franca is, in view of the limited lexicon, something of a risk and would probably produce nothing more than the standard description of a pidgin.[88]

Script as code is also a feature of the archival residue from medieval Spain. Just as Jewish languages could, and should, be written in Hebrew letters,[89] so Muslim languages were conventionally recorded in the Arabic alphabet. When these came to include Spanish vernacular, as in the kharjas of Arabic strophic poetry,[90] the convention could easily be extended to prose, as in the notarial documents of the later Morisco communities.[91] Employment of Arabic script was accompanied by a fair range of lexical and especially syntactic interference in the vernacular (aljamìa).[92] But the Arabic Vorlagen themselves exhibit a confluence of juridical formulae, of which one set at least (Latin, Arabic or Romance) is likely to have been calqued.[93] In conveyancing procedure there is admittedly a natural sequence that would determine format quite independently of cultural contact, but the known symbiotic data of Iberian, as of Sicilian, history in the medieval period permit conjecture that such contact was the rule not the exception. The remarkable prestige of Arabic (language and hence script!) is documented more than once in the complaints of Christians (e.g. Alvaro of Cordoba *ca* 860) and Jews (e.g. Salmōn b. Yerūḥīm *ca* 960) that their respective coreligionists spent too much time and effort acquiring Arabic and too little in mastering Latin and Hebrew.[94] Chancery products in Spain, whether of Muslim, Mozarab or Morisco provenance, would reflect that prestige, even though the Arabic itself might exhibit interference (again, especially syntactic) from the local vernacular.[95] For such reciprocal effects the locus could be a single notary (Muslim or Christian) whose bilingual competence permitted service to both communities, in which for certain kinds of litigation the same formularies were employed, e.g. property transfer, debt collection, promissory notes, and even marriage deeds.[96] Aljamía was both an emblem and a channel of cultural diffusion.

Common, and possibly crucial, to all these codes is their historicising dimension. Orthography tends to be morphophonemic, that is, etymological rather than phonetic. While that is true of any orthography (consider English spelling!), it has been argued that for Akkadian this is more pronounced in the peripheral dialects.[97] To infer from such data a scribal consciousness of a special idiom or of a familiar idiom in special circumstances may be presumptuous, but it is a presumption supported by a range of other factors, e.g. chancery context, bilingualism or diglossia, juridical formulary, school rhetoric, etc. Like the generous use of CV = C in final position (see above), historical orthography is conservative, even archaic, and not unexpected in the kind of writing employed to express authority. An analogy in West Semitic would be scriptio plena or, say, the Arabic definite article, but it is impossible to describe either as a peripheral phenomenon, at least in a geographical sense. If, however, the notion of cultural space is evoked, with the concomitant perception of language as barrier or catalyst to communication, peripheral phenomena can be redefined. What Bakhtine has described as the "hellenistic effect": the inevitable product of polyglot competence that affects performance even in the native idiom, can be observed in the residue of chancery practice.[98]

The data are certainly linguistic but also, as I have suggested, *visual*. In the composition of documents, whether for epistolary, juridical or accounting purposes, format is dominant. Since the several components and their sequence exhibit remarkable stability, description can be generalised in the now (more or less) accepted vocabulary of medieval European diplomatic:[99]

Protokoll :	invocatio
	intitulatio
	devotio
	inscriptio
	salutatio
Message :	arenga/proemio
	expositio/promulgatio
	petitio/narratio
	dispositio
	sanctio/comminatio
	corroboratio
Eschatokoll:	subscriptio
	testificatio
	recognitio
	datum
	apprecatio

Inclusion of all these depends of course upon the type of document issued: a letter, for example, might well contain a reference to petition, but almost certainly not witnesses' signatures, whereas a property conveyance would contain the latter but probably not the former.[100]

Absent from this inventory is one notable feature of pre-Roman epistolary format: the messenger formula. While its eventual disappearance can probably be attributed to the fact itself of writing, inflexions of the verb "to speak", whether imperative, preterite, perfect or participial, persisted for centuries as a fixed element in chancery diction and seem to reflect explicit instruction to the message-bearer.[101] A shift from imperative to the other aspects/tenses (e.g. Akkadian qibi/iqbi) might well signal a change from aural to ocular reception, but that is hardly necessary. The biblical formula of prophetic address (koh 'amar) exhibits the aspectual shift in what must still have been oral transmission.[102] And Ugaritic usage is sufficiently ambivalent to justify a participial or gerundive (rgm = lemor?) reading for what was after all written transmission. Instead of elimination, one could propose subsumption of the formula into some other component of the text, for example, the arenga, especially as characterised by rhyme.[103] That a part at least of the communication might be better served by hearing than by reading is likely for any ceremonial reception and would be signalled by implicit instruction for delivery. Analogous accommodation might be found for the cuneiform prostration formula (Akkadian preterite amqut; Ugaritic perfect qlt), never imperative and hence always a reference to the originator.[104] Eventually deleted (or absorbed into the salutatio?), its hyperbolic servility ("at the feet of my lord I fall seven and seven times") cannot but remind of the medieval Christian servus servorum Dei, of course a devotio and hardly token of humility.[105] On the other hand, its explicit allusion to (divine) source of authority is not so clear in the cuneiform model. Of interest is the fact that it is also not an instruction to the message-bearer, and I am inclined to suppose that this may have affected the shift of verbal inflexion in the messenger formula itself. Ultimate deletion of both formulae can only be dated e silentio: neither is attested in Phoenician, Aramaic, Hebrew or Greek, from which it is just possible to infer a lapse related to the supersession of cuneiform script(s). In an argument for continuity of chancery practice that conclusion is not quite satisfactory. The obvious alternative is acknowledgement of lacunae.

As always, these are plentiful, and occasionally crucial. To the context just depicted, for example, may be adduced some marginally pertinent data. An Aramaic congener of the Hellenistic prostration formula (proskynema), itself allegedly derived from a Demotic Vorlage, is fairly exhibited in the Hermopolis papyri (5th century BCE).[106] Common to the Egyptian, Aramaic and Greek formulae is invocation of the deity by originator on behalf of addressee, hardly the function of the cuneiform version. Even if all the key verbs (fall/make obeisance/bless) shared a metaphorical value and identical agent (originator), straightforward transfer seems unlikely. Nor does the imperative messenger formula, apparently contained in the only specimen of a Phoenician letter (Saqqarah) and conjecturally in a Hebrew papyrus from Murabba'at, quite demonstrate continuity: dated respectively to the 6th and 7th centuries BCE, both may be easily construed with participial and/or epistolary perfect inflexions of the verb "say" ('mr) and thus thought to conform with contemporary practice.[107] Of some interest, at least so far as the proskynema/berākhāh formula is concerned, is the input of Egyptian chancery usage, hardly surprising but worthy of remark for the history of a Levantine tradition so long dominated by cuneiform models.

Now, "domination" could be misleading. Even for the Bronze Age innovative techniques are documented (e.g. Amarna) and the stability of constituent parts noted above in their Latin version owes nearly as much to logic as to emulation. That the substance of a communication should be enclosed by introductory and concluding punctuation is not unexpected. Further, that this enclosure, however locally determined, should vary so little from place to place must be seen as the normal response to similar needs. As I have several times indicated, the only control in measuring variation is specificity. Besides insertion/omission this would include phrasing (diction) and sequence. Spatial position may be significant: for example, the proskynema/berākhāh element is in Aramaic and Greek documents part of the greeting formula (salutatio) but semantically an invocatio. Location of this, explicit acknowledgement of the deity, at the head of the text is monotheist and regularly attested in medieval Christian and Islamic documents, as verbal phrase or cipher (monogram) or sign.[108]

Invocatio

Emblem of (divine) authority, the formula is also a cultural symbol, its effect the product of position and design. The more elaborate executions were employed in correspondence with foreign rulers, with a descending curve of embellishment for internal and routine affairs.[109] Phrasal forms include in dei nomine, in nomine domini (Jesu Christi), in nomine sancte trinitatis and Greek equivalents, which could be compressed into ligatured initials or represented by a cross.[110] The Arabic version in all Muslim chanceries was the basmala (= in dei nomine), but often replaced in Ottoman documents by the pronoun huwa ("he") with an appropriate predicate ('azīz/ ḥayy) or stylised as a monogram.[111] Undoubtedly of East Roman origin, the formula was a feature of most medieval Mediterranean chancery products for any purpose and of whatever origin. Diffusion from a single source is easily conceived.

Prayer as rhetorical address (oratio) is of course ubiquitous and ancient, its application to secular occasions probably talismanic and precautionary. Beneficiary of the chancery invocatio is not the addressee but the originator, an orientation that distinguishes it from the pre-Christian blessing formula (see above). Unlike the devotio (dei gratia) it is neither assertive nor even declarative, but rather, a petition in aid of the writer's own prosperity. In cuneiform and Egyptian models, because the invocatio is a greeting it is logically placed after the address (inscriptio).[112] Admittedly, the "logic" is nothing more than practical and might yield to the more important demands of format. For example, in some Ottoman documents of the 16th century concern for the visual salience of a devotio formula (by the grace of God, I who. . . .) meant relocation at the head of the text, and its conjectural reading as a second invocatio. That practice, traced by V.L. Ménage to Far Eastern models (and vertical script), confirms the significance of layout (and ocular impact) in the production particularly of foreign correspondence.[113] By means of "elevation" (with horizontal script = marginal "extrusion"), formulaic components could be highlighted to serve as political statements. For the overall design the experiment resulted in mild untidiness and possibly some confusion. It may be observed that in late Bronze Age chanceries prominence (=primary position) was allocated to the seal, which contained the originator's titles and accompany tokens of divine authority, i.e. the intitulatio and devotio formulae. In Islam and Christendom these would have to surrender priority to independent acknowledgement of the only deity.

Intitulatio

All letters and most other types of chancery document contain a reference to their originator. This may be, and in the cuneiform tradition was, explicit in the so-called "messenger formula" (see above). There the designation seldom exceeded proper name and regnal status ("king of . . .").[114] Occasionally, in Middle Assyrian and later, a term referring to the message itself (e.g. awat/amat/abat = "word"; ṭuppi = "tablet"; cf. Ugaritic thm and Akkadian ṭēmu = "message"?) might be inserted into the formula in construct with the name of the originator, but more common was the adverbial umma/enma ("thus" say/said . . .). Though it cannot always be determined, sequence of originator and addressee in the formula appears to be in descending order of respective rank, that is, the superior party is mentioned first.[115] The relationship might be made explicit by addition of an epithet "your father/brother/son/servant" etc., seldom if ever a reference to actual kinship.[116] These marginal refinements, even when enhanced by such embellishments as šar šarrāni/mātāti/kiššati (king of kings/lands/universe") etc., hardly match the titulature of the later Byzantine and Islamic courts. Nor does the intervening West Semitic documentation fill the lacuna.[117] Neither Aramaic nor Hebrew, and certainly not Phoenician, letters exhibit an expansion of the basic "from/ to. . .to/from" formula to support a postulate of cumulative development. But those texts, mostly ostraca and papyri, lack a proper chancery context and might thus exhibit little more than rudimentary conventions. The Aramaic exception, the Arsames collection on parchment, is curiously unhelpful in precisely this respect.[118] Though there is no obvious reason why Achaemenid administrative officers should correspond in a format more appropriate to private letters, the few seal impressions found with the documents do not reflect an imperial chancery.[119] If indeed the employment of seals, alluded to above, were thought to be a possible source of titles in the chancery letterhead, it is the cuneiform evidence that is most persuasive. While patchy and not uniformly quantified, Gelb's typology reveals, especially for the Sargonid (*ca* 2335-2150 BCE) and Ur III (*ca* 2115-2005 BCE) periods, a proliferation of names, titles, epithets, professional designations and blessing formulae in seal legends.[120] Since the use of seals varied widely, in time, in place, and according to the kind of document issued, establishment of a link between the modes is not straightforward. To begin with, a common function would need to be ascertained. While seals were, and are, used to ensure custody, to signal identity, and as mark of authentication (in addition to their votive and ornamental values), the chancery intitulatio is an assertion of authority. Admittedly, it serves also to identify the originator, but that is achieved in other ways as well (see below) not intimately related to the long catalogues of territorial claim familiar from the medieval Mamluk and Ottoman chanceries.[121] The notion of authority is of course implicit in sealing, perhaps explicit when employed on legal documents, of which the purpose might indeed be authorisation (=legitimation).[122]

Apart from, or just possibly consonant with, its versatility, the seal exhibits greater formal variety: whether stamp or cylinder, inscribed or not, of precious stone or ceramic, of more or less quality in design and execution, the range far exceeds that of even a flexible chancery protokoll. That would hardly be evidence against the transfer of at least one motif (i.e. title), but there are other considerations, of which one would be position of the seal impression (if applied) on a tablet. Distribution of this, or these (in the case of several witnesses), also varied across the obverse or margins of the tablet or envelope (where one has been preserved) of Mesopotamian origin.[123] For Late Bronze specimens, on the other hand, whether Hittite (stamp) or Ugaritic (cylinder and stamp), a tendency to central or upper-face position is apparent.[124] These are "royal" seals, that is, identifying/authenticating the products of a state chancery, on which an intitulatio would be not only appropriate but expected. By that time (ca 1500-1200 BCE) the modes of validation had clearly merged, or at least achieved a sensible overlap.

Devotio

To the Christian versions dei gratia, fidelis in Christo, pistos en christo to theo, may be compared the Muslim ḥamdala, tawfīqī billāh, tawakkaltu 'alā'llāh, etc., all of which signify divine confirmation.[125] Less petition than assertion, these formulae may have possible precursors in cuneiform seal inscriptions that indicate the owner's service to particular deities.[126] Now, any votive inscription might then be thought relevant, irrespective of its literary or indeed architectural context. While that would be generally true, it does not quite explain the precise location of the devotio formula as appendix to the originator's titles. A matter of syntax in Latin and Greek ("by the grace of God, I . . ."), the formulae are in Arabic disjunctive, though a macaronic version (Allāhun 'ināyeti ile, ben . . .) in a 16th century Ottoman document suggests a calque of Latin dei gratia with embedded syntax.[127] In the Mamluk chancery a formula frequently employed at the conclusion of the intitulatio is a'lāhu allāh ta'ālā wa-sharrafahu wa-anfaḏhahu wa-ṣarrafahu ("May God Almighty elevate and ennoble him, grant him efficacy and power of disposition"), which is not a devotio but an invocation.[128] It could also be a reference not to its originator but to the

document itself (i.e. hu = kitāb/marsūm), an interpretation
that would support a view of the devotio as adapted (!) from
Christian chancery practice. Like the leading invocatio, this
formula emerges as a separate identifiable constituent from a
tradition of interrelated motifs that comprised both despatch
(messenger formula) and authentication (seal). What both
constituents proclaim is the vicarious quality of regalian authority, a view matured in the biblical matrix, from which both
Christianity and Islam derive. But the relatively few extant
Hebrew letters do not exhibit either of these, an unfortunate
accident of archaeology no doubt.[129] A tangential but certainly
interesting phenomenon contained in a few Aramaic papyri
(Hermopolis/Padua *ca* 500 BCE) is the "temple greeting" in
initial position (i.e. preceding the address) and referring not to
the deities of the originator but to those of the addressee.[130] As
such, it constitutes a salutatio, but its unusual location at the
head of the text may be related to an as yet undocumented
Hebrew practice.

Inscriptio

Depending upon respective rank, name (and titles) of the recipient might follow or precede those of the originator. Sequence
was also affected by the nature of the message, whether petition
or order, reply or initiative, official or casual, etc.[131] Without
accompanying epithets (e.g. "my lord/your servant/my broth-
er" etc.), clarity in this matter is seldom possible. If the historical
context of certain cuneiform archives, e.g. Amarna and Ugarit,
does appear to support a consistent sequence pattern in terms
of rank, that is not sustained in Iron Age documentation except
possibly in the Arsames collection.[132] The conventions revealed
by study of the later Christian and Islamic chanceries naturally
confirm a sequence based upon rank: in the utterances of
emperors, kings, bishops, sultans and caliphs the intitulatio
must precede the inscriptio. This was a principle well grasped
by the earliest authorities in the Muslim community: the despatches of not only a provincial governor (Qurra b. Sharīk in
Egypt) but also of the prophet Muhammad (to the Byzantine
and Sassānid emperors) have the originator's name immediately after the invocatio (basmala).[133] Of some marginal interest
perhaps is occasional evidence of alteration of the sequence by

translators for reasons of local propriety, as in the Italian version of an Arabic letter from Cairo to Venice, dated 1473.[134] Chancery protocol was easily transmitted, acquired and, where deemed desirable, adapted. Titles allocated to addressees were inventoried in scrupulous priority, especially in the Mamluk and Ottoman chanceries, from which an international scale of rank could be calculated.[135] This information, easily accessed and calqued, was stored in formularies of the sort compiled by Qalqashandī in Egypt (see above) and by numerous clerics in medieval European chanceries, e.g. the Merovingian Marculf.[136] To such an extent did these holdings perpetuate themselves that one finds the same formulae, the inscriptio for instance, in use across a wide area for several centuries.[137] That was probably facilitated by issue of the type called litterae apertae/patentes (cf. Arabic sijill manshūr/maftūḥ) addressed "to whom it may concern", a category of document whose flexibility permitted extension to a considerable range of official occasion.[138]

Salutatio

In the alphabetic tablets from Ugarit which consist entirely of formulae and thus probably served as scribal models, it is the greeting that is best and most variously exhibited. The cuneiform tradition was well established: syllabic versions are also rich and nicely elaborated, in particular specimens from the Middle Babylonian period (c. 1600-1200 BCE) to which the products of Ugarit and Amarna belong.[139] Absence of a salutatio in the earliest extant Akkadian letters, if not merely a fortuitous result of archaeological discovery, could indicate a terminus a quo during the Old Babylonian period (c. 2000-1600 BCE). The basic form is an invocation (see above): DN + liballiṭūka ("may the deity . . . grant you life"), for which is attested an extensive inventory of divine names.[140] This could be amplified by a series of non-invocational formulae, e.g. lū šalmāta/lū/baltāta/lū dāriāta ("may you be well/live/persevere"), which were seldom independently employed. Characteristic of Middle Babylonian chancery style is a collective reference to deity, i.e. ilānu liṣṣurūka ("may the gods protect you") but also, in examples from Amarna and Ugarit, the aforementioned prostration formula. Co-occurrence of the two phenomena is probably fortuitous, though the collective reference is also anonymous and hence transferable to the addressee's local pantheon, a gesture consonant with the image of prostration.[141] But the two do not appear to coalesce: the cuneiform prostration formula is not attested in the first millennium BCE. It is the invocation (=blessing) that most resembles the Hellenistic proskynema, whatever the direct descent of that formula.[142] The standard Ugaritic version of the Akkadian reads ilm tgrk tšlmk ("may the gods protect and give you peace") in which occasionally, as also in Akkadian, the gods invoked may be identified with a particular place but seldom individually named, contrary to earlier and later practice.[143] Extension of the blessing by such courtesies as hnny 'mny kll šlm ("here with me all is well") and tmny 'mk mnm šlm rgm ttb ("send word of your well-being there") also reflect Akkadian patterns, e.g. šalmāku ("I am well"), ana šulmika aspuram ("I am writing about your well-being"), šulumka šupram ("Write of your well-being").[144] The Ugaritic corpus, as indeed that of Amarna, illustrates the easy transfer of Mesopotamian phraseology, hardly modified for use in the Levant. Occasional innovation and/or deletion, like the prostration formula, would signal a change in style rather than discontinuity. For the salutatio persistence over two millennia of derivatives from the root šlm ("peace/prosperity/well-being") found apt equivalence in the Latin term, and precisely in this context.[145] The Arabic cognate (salām) could be so employed, both at the beginning and end of a letter and modified according to the addressee's religious affiliation, but the salutatio slot as such was regularly expressed as an invocation (du'ā), e.g. abqāka allāh ("may God make you endure") or akramaka allāh ("may God give you honour").[146] These and similar formulae, usually in Arabic (!), were customary in most Islamic chanceries, and exhibit thus the cuneiform tradition virtually intact. Possibly more than virtual: reappearance of the prostration formula in Egyptian documents at the beginning of the 12th century has been remarked, but not its cuneiform origins.[147] The Arabic version al-mamlūk yuqabbil al-'ard amāma 'l-maqām al-'alī ("the slave kisses the ground before the noble station") is of course not a verbatim rendering of the Akkadian/Ugaritic "at the feet of my lord I fall", and could indeed signal an innovation in Fatimid court ceremonial. But Qalqashandī offers variants, e.g. 'ataba (threshold) and mawāṭi' (footsteps), in his observation that this ancient practice (not more closely identified), discontinued in Islam, was merely a chancery metaphor (isti'āra) introduced by scribes under foreign influence.[148] It may, for that matter, never have been more than metaphorical, but nonetheless evidence of concern for protocol. Actual prostration (sujūd) is in Islam reserved for the deity.

Arenga

A preamble to the text containing general statements of authority, responsibility and concern for affairs of state and commonweal was a matter of justification and public address (harangue), characteristic of decrees and contracts but often inserted in official letters. The imagery, implicit in the invocatio, intitulatio and devotio (all of which refer to the properties of divine-regalian authority), is overtly benevolent but equally a symbolic affirmation of power to effect the provisions (enactments or promises) that follow.[149] The history of this embellishment is opaque: absent from extant specimens of Aramaic, Hebrew and early Arabic, the formula appears in Fatimid decrees of the early 12th century.[150] But since rhyme and uniform phrase length are there clearly evident, it is tempting to suppose a prior period of development, if not in chancery business itself, then in the earlier schools of rhetoric, in which after all epistolography was a major art form. I refer to the often celebrated and much analysed rasā'il of the 8th century belletrists Sālim, 'Abdalḥamīd b. Yaḥyā, and Ibn al-Muqaffa', whose production intersected and reformulated the bureaucratic utterance of Umayyad and Abbasid chanceries.[151] In the corpus attributed to 'Abdalḥamīd, e.g. his "instructions to secretaries" or the code of conduct from the caliph Marwān to his son, the components of the arenga appear, expressed as duties to God and to His creatures.[152] Politicisation of these had occurred outside the chancery, in the public address (khuṭba) associated with the Friday mosque service. Indeed, khuṭba would be a fair equivalent of the medieval Latin arenga, and in chancery usage the introductory portion of diplomas of investiture was so designated.[153] Now, the role of Hellenistic models in the development of Arabic epistolary prose is a matter of some dispute, and the earliest specimens of khuṭba are not epistles but literally "harangue" (oratory). On the other hand, the significance of the arenga in Byzantine chancery practice is unlikely to have been borrowed from Arabic, but read rather as witness to Hellenistic rhetorical tradition.[154] That such should eventually impinge upon documentary format was, in the light of a shared concern with the nature of authority and social order, inevitable.[155] Genre overlap is of course a perennial feature of literature, observed even for the early second millennium in Mesopotamia where the convergence of epistolary style with that of date formula and display inscription contributed to the elaboration of chancery prose. In Neo-Assyrian commemorative inscriptions, the motifs appropriate to apologia and res gestae are precisely the arenga ingredients that came to occupy a formulaic slot in official correspondence.[156] A Fatimid specimen would illustrate adequately the imagery:

"he who clothes the world in the goodness of his perception with splendour and beauty, and dispenses upon all the laden clouds of his bounty, and conducts affairs in exemplary order, and restores the patterns of equity, and perfects their harmony and congruity"

where the proclamation of justice serves as preface to the message about to be uttered.[157] Absence of this element in, say, the cuneiform texts from Amarna and Ugarit or those few preserved in Aramaic and Hebrew is probably fortuitous, though from the extensive corpus of medieval Arabic chancery documents, one might infer that the arenga was an optional flourish.

[Segmentation]
While every formula marks a textual division of some kind, major transitions as for example between protokoll and message may be more mechanically signalled: e.g. by horizontal lines (as in cuneiform tablets), spatial layout and different scripts (as in medieval Islamic chanceries), or by fixed and often fossilised phrases. The arenga itself, when inserted, may indicate the onset of message, preceding as it mostly does mention of the occasion for writing (expositio/promulgatio). But even here, punctuation may be reflected in an adverbial phrase, such as Arabic wa-lammā ("when therefore") or ammā ba'du ("now to the matter") or fa-inna ("thus").[158] The practice is ancient: Akkadian anuma/enuma, Ugaritic ht/wht, Aramaic k't/wk't, k'n/wk'n, k'nt/wk'nt, Hebrew w't/w'ttā, śe have that functional value, amongst others (!), and are mostly in place.[159]

Omission in the Lachish ostraca, where the body of the letter is introduced by the formula my 'bdk klb ky ("who is your servant but a dog that . . ."), must be a local convention but not inappropriate to an address from inferior to superior.[160] The Semitic tradition is thus unbroken, at least with regard to syntactic formality, though the semantic value of these phrases is not identical. While layout is obviously a visual property, it might be thought that fixed phrase is also a feature of writing, in which for orderly perception the stereotype (cliché) meets the reader's expectation. Of the documentary components so far reviewed all must have been anticipated by a recipient, and more or less in the proposed sequence. Exceptions, omissions and variations may occur, but seldom in such degree as to distort perception.[161]

Expositio

Reference to the immediate circumstances of utterance is a narrative form containing historical detail of previous correspondence, of an envoy's arrival, of a claim or request submitted, or simply of an event provoking response/action. As such, only its position is strictly formulaic, content variable as appropriate to the occasion. Yet even there range of expression is not unlimited, and tends to cluster in categories of declarative syntax ("it has come to my attention. . ."), e.g. u aššum amati sa aššatika ("as to the matter of your wife"), aššum uqni ša ana šarri tašpura ("on the matter of the lapis lazuli about which you wrote to the king") in Hittite letters to Ugarit; ky lik bny lht akl 'my ("since my son has sent me a message concerning food"), ky likt bt mlk thmk ("since you sent your message to the palace") in Ugaritic letters.[162] Achaemenid Aramaic exhibits PN šelah 'alay ken'amar ("So-and-so has sent word to me thus") and Arad Hebrew kṣ'ty mbytk wšlhty 't hksp ("when I left your house I sent the money").[163] Despite the often elaborate preceding formulae, the style of introducing business might be deemed abrupt. This was maintained in Arabic epistolography, e.g. fa-inna PN qad akhbaranī anna lahu 'alā PN ("so PN has informed me that there is owing to him. . . .") or fa-anẓur alladhī kāna baqīya 'alā PN ("so check what PN still owes").[164] When an imperative is employed, not at all uncommon, the referent is only tacit and, especially after a formulaic introduction, makes the transition even more abrupt. The effect is that of the preprinted format with slots to accommodate specific detail, clearly a venerable technique. Its utility in the mass production of chancery "blanks" may be elsewhere detected, even, perhaps surprisingly, in the matter of signature (see below). In Mamluk documents the standard expositio was literally a "promulgation", e.g. nuwaḍḍiḥu 1'ilmihim or nu'limuhum ("we hereby inform them"), whose origin may be located in the language appropriate to decrees.[165] But the regalian spirit of that chancery, as of the Ottoman, would entail some blurring of genres for which scribal personnel engaged in parallel tasks must have been responsible. Like decrees, letters were composed as autocratic expression: the tone was curt and the imagery deliberate.[166]

Petitio

Itself an independent genre, this component is also often a referent in the expositio, as event or as verbatim insertion.[167] The mode of incorporation (narratio) is illustrated in the grant of commercial privileges from Murād III to Elizabeth I (May 1580), where the latter's petition is encapsulated in the expositio.[168] The principle is archival: cross-reference as aid to filing and maintenance of a continuous record. Other means to that end included dockets, labels, and physical juxtaposition, but none would be so secure as the textual inclusion of previous stages of the same transaction. Its effect upon drafting might be considerable and could generate a decree consisting entirely of petition and a single dispositive formula (see below). Evidence for the antiquity of this style is elusive. From the Akkadian tablets at Ugarit are several which contain reference to previous and ongoing transactions, e.g. concerning a delayed consignment of lapis lazuli to the Hittite ruler (see above) and an acknowledgement of oaths required in writing.[169] More significant are instruments of treaty negotiation between Ugarit and external powers (Hatti, Amurru, Uśnatu) quoting earlier communications and decreeing their implementation.[170] Here the provision is juridical as well as archival, since even this patchy documentation exhibits concern for authority in writing. In the absence of complete records for these negotiations, it is possible to read the ostensibly verbatim citatation (iśpurama/iltapra . . .) as rhetorical flourish, but in the light of later medieval practice that seems unduly cautious. According to Bresslau, the notarial application of this device (insertio), specifically for confirmation or renewal of earlier dispensations, is not attested before the 10th century.[171] But there is a shared impulse to establish authority by reference to precedent as ipsissima verba, record of which is a custodial obligation. Hence the archive.

Dispositio

It might be expected that the centrepiece, indeed propositional fulcrum, of the chancery instrument be also visually salient. But except as clause (or paragraph) head this is not so, and in format the dispositio yields pride of place to the sign of authentication (signature). Here, the formal factor may contain a functional value, since in some medieval Christian documents the dispositio is absent, in others quite explicit (e.g. fieri iussimus).[172] I have earlier referred to a practice in medieval Islamic documents to fuse this element with the request (petitio) that provoked it, by recourse to a single verb of command (e.g. rusima, rasamnā bihi = fieri iussimus).[173] Even when elision does not result in syntactic dislocation, from calques and other evidence of translation the shape of a petition can often be reconstructed. The matter of "original" and "translation" will be treated in the following chapter. Composition of the dispositio from ambassadorial instructions and memoranda has frequently been noted, and could be interpreted as further evidence of an archival impulse (see above).[174] But equally significant is the procedural basis of such transaction, which would neutralise extensive borrowing of external material (e.g. the petition) by merely appending a command, itself a reflex of the authority invested in signature. The whole process suggests a time-saving device with the additional advantage of minuted negotiation, and might even help to explain the low visibility of the dispositio as such. Now, while it would, I am sure, be unwise to press this argument too far, it is supported by the format of medieval chancery documents which contain that element, e.g. treaties, contracts, and decrees. Letters may, if in reply to petitions.[175] Of course much, if not most, of chancery material is not dispositive, but evidential: the record of an act in law. There the principal components are expositio, witness, date and place of enactment, mostly if not always in that order, and tend to dispense with the formalities of address (protokoll and arenga).[176] The purpose of such documents is testimonial: memorandum and affidavit, the record constituting its own validation. Chancery functions not as originator but as public repository, a role of which the medieval version at least is thought to derive from Roman practice. The documentary typology is, however, much older, even though not always confirmed by archival location. At Ugarit, for example, a quittance for emancipation might consist of date formula (ištu ūmi annim: "from this day"), narrative of the transaction (=expositio), duration clause (adi dāriti: "forever"), witness (šību) signatures, name of scribe (tupšarrum), and reference to authentication (kunuk: seal).[177] In litigations, reference to place (ana pani PN: "in the presence of PN"), procès-verbaux, oath (māmītum), and sanctio formula (ša iragum tuppu annu ile'esu: "who ever protests, let this tablet prevail") may also be included.[178]

Sanctio

The Akkadian example adduced above is common, if not quite explicit in its reference to sanction. More elaborate versions occur including the names of deities as guardians of oath (bēlū māmīti).[179] And these, who will know who modifies/contravenes the terms of the decree (ša abate tuppi ša rikilti annati ušašna-a lu idušu), may be invoked to destroy his family, property, etc. (qadu mimmušu lu ḫaliqušu).[180] Conversely, they may be invoked, in case of compliance, to preserve all this (qadu mimmšu liṣṣurušu), which is rather different, but not infrequent in medieval Christian documents.[181] Curse and blessing formulae belong of course to a well-attested chancery tradition, of which the reflex in scripture has been much studied, especially in the context of treaty terminology and biblical covenant.[182] I think "chancery" tradition is probably right, though these formulae seem integral to the law-code (e.g. Ḥammurabi), the prophetical "lawsuit" (Hebrew rîb) and the controversies of Psalter and Wisdom literature. Sanctio imagery is basically forensic: oath, penalty and reward. Its recurrent association with divinity reflects an acknowledged source of authority, to which the conventions of trial, verdict and sentence would then be attributed. Chronological evidence of this, in whatever literary form, is really uninterrupted, so that its exclusion from later practice would require explanation. In Mamluk documents variants of qawlan wāḥidan wa-amran jāziman min ghayri rukhṣa wa-la tahāwun ("an unambiguous decree in respect of which neither license nor negligence will be tolerated") are standard, with occasional reference to penalty, e.g. wa-man imtana'a 'an al-qiyām. . . yuḥmal ila'al-abwāb al-sharīfa ("whoever evades compliance . . . will be brought before us").[183] It is indeed specification of reward and/or penalty that in Arabic chanceries is attenuated to an extent that makes of the formula merely a phrase of exhortation or emphasis (ta'kīd).[184] In a culture so explicitly monotheistic and legalistic as Islam the sanctio might be expected to exhibit a panoply of divine authority. Departure from the Semitic tradition, at least as preserved in cuneiform texts and Biblical Hebrew, could be read as displacement in favour of pious formulae distributed elsewhere in chancery format, e.g. invocatio, devotio, and apprecatio (see below), particularly the latter as conclusion. But the sanctio belongs to a certain type of document, which makes discontinuity difficult to illustrate. The extant Aramaic and Hebrew letters would hardly (and in fact do not) contain the formula, but the Aramaic legal papyri do.[185] On the other hand, the most common of the cuneiform examples adduced above does little more than draw attention to the decree itself. And that is approximately the value of the next component.

Corroboratio

Strictly defined, this formula is a reference in the text to the document's sign of authentication. That could be a signature (hence: manus nostre subscribcionebus subter eam decrevemus roborari), cipher (signaculum manus nostrae), or seal (sigillo nostro corroborari precipimus), or a combination (manu propria subter firmavimus et anuli nostri inpressione signavimus).[186] Its origins would be related to a supply of chancery "blanks", to which I have already alluded and whose pre-inscribed format (perhaps with seal, possibly even date) required the personal confirmation of originator.[187] While that arrangement, in the interests of mass production and prompt response to events, is easily documented for medieval chanceries, similar data in earlier texts might not support the same conclusion. Whether, indeed, from textual reference to the seal(s) in cuneiform tablets a pre-cast ready supply of these can be inferred is at best doubtful. At Ugarit such reference is frequent, if not the rule.[188] But unlike paper, pre-sealed clay would have to be moistened to take further impressions: though sealing might well precede writing it is likely that these were stages in a single process, occasionally quite explicit, e.g. inanna PN šanutišu ikunk ("now PN has sealed its duplicate").[189] The formula can nonetheless be defined as a chancery convention, of juridical rather than practical moment. In the Mamluk chancery a phrase of the type wal-khaṭṭ al-sharīf a'lāhu ḥujja fīhi ("and the noble script above is proof of it") or variant wal-'alāma al-sharīfa ("the noble sign") was employed very probably to both ends as appropriate.[190] The common denominator is personal intervention in what had become a fixed and to some extent mechanical procedure for public expression of authority. Certainly seal and sometimes signature were the responsibility (pro cura) of designated chancery officials whose remit could vary according to opportunity, ambition and political context. Autocratic assertion and entrenched bureaucracy would conflict, generating marginal circumstances in which ad hoc measures were gradually formalized. But application of this hypothesis may be limited: other modes of "corroboration" are attested. In the Egyptian Aramaic legal papyri both dictation clause (including name of the scribe) and witness list serve that purpose, though neither of course is identical to the formula discussed here.[191] What they share is validation by reference to named persons whose signature/sign is thereby vested with legal force (see below: subscriptio).

[Segmentation]

Like the arenga, corroboratio signals a major transition in the sequence of chancery formalities. Depending upon layout its referent may precede or follow, and from the medieval Latin rubric "subscriptio" it would seem that the latter was envisaged. Indeed, all the concluding elements (eschatokoll) could, and at various times did, express authentication of the document's content. But amongst these the principal, a "signature" incorporating name or title or both, might be set on any part of the instrument, say, in any one of the four available margins, that would make it conspicuous. Spatial allocation was thus flexible but also signalled by a textual reference, appended usually to the substantive portion (message) of the document. Order of the following components might vary: the date, for example, and place of enactment (where specified) could appear at the head of the text, especially in contracts. Witness signatures (testificatio) would invariably (and obviously) be appended to the object of their testimony. But however arranged, the concluding formulae exhibit a procedural device to insure against addition, deletion and modification: that is, by depicting enclosure of the transaction. Reference back to its source of promulgation was one amongst several means of achieving that.

Subscriptio

The rubric is inclusive: all signatures, whether of originator, scribe, chancery personnel (registration), notary, or witness, whether personally inscribed/impressed or delegated (proxy), contribute in some way to authentication of the document. Such marks may serve to distinguish genuine specimens from forgeries, original from copies (for archival use), but their purpose is juridical: to create or to confirm an act in law. Since much of that is accomplished by the format itself, that is, technical terms and arrangement of parts, the insertion of personal names might seem gratuitous. But because the text never quite achieved autonomy, a validating agency had to be imported: signature is the visible deposit of oral utterance, traces of which may be seen in the originally imperative "messenger formula" (see above) and, as I have already suggested, in the corroboratio. Bureaucracy is thus not absolutely anonymous nor alone adequate to promulgation of law.[192] To that end formulaic composition is a necessary but insufficient means. But like the range (and number) of signatories, the modes of signature were not unlimited. As in other components of the chancery text, here too a reductive typology is discernible: most configurations appear to evolve towards a ligatured pattern of letters and/or other (vegetal, geometric) motifs to produce a cipher (monogram) whose design is probably a reflex of the earliest attested signature, the stamp seal.[193] Originally a proprietary token, that device might contain name, title, invocation to deity, and pictorial imagery associated with the person/office/rank of its owner. These elements could be more liberally and attractively displayed with a cylinder seal, historically related to the use of clay and cuneiform syllabary.[194] Here the inscription is mostly adjacent to the image and often framed in vertical lines, a layout made possible by reserving a broad field for application of the cylinder and precluded to the stamp seal. Of extant specimens/ impressions of cylinder seals only a minority bear inscriptions, but all those from the chancery at Ugarit do. It might seem that identification of the seal owner/user would require an inscription of some sort, but despite considerable evidence of erasure and re-cutting, the overwhelming majority of uninscribed seals would indicate the contrary.[195] It was visual imagery that generated production and use of the seal as "signature", and this feature was easily transferred to and retained in writing (cf. paraph). An additional stimulus from the cuneiform tradition was the seal as instrument of divine authority in political transactions, e.g. of the god Assur, preserved in the chancery (bīt ālim?) and affixed to the vassal treaties of Asarhaddon. There the attendant imagery (kunuk šīmāti: "seal of destinies"; markasu: "bond") is at once administrative and cosmological, a recurrent theme in the lexicon of chancery practice.[196] Now the evolution from seal to handwritten ligature was not linear but orbital. Between the cuneiform designs and the densely patterned devices of the Turkish chanceries a number of byways intervened. These were mostly pious formulae, of scriptural derivation, conspicuously inscribed with a broad nib and centered in a separate line of text. In Arabic documents this could be either at the head of the text (below the invocatio) or at the end.[197] There was regional, and some individual variation, but a single formula could become the chancery hallmark for an entire dynasty, e.g. the Fatimid al-ḥamdu lillāhi rabbi'l-ʿālamīn ("Praise to God Lord of the Universe" = Qurʾān 1:2). Though the evidence is severely lacunar, e.g. for the Rashidun, the Syrian and Spanish Umayyads, the early Abbasids, Stern argues that the "classical" Islamic signature (ʿalāma) was precisely the pious motto or legend, formulae that would in my inventory of components correspond to invocatio, devotio or apprecatio. But the allocations are not mutually exclusive, since even the date formula may serve as "signature" (see below). The fact is, however, that the earliest Muslim documents, the Egyptian papyri, often bear seals as device of authentication, and that is less a surprise than application of a pious phrase in this function.[198] I mean the handwritten motto or legend as signature, since seals themselves might, and often did contain such inscriptions, and I have referred above to inscribed Bronze Age seals as equivalent, if not source, of the medieval invocatio. Apud Qalqashandī the Arabic evolution was from signet (khatam) with name only to name combined with motto to motto only, apparently a Persian legacy.[199] The distinctions, however, are blurred and probably not reliable. The transfer of one or both types of seal inscription to writing might exhibit a distinction between seal as custodial (Versiegelung) and seal as signature (Untersiegelung), with the latter adapted to the rest of the chancery format. Appearance there of the name of the originator in the intitulatio could explain choice of the motto as authentication. This technique was rigorously maintained in the Muslim West, amply illustrated in the Saadian chancery of Morocco (1553-1666), where a tendency to replace the handwritten motto al-ḥamdu lillāhi waḥdahu ("Praise to God Alone") with a stamp seal (ṭaba'a) containing the same inscription becomes evident in the later years of the dynasty.[200] But the seal may never have disappeared from western usage, e.g. in the chancery of the Spanish Umayyads.[201] A further tendency, especially visible in the contrast between Fatimid and Saadian signatures, is the calligraphic elaboration of the motto into a convolute embellished with floral and other motifs. It may be, and has been, argued that this development derived from seal imagery, specifically exhibited in the eastern Turkish (Seljuq) adaptation of the tribal cattle-brand (tamgha).[202] As description of Islamic chancery practice that is surely plausible, but the phenomenon is attested much earlier in both the cuneiform and hieroglyphic traditions, whatever the *use* of seals in the latter.[203] The operative factors seem to be change in writing materials (from clay to papyrus to paper) and selection of regnal attribute (name, title, religious doctrine). Employment as signature of the date formula itself (kutiba fi'l-ta'rīkh), of a corroborative phrase (e.g. ṣaḥḥa dhālika), or even of a combination like ṣaḥḥa fi'l-ta'rīkh ("Correct on the date") evaded the matter of seal altogether.[204] But the Turkish contribution can hardly be discounted: the extended shafts of the Mamluk ṭughrā, as well as the even more ornate Ottoman versions, are sufficiently proximate to the Seljuq writing of SULṬĀN to make derivation a reasonable conjecture.[205] The Mamluk signature ('alāma), on the other hand, suggests a ligature allied to seal inscriptions.[206] It is also neither motto nor title, but proper name, and thus conforms with the Roman and Byzantine versions of medieval Christian practice. Standard Latin was Ego PN subscripsi often accompanied by a sign of the cross, and Greek PN en christo to theo pistos, both frequently composed as monogram.[207] Both contain of course a motto of sorts, or at least a declaration of faith, and the cross itself could serve as structure for the monogram.[208] A further rapport was the use as signature in both Latin and Greek documents of the legimus formula ("we have read"), functional equivalent of the ṣaḥḥa dhālika ("that is correct") entry referred to above.[209] But these characteristics shared by Mediterranean chanceries are generic not verbatim: to list them as calques rather than merely parallels might be thought extravagant. For example, the seal (sigillum) was a more frequent and widely distributed phenomenon in Christian than in Muslim chanceries, probably the result of, or possibly the reason for, its specialised juridical value. As custodial mark, the practice was Roman but so similar to the function of seals in the cuneiform tradition that some linkage, say, via Aramaic usage, is a matter for serious speculation.[210] As sign of authentication, the evidence is later and not unmixed with its simpler role as identifying mark, that is, as rudimentary "signature" in addition to a handwritten one. Bresslau located the transition from that arrangement to one in which the seal served as sole authentication at the beginning of the Carolingian period, characterized by diminished literacy.[211] The spread of this practice to other, e.g. episcopal, chanceries had of course nothing to do with lack of literacy but was simply a product of emulation.[212] Procedural refinement was related certainly to the distribution of Chancery tasks (e.g. recognitio) and the increasingly formalised role of notary and witness (testificatio), but probably also to the differential production of seal types.[213] This observation is not quite frivolous: the appearance of seals on documents from the Mamluk chancery, not as signature but as heraldic emblems marking paper joins, exhibits incorporation of an extraneous genre into the format.[214] Essentially proprietarial and decorative, these could be invested with normative value only by virtue of guaranteeing the physical integrity of the text. As such their function is custodial rather than juridical, comparable to clay envelopes, cord sealings and the like. The proliferation of signs, originally conceived for quite different purposes, would affect the range of seal imagery and application. Parties, whether principal or tributary, to a transaction were more readily identified by a distinctive image than by a possibly illegible signature or simple stroke of the pen.

Testificatio

Witness, expressed by mention, by signature, or both, is a recurrent feature of at least certain kinds of document from the earliest specimens onward. There must have been as there is still, a distinction between witness as party to a transaction and as guarantor of its legality. It would be tidy if, in the cuneiform tradition, Akkadian šību referred exclusively to the latter category, but that is probably not so.[215] Etymologically, the term (šību = "elder") might seem to convey the notion of professional or positional qualification to "witness" and hence of disinterest.[216] West Semitic yph (Ugaritic, Hebrew) is of quite different origin but does render "witness" in legal contexts.[217] In Aramaic and Arabic yet another root (sh.h.d) is employed to that end, that is, to render "witness" as guarantor. The concept of testimony is thus easily established, its precise juridical value less so. The dominant context is the type of document generally called evidential, in which a transaction is recorded as having taken place.[218] The instrument, itself is not thereby authenticated, unless one of the signatories is notary or scribe. For such texts authentication lies in explicit reference to originator, which might be a signature or corroboratio formula. In the Aramaic papyri from Elephantine, however, the numerical distribution of witnesses between types of contract suggests a formula specific to validation, that is, either four or eight signatures, though the respective typologies are anything but clear-cut.[219] Of some interest is the fact that contemporary (Persian period) Demotic legal texts exhibit a roughly similar distribution. Whether in either set it is these signatures that validate the text is something of a problem: both contain also date formula and scribal signature, and the Aramaic documents have in addition a dictation formula, which from the point of view of chancery practice seems a more likely mode of authentication.[220] Witness to a signature, tantamount to corroboratio, is found in a curious context generated in part by the Mamluk chancery: two Arabic testimonials appended to the Italian text of a treaty drafted in Venice in 1507 refer explicitly to the signature in Latin script of the Egyptian envoy Taghri Berdi.[221] The formula ashhadanī 'alayhi PN (titles)...al-wāḍi' khaṭṭahu a'lāhu ("PN has summoned me to bear witness for him to the signature he has written above") is the only formal acknowledgement of Egyptian participation in the type of contract known as instrumentum reciprocum, which would still require ratification in Cairo. The witnesses themselves, though members of the envoy's party, were external guarantors, demanded by the Mamluk chancery. In medieval Latin documents that was also standard practice for private transactions, which had to be registered and publicly validated.[222] There however, and particularly in Frankish chanceries where the office of notary was less developed than in Italy, the practice was extended to royal decrees. Bresslau interpreted this as an evolution from interventio: the role of advocacy and mediation by privileged members of court, whose position acquired political significance in cases of minority and regency.[223] In terms of format such signatories were indistinguishable from witnesses whose presence thus served as much to authenticate the decree as to attest the transaction that provoked its issue. A distinction of function, if such there was, is not always clear unless the signatories can be identified as belonging to regalian retinue or, say, as not having actually "witnessed" the transaction. Latin testes thus shares the ambiguity noticed above for Akkadian šību. In the Judaeo-Arabic affidavit of 1187 (Syracuse) witness is certainly to the transaction, but the selection of signatories may represent a communal institution (zeqēnīm = gerousia) invested with authority for precisely that purpose, as is attested in other parts of Norman Sicily.[224] A *number* of witnesses, and it varied considerably, would evoke the notion of consensus and a concomitant diminution of autocratic utterance. But other formulae of validation, internal to chancery procedure, had a different effect: by extending authority to the format itself.

Recognitio

Designation of specific chancery personnel was explicit acknowledgement of the mechanics of production. In respect of the Elephantine papyri I have mentioned the dictation and scribal formulae as features of validation internal to the text. The process of inspection/authentication (recognitio) in the late Merovingian period, a duty assumed by the head of chancery probably in times of political instability, represents a more comprehensive mode of scrutiny. Variously entitled cancellarius, protonotarius, notarius or simply magister, that officeholder was invested with responsibility (pro cura) for drafting, employed on diplomatic missions, and more often than not recruited from the prelacy.[225] But the evolution and proliferation of chancery office was hardly uniform: its history exhibits considerable local variation reflecting sharp division of labour of the sort noticed at the beginning of this chapter for the medieval Egyptian chancery.[226] Subordination of such functions as dictation (abbreviatura) and preparation of fair copy (grossare litteras) to the overarching supervision of cancellarius was inevitable and enshrined in the formula iussus recognovi.[227] Even though accompanied by signature/seal manifesting personal intervention (see above), it is the salience of formulae that characterises the medieval chancery document. Format stresses office rather than incumbent, function rather than personality. This is particularly marked in the modes of authentication: the formulae legi/ legimus and Arabic ṣaḥḥa, for example, could occur as countersignatures, that is, as corroborative of the originator's own, inscribed by cancellarius or subalterns.[228] Internal procedure furnished several stages of validation, much of which derived from the preparation of private contracts whose status in law required chancery inspection.[229] Better possibly than "inspection" would be "prescription", for chancery was a model of the chambers and procedures of magistrate and notariat, disseminated via an extensive corpus of formularies (Latin formularius; Arabic 'ilm al-shurūṭ), less voluminous than but addressed to the same questions as that of Qalqashandī.[230] These were the common property of judge and notary, whose rules for drafting, recruiting witness, taking oaths and securing depositions generated a uniform style of written law. The concept of recognitio is an enabling one for the delegation of authority and thus presupposes an acknowledged source of power. Since these are features of pyramidal and hierarchic organisation, it would be reasonable to infer that the mechanism of diffusion was the formulary itself. Conversely, the fact that "procedure" was tangible and could be acquired meant that a code of practice was the very instrument that facilitated centralisation of authority. Of course these are complementary hypotheses and do not support a unilinear narrative of historical development. In contracts from Ugarit, for example, a range of almost mutually exclusive officeholders appears to fill the role of validating authority, e.g.

šarru ("king"), šākinu ("vizir"), and šību ("witness"/"elder").[231]
An explicit formula of delegation corresponding to recognitio
is, however, indiscernible. That may indicate dispersed and
autonomous jurisdictions, but in the light of territorial extent
and archival findspots that seems unlikely. Internal reference
to the legal force of the document is frequent enough (e.g.
sanctio and corroboratio) to reflect a perception of form as
binding, whatever the source of actual authority. Ugarit would
thus exhibit a polity not yet centralised but whose institutions
shared certain formal conventions. Proximity made for cohesion
and coherence.

Datum

Though one reason for dating a document ought to be archival
(i.e. to facilitate storage and retrieval), history of the practice, so
far as it can be traced, reveals rather a juridical purpose. Roman
practice made the dating of contracts obligatory, only later (12th
century) extended to letters.[232] Whether the procedure was
initially addressed to recording the transaction or to validating
its written form or even to indicating its promulgation (i.e.
despatch/delivery to parties concerned) is not altogether clear:
the formulae actum and datum seem to overlap.[233] The incidence of dated contracts is of course much older: matters of
endowment, property transfer (sale/purchase/lease), assignment of rights, marriage and divorce were dated, in Bronze Age
(Akkadian and Ugaritic) and Iron Age (Aramaic) transactions.
From position of the date formula, which fluctuated between
beginning and end of text, it is difficult to insist upon the
priority respectively of transaction or of instrument: variation
may be cultural (Aramaic as contrasted with Assyrian) or local
(Italian contrasted with Germanic).[234] In the Byzantine chancery
normal position was final.[235] That practice, shared with Islamic
chanceries, might well have been related to employment of the
date formula as "signature", to which I have alluded in discussion of subscriptio types.[236] Admittedly, that functional colliga-
tion might also have resulted in an initial slot for the date
formula, but where such is rigorously observed, as in the
Aramaic legal papyri, the conventional modes of authentication
(i.e. dictation clause, scribal signature, witnesses) appear at the
end of the document. A reasonable inference would be that

initial dating was specific to contracts, a practice long retained in western (e.g. Sicilian) texts, confirming the likelihood that its purpose was to record the transaction therein contained.[237] The contribution of chancery rhetoric ought not to be overlooked: the phrase "from this day" (Akkadian ištu ūmi annim; Ugaritic l ym hnd; Aramaic men yōma' zenah) may figure as incipit without a calendrical date and thus exhibit a general formula for legal efficacy unspecified.[238] It must seem that this is a reference to the instrument itself rather than the transaction, which would have to be chronologically fixed in another way, e.g. Akkadian eponym (limmu) dating, Aramaic be + date, Arabic bi-ta'rīkh + date, etc. Instances of anterior, posterior and discrepant dating have been noted, and can mostly be explained by the use of prepared formats in the chancery for special occasions. A curious specimen was a Florentine-Egyptian commercial treaty of 1497, dated after the death of the ruler whose cipher appears at the head of the document.[239] A wish to conceal the decease, defer the succession, or an unexpectedly protracted negotiation might explain that case, but more generally significant was the provision for adjusting components to fit a policy decision. Like medieval Latin ones, cuneiform *letters* were not regularly dated. Aramaic usage varied, as did Egyptian epistolography in this respect.[240] Since Byzantine and Arabic letters were dated, it may be that an East Roman prescription (Constantine, Justinian) for decrees and the like came to be generally applied to all chancery products. According to Muslim tradition at any rate, invention of a hijra calendar was intimately related to chancery (dīwān) practice as established by the caliph 'Umar.[241] The model for both would have been Hellenistic (Seleucid world-era), imagery appropriate to imperial administration. An archival dimension was thus acknowledged.

Apprecatio

A concluding prayer to balance the invocatio is almost certainly witness to Christian piety and Roman symmetry. Its earliest attestations are medieval, Byzantine and Islamic. Like the date, recognitio and legimus formulae, the apprecatio could serve as validation, inscribed manu propria by originator or chancery official. Christian versions varied but slightly: divinitas te servet, deus te incolumem custodiat, valete in Christo, bene valeas, merely amen, or a cross.[242] Islamic ones included a range of benedictions, e.g. ḥamdala, taṣlīya and ḥasbala, most of which might also appear elsewhere in the format as transition or segment markers.[243] Terminal sigla, i.e. ha' (=intahā: "finished") and ḥr (?muḥarrar: "recorded"), were probably inserted by the scribe.[244] In most texts these formulae began a fresh line, were indented or centered, arranged in short as linear culmination of the documentary framework. The closure thereby signalled was also semantic (i.e. valedictory) and juridical (i.e. delimiting), but primarily visual: the space was "blocked" (Qalqashandī used the expression li-sadd al-bayāḍ). Internal chancery instructions, e.g. for proofreading, registration, despatch, etc., might well be entered on the lower edge or margins of an archival copy, on the reverse or attached (i.e. epigraphs/ dockets). This practice, attested also for cuneiform tablets, did not seriously affect the format of an original intended for despatch or display.[245]

Now, from this *deliberately synoptic* survey of components it might just be possible to reconstruct a chancery document, but one that would correspond to no extant specimen. What I have sought is to identify the channels of transmission for calque and continuity in chancery practice. These are nearly but not absolutely constant: e.g. the attenuation and disappearance of the messenger formula, the emergence of recognitio and apprecatio, and some variation in layout attest to an evolution in style. Here, the major factor is prominence. For example, date and signature tend to appear either at the head or the end of the document. Since each may figure as validation (of the transaction, of the instrument itself, or of both), it could be inferred that high visibility lay at either end of the format (approximately: "letterhead" or "bottom line") but not in the text block. While medieval documents were framed by benedictions (invocatio and apprecatio), these were of reduced salience precisely because they constituted a framework. Visual expectation in the course of scanning would be arrested only by the absence of these embellishments. Signature and date, on the other hand, would be crucial to even a casual reading. That these (and other) significant slots yield a mechanism for tracing continuity will, I trust, be conceded. Diachronic analysis requires first to locate the points of contact.

Typical contexts are the polyglot chancery and adoption of a lingua franca. Case studies have begun to accumulate, some of the best being analyses of the Aramaic legal papyri from Elephantine.[246] The status of Aramaic as lingua franca during the Achaemenid period (539-333 BCE) is well-known and the history of Egypt during the following millennium provides a context for the evolution of documentary style. Here, localisation is important: neither the Aramaic of the texts analysed nor the Akkadian of the imperial tradition which they reflect nor the Arabic in which the formulaic deposit finally came to rest was native to Egypt. That region, with a different legal and linguistic tradition, could be a useful control matrix for assessment of the injection, blend and eventual consolidation of alien ingredients. Indeed, considerable work on these documents has been so formulated, with due attention to the distinction between parallel development and historical dependence.[247] Demonstration of the latter, which I have regularly designated calque, may be elicited from the sequence of components, but is more reliably based on their semantic and functional equivalence. Thus, Yaron's analysis of the date formula (day-month-year etc.) is valuable but acknowledges the limited permutations this could assume.[248] On the other hand, Muffs' painstaking study of the remuneration clause (ṭyb lbby: "my heart is satisfied") confirms its Akkadian origin (libbaśu ṭāb: "his heart is satisfied") and offers persuasive argument for Aramaic influence on Demotic Egyptian: dj.k-mtj h3tj (.i) ("you have satisfied my heart").[249] It is of course not merely the etymological continuity vs discontinuity/innovation that support the reconstruction, but the identical function (Muffs: Entgeltlichkeit) of all three versions of the formula in conveyance transactions. The study is undoubtedly a paradigm for all such in the matter of calque and conceptual transfer. Perpetuation of the formula in Arabic (ṭyb nafs/rḍy qlb: "(his) mind/heart was satisfied/pleased") well into the Middle Ages for conveyancing attests clearly to continuity of the idiom, and probably from Aramaic rather than as translation from Demotic, Coptic or Greek. It would seem also that its functional value in Arabic contracts was not volition but remuneration, as Muffs has shown for its Semitic cognates.[250] Some three millennia exhibit an impressive life for a legal formula and in this instance at least can hardly be attributed to parallel development.

Admittedly, a major segment of this chancery tradition is preserved in Demotic, Greek and Coptic: attested in both translations and bilingual instruments. There, the sequence of constituent element is irregular, and many of the technical terms (e.g. for defensio/quittance) are calques (=loan-translations) rather than cognates, but that could, and did, also happen within the Semitic lexicon.[251] In Egypt local variation, despite the convergence of several cultural traditions, was remarkably limited. An instance is the contrast between subjective (first person) and objective (third person) formulation in the narrative which constituted the business being transacted: Demotic, Aramaic and Greek texts are subjective, while Arabic contracts tend, like most Akkadian examples, to be cast in objective style.[252] That is an important difference, but not one from which historical dependence could be inferred. In any case, neither Akkadian nor Arabic is exclusively objective in contractual language and, as in the possibilities for expression of the date formula, mentioned above, choice is not great. Rather more important is the fact of *lingua franca:* neither Demotic nor Coptic could be described as such, but all the others were and thus exposed to a spectrum of usage that could only be constrained from time to time by strictly local practice. That is to say that scribal habits might be anchored to a specific curriculum, irrespective of its historical and geographical origins. For Aramaic scribes at Elephantine, Mesopotamian and Syrian models would not have been altogether absent (i.e. ignored or forgotten), but the presence of Egyptian formularies must have impinged.

Ugarit offers another fixed point in mapping the trajectories of chancery practice. I have mentioned the scope of experiment there.[253] Its major technological achievement was production of a cuneiform script for the Canaanite language known to modern scholarship as "Ugaritic" but of which knowledge and practical use far exceeded the territorial boundaries of the north Syrian port. Since the acknowledged lingua franca was Akkadian, the Bronze Age precursor of Aramaic in the next millennium, application of the new technology deserves some attention. Conventional wisdom and the evidence so far available allocated Akkadian to international instruments and Ugaritic to domestic records. But this division is only approximate: a fair number of local (Syrian) transactions are expressed in Akkadian and some communications to and from foreign parts in Ugaritic. An inventory is now available in the Concordance

published by Bordreuil and Pardee.[254] Since the excavation
numbers include fragments, a quantitative analysis of tablet-
script distribution is somewhat arduous: the entries for Akkadian (syllabary) and Ugaritic (alphabet) are approximately even
(*ca* 1800). The few eccentric instances of mode reversal (i.e.
Akkadian/alphabet and Ugaritic/syllabary) I have mentioned
above. Hurrian is mostly, but not exclusively, represented in
syllabic, Hittite and Sumerian exclusively so. Egyptian and
Cypro-Minoan may be regarded as having been produced
outside Ugarit. Of interest for chancery practice are three
groups of documentation: Akkadian inscriptions on Ugaritic
tablets, Ugaritic inscriptions on Akkadian tablets, and several
artifacts inscribed with Ugaritic but found outside Ugarit. I
shall deal first with the last group.

It would no doubt be extravagant to argue that the findspots of the (so far) nine artifacts attest to widespread knowledge
of Ugaritic. Strictly observed, only two (Tell Sukas and Taanakh) are tablets, a third (Bet Shemesh) a circularly inscribed
amulet.[255] The two texts from Kamid el-Loz, as well as those
from Qadesh and Sarepta, are sherds and their inscriptions
indicate either ownership or dedication.[256] Tabor is a bronze
knife blade and Hala Sultan Tekke (Larnaca) a silver bowl.[257]
Moreover, the findspots represent destination (or at least final
resting place), not the origin, which might have been Ugarit. In
fact, Tell Sukas seems to contain a list of personal names each
followed by an allocation ("one"?) of a type well-known from
the city's archives. Taanakh has been read either as an invoice
for grain/flour or receipt for payment of a fee. Both tablets
could be read as generated by juridical or mercantile activities
in Ugarit. The very fragmentary text from Bet Shemesh is
probably an apotropaic fertility formula, brought or sent from
Syria to Palestine. A similar origin and despatch may be
postulated for the other materials, none of which contains a
"message" in any normal sense of that word. While the Levantine dispersion of these artifacts can hardly be surprising, there
are a few features of some epigraphic interest. One of the Kamid
el-Loz inscriptions, as well as those from Qadesh, Tabor and
Hala Sultan Tekke, read from right to left in the manner of West
Semitic linear scripts. Further, all but Tell Sukas employ a
modified cuneiform script with reduced consonantal inventory
and certain deviant shapes. Finally the repoussé style of Hala

Sultan Tekke, though clearly alphabetic cuneiform, bears an uncanny resemblance to Cypro-Minoan script. Now, the so-called "reduced" alphabet, exhibiting coalescence of ghayn/ 'ayn, th/sh and het/khāf, variant letter forms and right to left direction, is also attested at Ugarit.[258] These tendencies towards Phoenician linear might be thought, since they comprise so little of the full Ugaritic corpus, to confirm the chronological priority of the latter. But they are not always so interpreted, and the possibility that the thirty consonant cuneiform alphabet exhibits an expansion of the "reduced" (hence, a misnomer!) version has been mooted.[259] There are too few specimens of this version for substantive proof and no evidence at all that they are earlier than the conventional alphabetic texts from Ugarit. A further dimension must be signalled: the Sarepta inscription exhibits the "reduced" alphabet but is written from left to right in normal cuneiform style. This departure from the collocation of features described above is further distinguished by lexica unfamiliar in Ugaritic (i.e. p'l = "to make" and agn = "basin"), which has led both Greenstein and Bordreuil to read the text as Phoenician.[260] While caution is certainly necessary, data of this kind would seem to confirm that Phoenician linear was a later development. In the Bronze Age it had to be written in cuneiform. Deliberate diffusion of that script for general use cannot really be inferred from these artifacts, save for the stylistic adaptation to Cypriot models on the silver cup from Hala Sultan Tekke. Even that could have been inscribed by a craftsman at Ugarit, where several specimens of the script have been found.[261]

The two other kinds of scribal evidence from Ugarit which seem to me relevant to analysis of literacy in Canaanite are reflected in the incidence of chancery "dockets". Some twenty tablets composed in Ugaritic (alphabet) contain lines of Akkadian (syllabary), inscribed usually on the edge or at the bottom of the text. The texts themselves are exclusively administrative: conscription and beneficiary lists, allocation of rations, equipment, pay and taxes, census records, and one inventory of tribute for the Hittite ruler (RS 19.017).[262] The Akkadian epigraphs are summaries of the allocations (numbers + naphar = "total"), brief descriptions of the commodities (quantities: gur/ gín + name: zì = "flour"/kubabbar = "silver"/dug = "cask" + gestin = "wine"), of the recipients (tuppu sabē ša qašāt = "tablet concerning archers") topographical reference (āl Alašiya = "city of Cyprus") and the like. Practical use as *archival index* would explain their location on the tablets, and also suggest that the language of reference in the chancery was Akkadian. If that were in fact so, one might have expected rather more use of this device. The reverse mode is also attested: two instances of Ugaritic inscribed on Akkadian tablets,[263] and a dozen loose alphabetic "tags" which probably served a similar purpose.[264] Neither category of docket is in sufficient quantity to illustrate an archival reference system, though it would be surprising if none existed. From the balance of linguistic evidence it is also impossible to infer the dominant mode of communication.

For the Levant in the Late Bronze Age a network of international relations can be extrapolated from archaeological findspots. From Ugarit to Amarna and including Alaśiya these number some three dozen for which Akkadian witness has ben found.[265] These are mostly letters, whence one may infer a degree of cuneiform literacy, or literary (Amarna and Megiddo) and lexicographical (Aphek) exercises, from which one could postulate a scriptorium. The Ugaritic network is less extensive, as far south as Bet Shemesh but also includes Alaśiya (Hala Sultan Tekke). These are mostly not letters and thus, as I have conceded, hardly witness to literacy in Ugaritic (see above). And yet, those which are letters, or administrative documents (Tell Sukas and Taanakh), must, unless they are archival translations from Akkadian, have had some function in establishing or maintaining contact. Two sets of correspondence, each containing both Akkadian and Ugaritic components, will be adduced in support of this postulate.

It might be supposed that contact between Tyre and Ugarit would be expressed in a Canaanite language. Indeed, two letters in Ugaritic confirm this expectation. The first, from the ruler of Tyre, reports the foundering in that harbour of a ship bound from Ugarit to Egypt, the result of severe sea weather. It was taken in charge by the salvage master, repaired and despatched to Akko.[266] This suspension of the lex naufragi was an amicable gesture, or perhaps a convention of international law, from one ruler to another. The second letter, poorly preserved, is a report to the ruler of Ugarit from his officer, one Ṣpṭ B'l, concerning a transaction (unclear) with the ruler of Tyre.[267] Some clarification appears from two further letters, preserved in Lattakiya but probably (?) excavated in Ugarit and written in

Akkadian.[268] One, from the ruler of Tyre to the ruler of Ugarit, mentions Špṭ B'l as in default of payment, and the other, from the latter's business partner, Dagan Bel, describes the commodities involved and includes several further demands. Since a portion at least of the business is related to Emar and countries to the East, Dagan Bel might well and more naturally have written in Akkadian. But that would hardly explain the language of the first letter. The fact that the Amarna letters of Abimilki of Tyre are of course Akkadian might account in part for a chancery convention.[269] But no such blurring of genres could justify regarding the two Ugaritic letters from Tyre to Ugarit as translations from Akkadian.

The second set of correspondence is rather more complex. As for Tyre, so for Alašiya and Ugarit the Amarna deposit is Akkadian.[270] Between Alašiya and Ugarit four further letters, two in each direction, are also in that language.[271] The first, in which Niqmad of Ugarit addresses the ruler of Alašiya as "my father" (abuya) and refers to himself as "your son" (mārika), concerns a transaction for oil sold from Ugarit. The second, from Ešuwara, governor (?) (maškim gal) of Alašiya, to the ruler of Ugarit warns him of a hostile naval force nearby. In the third, the ruler of Alašiya (unnamed) advises 'Ammurapi of Ugarit to muster defence against (the same?) enemy fleet. In the fourth, the ruler of Ugarit (unnamed, but = "your son") informs the ruler of Alašiya (unnamed, but = "my father") that the naval attack has now been launched upon his land and that he is helpless, his army occupied in Hittite territory and his fleet stationed in Lycia. This exchange, at least the last three letters, has naturally provoked a good deal of historical speculation about the invasion of the "Sea Peoples" and the destruction of Ugarit.[272] My concern here is with the contact language. The two Ugaritic rulers are well attested, in both syllabic and alphabetic texts.[273] The only name from Alašiya, the writer of the second letter Ešuwara, is Indo-Aryan or Hurrian.[274] One can only guess at how a Hurrian came to occupy high office in Alašiya or whether the four published (but unread) Cypro-Minoan tablets discovered at Ugarit could have emanated from this quarter.[275] In the polyglot context here adumbrated recourse to the acknowledged lingua franca is hardly unexpected. The two letters *from* Alašiya do exhibit some eccentricities (e.g. enclitic -ma to conclude a series) but mostly conform with the usage of peripheral Akkadian (e.g. umma + genitive = Ugaritic thm in stat. const. = "message of..."). Now, the Alasiya dossier could be increased by two alphabetic texts from the archives at Ugarit.[276] The case for the first is circumstantial: one Pgn addresses the ruler of Ugarit (unnamed, but "my son" passim) from "your father" (conjecture abk) requesting that food be sent by ship to him in his current plight.[277] Only fourteen lines can be read (of a total twenty-five) and half of those are formulaic (inscriptio/messenger/salutatio), but which at least confirm the chancery origins of the letter. The link with the Akkadian correspondence is formal ("father" and "son") and possibly contextual (hardship). The tablet is one of some dozen letters in a collection of approximately seventy-five documents discovered in the celebrated "kiln" of Court V in the Royal Palace.[278] These, all alphabetic and apparently being fired at the very moment of Ugarit's destruction, have generated a putative "last days" chronology (c. 1190 BCE). Even more important is the inference that location in the kiln must mean outgoing documents or archival translations (sic!) of incoming ones. Apart from uncertainty about the débris in Court V (i.e. whether or not fallen from upper chambers), the fact that the letters from Tyre (see above) were also found there ought to counsel caution in this matter. On the other hand, Pgn has not yet been identified. The second proposed addition to the Alasiya dossier is rather earlier. While neither originator nor addressee is unequivocal, it contains reference to "all the gods of Alasiya (kl il alty)", the Egyptian pharaoh Nmry (Nimmuriya = Amenophis III 1413-1377 BCE), is written in Ugaritic and was found there.[279] The text consists of two fragments from the upper left corner of a much larger tablet and offers some two dozen lines, none of which is complete. The inscriptio reads "to the king my lord", the intitulatio "message from the chief of . . .your servant", and the salutatio includes, besides the prostration formula (see above) invocations to the gods Špš, 'štrt, 'nt, those of Alasiya, and Nmry. The title of the originator has been interpreted "harbourmaster" (rb miḫd), "seal-bearer" (rb mišmn) and "centurion" (rb mit), and the "king" mentioned five times in the text identified with the addressee, assumed not unreasonably by all to be the ruler of Ugarit. What can be gleaned of the transaction suggests procurement of ships by a merchant (otherwise unspecified), for which approval is sought from the addressee. It might seem from the address ("my lord". . ."your servant") that the originator was an official commissioned from Ugarit. On the other hand, the epithets may be mere courtesies of rank (see above), but quite unlikely if the sender were Egyptian and the text a translation from Akkadian. But if the merchant were Egyptian and the originator a Cypriot official, a letter to Ugarit could well have been composed in the dominant Canaanite language of that period. The invocation of both Canaanite and Alašiyan deities might be thought to confirm that interpretation.

The hypothesis of archival translations at Ugarit begs the question of their purpose or necessity. I have mentioned the only two instances of paraphrase so far discovered: the "pantheon" (from Ugaritic to Akkadian!) and the Hittite "tribute list" (from Akkadian to Ugaritic).[280] There was also a fair amount of graphic experiment and lexical tabulation, but no bilinguals as such. Indeed, a scriptorium characterised by intensive training in the cuneiform tradition might be expected to produce texts in several languages, but not to require cribs. Invention of the alphabet there would certainly generate some scribal exercises, but not affect the production of fair copies for despatch and storage. Some contamination was of course inevitable. In the diffusion of a *koine,* the transfer of concepts and attendant translation of words often exhibit décalage, of a sort that makes either one or the other the primary vehicle of change.

An example may be seen in the development respectively of substantive law and juridical terminology. Persistence of the Akkadian conveyancing formula libbašu tab across three millennia, mentioned above, is not a unique phenomenon but nonetheless one of some rarity. More often than not conceptual transfer is complicated by lexical modification. One well documented, and much discussed, instance concerns the notion of "guarantee/pledge", Akkadian qātatam ṣabātu ("to grasp hands") but also ḫubullu ("interest-bearing loan").[281] At Ugarit the Akkadian root erēbu ("to enter") generates erubu and urubānum = "earnest/pledge", consonant with West Semitic forms attested in Ugaritic, Phoenician, Hebrew and Aramaic.[282] In Arabic, both this spelling and one with initial glottal stop (as also in some Aramaic dialects) are found, the latter sometimes thought to indicate a return-loan from Greek arrabon or Latin arrabo.[283]

Contamination with South Arabian 'RB ("to import/offer") provides a further dimension to the semantic field represented in medieval Mediterranean lingua franca as arabun, arbon, arram, caparo, and caparrum. Derivation of all these from Akkadian ḫubullu is far-fetched but phonetically conceivable.[284] More significant is the fact that in Arabic juridical literature the technical term for "guarantee/pledge" is none of these, but rather, ḍamān or kafāla or rahn, the last of which has as primary value the meaning "pawn/hostage/mortgage". Chancery use of forms from the stem 'RB suggests an independent channel of transmission. Now, the precise referent in this vast documentation may not always be the same: a transaction named from a lexeme with the basic meaning "enter/offer" could be a guarantee, but also a loan, insurance or a hypothec.[285] In the Ugaritic texts at least most of these are possible readings, which is merely to confirm that substance and form did not evolve in unison. The absence of a corpus of jurisprudence at Ugarit, or in Phoenician, makes difficult a grasp of nuance, at exactly the chronological point of entry into the West Semitic lexicon.

A more disciplined trajectory is discernible in the Semitic term for "custom/toll". While from its earliest attestations Akkadian miksu was a technical term, its referents are multiple. Apart from a general meaning "share" and thus denoting quantity, the contexts are those of a publicly administered impost.[286] It was levied on both agricultural yield and on commerce (import/export/transit) in a manner that indicates contractual tax-farming. Although the basis for assessment is seldom clear, the impost is as often levied upon collectivities (e.g. towns) as upon individuals. Agency is identified with the mākisu (publican) or rab miksu (probably the same) in the Neo-Babylonian period, once with rab kāre (port authority). Evidence from Mari, Ugarit and Assur exhibits the preponderance of commerce over land yield, though the commodities taxed would of course include agricultural products. A gradual convergence of miksu with "tithe" (eśretu) is also attested at Ugarit, more in the context of a customs tax on trade than of an agricultural impost.[287] In West Semitic it is only the Biblical mekes l'adōnay (Numb. 31:28, 37-41), as a tribute to the Lord following upon the Midianite campaign, that perpetuated the Akkadian term. Ugaritic and Phoenician cognates are not known, but the Biblical image was preserved in Syriac versions. It was also there, as in New Testament Greek (telónes) and Talmudic Aramaic (mōkhēs), that the notoriety of the "publican" as cheat and thief was established. Finally, the Judaeo-Christian version culminated in Islamic usage, where the term maks, originally the pre-Islamic Arabic designation of market imposts (!), became the general one for all non-canonical taxation.[288] In the evolution of West Semitic tax law the original term for public impost has become marginalised to a point of juridical obloquy. The political environment in which this could occur was probably imperial (Seleucid/Roman), where tax-farming would have been especially susceptible to abuse.

My third example of conceptual/lexical décalage is one to which I have already briefly alluded: the expression of exterritorial identity in commercial law.[289] In nuce, an implicit feature in the earliest records of diplomatic contact, the status of envoy, whether court official or merchant or both, came to be articulated as institutionally conferred privilege. By the end of the medieval period both substance and format were as elaborate as they were ever to be. The stipulations of safeconduct included:

Security of person and property
Freedom of worship
Testamentary rights
Consular jurisdiction
Abolition of collective responsibility
Right of address to local authority
Protection at sea
Abolition of lex naufragi

Because they guarantee the others, the most important of these are consular jurisdiction and abolition of collective reponsibility. The underlying juridical principle is that of procuratio, by which liability for the conduct and affairs of its members is assigned to a single communal representative, namely, the "consul". His status might vary with the mode of appointment: whether despatched from the metropolis (missus), chosen by members of the community abroad (electus), or appointed by the local authority (hospitis). The somewhat enhanced status of the last category was traced to Islamic law, which specified that a general safeconduct (amān 'āmm) could only be issued by the local Muslim authority (imām) or his deputy (nā'ib).[290] For the most part a general safeconduct would reflect circumstances in which there was steady traffic in envoys/merchants or a resident alien community that required ongoing security and rights in civil and criminal law. That such obtained in the late medieval Mediterranean is well-known and copiously documented. Of interest here is the fact that the Arabic term for this arrangement (amān) is the one also employed (but qualified khāṣṣ = special) for the grant by any legally competent (mukallaf) Muslim to a single or restricted number of (non-Muslim) foreigners and equated with the ancient Arabian (pre-Islamic) concept of "protection" (jiwār). The achievement of Muslim jurists was to identify as traditional what was in fact a legal innovation to enable regular commercial and diplomatic activity. Dating this transition is difficult: for the Egyptian chancery Qalqashandī records as innovation the issue by the sultan Qalā'ūn (1280-90) of a general safeconduct in favour of oriental merchants with the opening phrase "It has been decreed" (rusima).[291] Explicit reference to a unilateral edict (marsūm) and address to an unspecified number of recipients would make the text something of a landmark in chancery practice, and its date corresponds to the invigoration of commercial contact after the Muslim occupation of the last Crusader fortress at Akko (1291).[292] Incipient modification of tribal jiwār by institutional amān is attested as early as the prophet Muhammad's "Constitution of Medina" and could account for the specific evolution of Arabic terminology.[293] The West Semitic root GWR is of course rather older, attested in Hebrew (Biblical ger = "sojourner/proselyte"), but also in not altogether clear sanctuary contexts in Phoenician and Ugaritic.[294] Except etymologically, none of this material is relevant to exterritorial status, for which Hebrew employed goy/nōkhrī and Ugaritic the Akkadian term ubru.[295] Mostly, however, the identity of foreigners is signalled by a gentilic or an epithet like mārū/awilū GN ("sons/men of...").[296] But whatever their designation, institutional regulation of the affairs of aliens is documented as early as the Middle Bronze period (Mari) and for Late Bronze, besides Ugarit, the Amarna corpus.[297] Movement of envoy (mār šipri) or merchant (tamkaru) was hedged with exemptions and immunities, but also security measures, provision for transport, nourishment and sojourn. Passports as such are not attested, but orders to expedite passage occasionally (e.g. Amarna no.30; cf. Arsames no.6).[298] In several Akkadian documents from Ugarit management of exterritorial rights is stipulated in both general terms (i.e. eventualities) and particular cases (i.e. litigations). These set out indemnity for loss of life (homicide) and of property (theft, embezzlement, bankruptcy).[299] One litigation concerning shipwreck may, like the Tyrian letter to Ugarit (see above), reflect abrogation of the general lex naufragi.[300] A significant feature of all these is their unilateral issue: they are edicts like those promulgated in medieval chanceries and probably the ultimate source of that format derived in Islamic law by a fictive pedigree from Arabic tribal jiwār.

Admittedly, the proximate model could be Rome.[301] Effective measures for the safety and control of foreigners could only be put in place by an authority whose jurisdiction covered the entire territory in which they might be found. Toll stations, immigration points, and the like are affairs of state, very seldom private property. These proliferated with the political fragmentation of empire but continued to benefit from the techniques of imperial administration. Such components as guarantee (pignus), impost (vectigal), safeconduct (mundeburdis), and the like are standard in all but the (hypothetical) closed economy. Their efficacy is a product of administrative attention to the mechanics of commerce, and would vary with the allocation of resources. While the scale of empire might ensure an abundance of these, it is clear from the cuneiform tradition that the technical expertise was also available to much smaller units. In the Ugaritic sector of this material the legal persona of "ruler" (mlk) seems dominant.[302] Salient in both syllabic and alphabetic texts, this feature should be (but is not always) regarded as juridical rather than political. That is partly owing to the regalian associations of West Semitic MLK (derived from Biblical imagery), partly architectural exegesis on the site itself (PRU = "le palais royal d'Ugarit"), and finally the concentration of archival data in chambers thought, on the basis of a single "king list" and a series of seal impressions, to have housed a dynastic monarchy.[303] To my knowledge, the possibility of reading yaqarum, the name of the putative founder of that

dynasty, as a title (="honourable/worthy", cf. Hebrew yāqār/
yaqīr) bestowed upon any/every occupant of the highest political office in Ugarit, was just once proposed.[304] There are,
admittedly, obstacles: yaqaru is attested as a proper name, in
Amorite and Akkadian, as well as at Ugarit (syllabic orthography only);[305] the legend on the so-called "dynastic" seal reads
yaqarum mār niqmadu śar ugarit ("Y. son of Niqmad king of
Ugarit").[306] To interpret Akkadian māru not as "son" but as
"officeholder" (cf. mār śipri = envoy) and Akkadian śarru not
as "king" but as rendering local mlk (ruler/chief) may indeed
be audacious, but surely possible. In any case, the "ruler" of
Ugarit figures prominently in chancery acts.

These include political and commerical agreements, deeds
of conveyance, contracts of marriage and succession, adoption,
exemption and emancipation, warranty and enfeoffment. His
presence, whether as party or as witness to the transaction, is
almost invariably signalled by application of the yaqarum seal.
The juridical principle must be one of *chancery* validation,
functionally similar to the legimus/vidimus/recognitio formulae of medieval documents (see above). That the yaqarum seal
was a sign of office rather than of dynasty might be supported
by the occasional employment of personal seals on chancery
documents, alone or in conjunction with the official emblem.
For example, that of Niqmad, inscribed in Akkadian (!), appears
at the head of two alphabetic texts;[307] of 'Ammiśtamru, inscribed in Ugaritic (!), on an Akkadian tablet, together with the
yaqarum seal.[308] Distribution cannot be related to the language
of the tablet: two Ugaritic texts are sealed with the yaqarum
device.[309] The evidence of other personal seals exhibits use of
alphabetic, syllabic, and even Egyptian hieroglyphs.[310] These
proprietarial devices would of course not be limited to chancery
use, whereas the yaqarum seal must be. It is thus the bureaucracy, not the dynasty (if such there was), that emerges as locus
of authority.

That the machinery of administration generates its own
momentum is a familiar phenomenon, and one to which I have
several times alluded.[311] A kind of "diplomatic revolution" in
the late 12th century Mediterranean attests certainly to increased traffic, but also to an altered perception of the paperwork necessary to support such activity. Not merely the

volume, but also the types of document proliferate: these include instructions to and reports from envoys, to and from resident consuls, letters from merchants and consuls, credentials and passports (safeconduct), petitions, procès-verbaux, and treaties, business records (account books, bills of lading and exchange, receipts, insurance policies and notarial records). Some of these, particularly the correspondence of consuls and merchants, are informative about areas quite outside the strict conduct of business and reflect a tendency to substitute written for oral reports.[312] But volume is also remarkable: during the period 1171-1516 some 60 commercial treaties were concluded and/or renewed between Egypt/Syria (Ayyubid and Mamluk) and western European powers, and a similar number between the latter and the several states of North Africa (Almohad, Ḥafṣid, and Marinid).[313]

Generally these treaties, or copies of them, were preserved in the municipal archives of Venice, Florence, Pisa, Genoa, Barcelona, etc., but not always. Some have been found in private collections, since transferred to public libraries.[314] The route thither points to original possession by merchant, envoy or consul, in whose papers it might easily, at the end of an overseas mission or posting, have been deposited. That probability is corroborated by the format of some at least of these documents. They are not bilateral "treaties" but unilateral "directives" addressed to officeholders in the Mamluk administration of Egypt and Syria.[315] It is in this type that the original request (petitio) of the European merchant community was adopted verbatim as the chancery decision (dispositio) conferring right of entry, trade and sojourn in the Mamluk dominions.[316] I have referred to this device, called insertio, in European notarial instruments, probably adapted from oriental usage.[317] The procedural advantage is clear: its immediate benefit was the accumulation of law by precedent. An important corollary was the diffusion of juridical terminology by calque. While the many lexical loans, between Italian and Arabic or Turkish and Greek, constitute the primary index to that diffusion, it was the substance and style of negotiation itself which generated the medieval lingua franca.

"Directives" were not despatched, but distributed. From customs offices (matjar) they passed to members of the resident merchant community (ṭā'ifa/jamā'a/jins) as vademecum for the ongoing regulation of trade. The format was either a complete text (marsūm) or an abbreviated version (murabba'a).[318] Since it was easier to handle, the latter form was preferred. Occasionally a copy for the local consul was specified, but not invariably, and one must conclude that the versions found in European archives are not "originals" but authenticated (!) copies for general use.[319] Preparation of these in the chancery, however, is signalled by the subscriptio ('alāma), of which examples, even if pre-inscribed, would be available only there.[320] From the Italian versions, which appear to have generated the language of the Arabic texts, it is just about possible to recapture the dialogue of negotiation. For example, the Arabic rendering of a letter of safeconduct from the Ḥafṣid ruler of Tunis, dated in Ramaḍān 767/June 1366, was designed to fill a single sheet of paper (customary in North African chanceries) in a manner that placed the concluding 'alāma (the conventional motto) at the top. An Italian paraphrase written in Maghribī script (!) for the benefit of the Pisan community to whose head it was addressed, dispensed with that formality.[321] It may be conjectured that the latter version, found in the municipal archives at Pisa, served the practical purpose of quayside communication. The conclusion would be that Tunisian officials understood but could not read Italian in Latin script. An alternative but less likely explanation is to regard the paraphrase as a scribal exercise, for which a more liberal resort to scriptio plena might have been expected.

    That particular mode of literacy is not surprisingly unique. But the increase of recorded transactions is general and cannot, I think, be attributed to chance discoveries. It was, rather, the diffusion of juridical authority and concomitant proliferation of scribal labour. For European diplomatic an index is the elevation and significance of the notariat.[322] From an earlier more or less undifferentiated equivalence scriptor: notarius, the latter office came to be applied to the public scribe whose services were available to anyone requiring an authenticated instrument in law. Diplomas of appointment for notaries become abundant from the 12th century on, from which one may infer a widespread employment. Now, lest one suppose that the impetus for a burgeoning Mediterranean bureaucracy was European, it is well to recall that in Islamic law the scribal profession was equally well established and certainly older.[323] Especially in commerce (tijāra) and the enforcement of marketplace regulations (ḥisba) procedure was explicitly documentary and the public scribe (kātib) a feature of the urban scene. Owing to the emphatically decentralised character of the Muslim magistracy (qaḍā'/naẓar fi'l-maẓālim) that function was broadly distributed. With supply securely in place, demand was bound to increase. That was of course not merely a result of the encounter of those two post-Roman cultures. It was primarily the *contractual* nature of this encounter, some centuries on from the casual embassy or uncalculated exploration in search of goods and markets. Scheduled sailing and pre-reckoned ladings were the product of ledgers, calendars and notarial records of capital shares, pledges, insurance loans and material orders. Only with storage of the requisite information was planning possible. It is the rational organisation of these data that characterises the medieval archive. For earlier deposits it is the impression of accumulation, rather than of allocation, that seems dominant. But that may well be an accident, for certain private, and inevitably smaller, archives do reflect an organising principle.[324] Also typical of the medieval archive is a remarkable span of coverage, visible because articulated in such detail. Any description of, say, the Venetian archivio di stato or of the Fondo Francesco Datini in Prato would illustrate that attention to inventory and rubrics.[325]

If there is a thread in this narrative it must be the displacement of agency by technology. The latter is a compound, mostly of techniques originally isolated, gradually juxtaposed and finally amalgamated in the interests of efficiency. For the chancery the result was an intelligible format and a set of standard procedures. For the transactions of diplomacy and commerce the result was internationally understood practice and increased productivity. In law convention replaced confrontation, in finance calculation superseded guesswork. While the evidence for this happens to be preserved *in* writing, it has been argued that writing *itself* was the operative factor.[326] That view has considerable merit, but I have referred to a striking difference in tone between the Amarna correspondents and that of the Venetians in Alexandria.[327] The separation in time comprehends the three millennia adopted as baseline for this study: the craft of writing was already at its beginning established and distributed. Its evolution had still to experience the alphabet and several systems of shorthand (e.g. the Roman Tironian notes), modifications that would certainly enhance its usefulness and probably accelerate the spread of literacy. They would not alone explain the diffusion of a juridical and administrative koine. It is, indeed, unlikely that any single factor could explain that phenomenon, but mutual expectations would have to figure somewhere in the process. These are generated by contact, stipulation and compromise, none of which is possible without a set of shared symbols. That is most easily perceived as the product of an inclusive political system (e.g. the Roman empire), but the actual historical development is probably the opposite: that is, the political system as product of mutual expectations. The evolution is anyway not inevitable. The Bronze Age "cuneiform culture", based on a common script, a nearly uniform code of international law, and a lingua franca, was never politically united. And the political integration associated with other lingue franche (Phoenician, Aramaic, Greek and Arabic) was, even if spectacular, short-lived. The technology in question is thus not only linguistic.

I have also alluded to a *semiotic* dimension.[328] It is in this respect that the salience of format can be captured, already exhibited in the earliest Sumerian accounts. Besides visibility, the tidiness of segmentation and symmetry could be easily conveyed and transferred across linguistic but also cultural barriers. Its symbolic value was thus immediately and universally accessible. Against that diffusionist exegesis it must be (and has been) admitted that many features of format are of spontaneous and independent origin, like the palindromic segmentation of "ledger" tablets in such distant areas as Hagia Triada (Crete) and Susa (Elam).[329] Where, as here, the likelihood of contact (across time and space) is minimal, it may be guessed that certain techniques are products of broadly similar local requirements, e.g. commodity registers. While the palindrome or bracketing (linear and columnar) would be limited to logographic signs, any numerical series would qualify and hence facilitate transfer at least of layout, for calculation and inventories. For business records a good deal of common ground is thus optionally available. If the syntax of numbers is largely signalled by determinatives ($+/-/\times/\div/=$), for lists it is merely a matter of spatial arrangement, whether of words or of lines or of paragraphs (e.g. indentation), as in the sequence of documentary components described above.

Since every system of notation must have originated in a specific cultural context, its semantic and phonetic range would in the first instance be monolingual. Application/adaptation to bilingual, eventually polyglot, circumstances exhibits a creative recycling of acquired goods. Some systems travelled better than others. This is not easily explained by reference to "systemic" advantages: neither Akkadian cuneiform for Hittite and Hurrian, or Aramaic "ideograms" for Iranian languages, or Arabic script for Persian, Turkish and Urdu, could be deemed an obvious choice. But in each of these instances the catalyst was, and perhaps had to be, bilingualism: the script accompanied acquisition of a second language. Admittedly, the remarkable proliferation of scripts based on Aramaic, especially in central and south Asia, is better depicted as a chain reaction rather than de novo return to source.[330] But that was precisely the advantage of an alphabet, which could be acquired by sound value rather than semantic equivalence. The diffusion of Phoenician forms in the Mediterranean exhibits a western counterpart to Aramaic. From the distribution of bilingual inscriptions it is hardly possible to infer that the adoption of phonetic signs required mastery of the language from which they were borrowed.[331] That is, invariably required: from *chancery* evidence, on the other hand, it is quite clear that script and language were inseparable in the initial contact. For Akkadian, as for Chinese in the Far East, it could hardly have been the graphic system that commended itself to potential users, but rather, the cultural weight of an established tradition. That factor is more than merely conceivable in the diffusion of Greek and Arabic, but here undoubtedly facilitated by the ease of phonetic transfer.[332] However, for the two modes of widest diffusion, Phoenician and Aramaic, available evidence points not to an accumulation of literary models, but to the simplicity of graphic adaptation. Of Phoenician at least that is likely to be so, since the only chancery tradition to which that language can be related is Ugaritic. Achaemenid employment of Aramaic, on the other hand, might be thought a possible model for emulation.

Now, a typology of scripts (e.g. pictograph, ideograph, logograph, syllabary and alphabet) must appear unduly mechanistic. Theoretically, any language could be recorded in each of these modes with a fair chance of intelligibility. That all these possibilities are not historically attested could be read as witness to economy of experiment and of course to diffusion rather than to infinite polygenesis.[333] If that were so, it is because technology transfer was anyway assured by established traffic patterns or because writing itself contributed to proliferation of these. In the most recently published taxonomies of script, Jensen identifies twelve foci (Schriftenkreis) and Haarmann fourteen (Schriftkulturkreis).[334] For a single technology both might seem extravagant, but the periods covered are five and seven millennia respectively, the latter including the Danube-Vinča culture and an argument for the sacral origins of writing.[335] Linkages, if conjectural, are plausible, e.g. Phoenician : Numidian, Aramaic : Brahmi, and could reduce the number of independent starts to few more than half a dozen. For that the obvious exegesis would be stimulus diffusion, provoking in turn the question of comparative stages in cultural development at reception of the stimulus. Haarmann's allocation of a separate Kulturkreis for Arabic and Cyrillic is of course consistent with his notion of sacral origins, but seems to me to impose a template on the whole enterprise that may be deceptive.[336] In this study I have sought the matrix of writing in business records and chancery format, its evolution in the spread of a juridical and cultural *koine*. While a sacerdotal input can hardly be denied, it is in my view more accurately, and altogether more conveniently, subsumed under a commercial rubric: the temple was a place of both business and worship.[337] Irrespective of aim, entrepreneurial activity is defined by nearly uniform traits. The category "missionary script" might possibly (?) be applied to Cyrillic, but certainly not to Arabic, whose origins were manifestly secular, as indeed were the agents of its propagation and of the Islamic culture with which it was eventually identified. That the history of Classical Arabic (language) is also that of the Muslim religion is not here being dismissed, but the script as vehicle of cultural uniformity was an administrative device. The vast corpus of mystical poetry in Persian, Turkish and Urdu (all composed in Arabic script) is evidence of its success. Earlier records of the first two languages were expressed in variants of the Aramaic (and confessionally neutral) paradigm, as structurally inappropriate as the Arabic. A fair amount of experiment can in fact be discerned in the marriage of script to language, as well as in subsequent modification to accommodate linguistic change. I have referred to the phenomenon at Ugarit, and ramifications beyond its territorial boundaries.[338] A detailed analysis is available for Hittite adjustments to Old Babylonian cuneiform, which affected not only script but format.[339] Both the selection and allocation of Akkadian signs (e.g. for Indo-European sibilants and gemination for voiceless plosives) and the employment of linear rulings as syntactic markers are distinguishing features of the Hittite syllabary, just as the (late) use of otiose Semitic consonants for vowels distinguished the Greek version of the Phoenician alphabet. In such examples of demonstrable diffusion, the convergence of script and cultural identity is secondary to the solution of practical problems.[340]

Adjustment of signs, whether to conceptual, phonetic or grammatical categories, is a mechanical process, innovative only where gaps must be filled. Genuinely creative moves, like the cuneiform alphabet at Ugarit and the Old Persian syllabary, exhibit a different stage in the accumulation of cultural emblems. Informing these products of scriptorium (or chancery) is a significantly rhetorical factor that does invest the notion of identity with some substance. Of the formulaic elements in a chancery text depicted earlier none is more eloquent witness to the role of rhetoric than the arenga.[341] Adopted from the field of public oratory, its place in epistolography (epistolaris sermo=ars dictaminis) appears not to have been secure before Late Antiquity. The earliest treatment of a specifically epistolary style, in the Hellenistic composition of one Demetrios (Peri Hermeneias), is a plea for casual informality and avoidance of declamation, of which Aristotle is there accused.[342] By the time of Alberic of Montecassino (1087 CE), his Flores Rhetorici could enshrine the art of rhetoric as central to the style.[343] Now, that testimony is considerable distance from the cuneiform letter, but not of course from the commemorative inscriptions of Neo-Assyrian monarchs. The achievement of the medieval "art" (Greek tekhnē; Arabic ṣinā'a) was to capture in a single treatise all the formulae, tropes and figures that might serve to pace and embellish verbal expression. Like the chancery manual, the handbook of rhetoric was indispensable to the display of authority. Eloquence required erudition, which meant recourse to ancient models, preserved henceforth as much for reasons of style as of content. Reference to these for the production of administrative prose might well attain to eloquence, but could also, as noticed at the beginning of this chapter, generate an obstacle to intelligibility. The standards of chancery rhetoric, designed (like calligraphy) to enhance the local culture, might seem to impede the catholic tendencies of an international koine. While Alberic's models include Boethius and Isidore of Seville, most are emphatically Classical: e.g. Ovid, Cicero, Sallust, Virgil, clearly sources of Latin eloquence whose niceties would have been lost on many, if not most, of his 11th century readers. Some 250 years later Dante could still compose his advocacy of the vernacular (De vulgari eloquentia) in Latin and describe Virgil as his model (lo mio maestro).[344] The observation (Curtius) that his Latinitas was more medieval than classical may be compared with the contemporary evolution of literary Arabic (al-fuṣḥā), asserted by practitioners to represent an immutable standard but in fact susceptible to the normal fortunes of linguistic change.[345]

Between the rhetorical ideal and the exigencies of communication emerges thus a significant tension, mostly resolved as compromise, e.g. glossing, annotation, transliteration and the like. The rhetorical style is forensic, its aim, after all, persuasion. Incorporation of this register into the chancery format may seem wayward, but the arenga at least suggests that it was not so perceived. Other components, like the greeting (salutatio), might also qualify, for there too a slot had to be filled from a range of epithets and miscellaneous courtesies.[346] The major shared feature, however, was arrangement of parts: the more or less fixed sequence of components prescribed for both oration and chancery instrument. That its origin should be the practice of the law courts is hardly unexpected. The substance itself of these matters might be thought to dictate a similar style of presentation: argument, evidence, judgment, and the emblems of authority. The extent to which this *koine* can be understood beyond the confines of a local culture has been the issue addressed in this chapter. While the focus was upon format, such factors as prestige and second language acquisition had to be acknowledged as contributory to a process that looks like diffusion. An exclusively semiotic mode of transfer could dispense with some or all of that, but even those sign systems associated with the most recent technologies require a manual of instruction in the user's language(s).[347] These systems are culture-bound only in the sense that culture = technology, and the semantic values of their components can be fairly easily acquired. The "language" inherent therein is stringently utilitarian and essentially not transferable beyond the dedicated domain for which it was initially designed. Within these limits, nicely illustrated by bar-codes and electronic data processing, a universally intelligible language is conceivable, but not, I think, one that would deserve the conventional description "lingua franca".[348] Reasons for this are historical and lie in the modes and materials of cultural contact so far adduced.

Natural languages in contact do not of course exhibit a tidy allocation of sign, phonetic value, and function. Their mutual state is one of discontinuity irregularly but persistently eroded by the fact of juxtaposition. Some areas of linguistic structure are more impervious than others to breaching or bridging (depending upon the metaphor employed), e.g. phonology and morphology. But even here such factors as degree of exposure and complementary lacunae in the phonemic inventories of the two (or more) languages can generate significant change. Lexicon and syntax are less resistent, undoubtedly because loan-words can coexist with indigenous vocabulary and because permutations of word-order are after all limited. Discontinuity is also compromised by the recognition of equivalence: in register, idiom and intention. To illustrate that feature of language contact I have dwelt at some length on the role of formulaic expression, characteristic of any usus loquendi but critical in the jargon of commerce and diplomacy. It is in the modes of transfer, set out as transcription, translation and transposition,[349] that may be discerned a scale of competence in rendering equivalent concepts.Though a fair amount of this activity might be deemed ad hoc, much if not most was prefigured by the existence of a perspicuous, and hence intelligible, format. That this *koine* could engender one or more lingue franche is the subject of the following chapter.

3

Lingua Franca

While it is probably true that at least one function of diplomatic relations was always procural of advantage, say, control of resources, it must by now be obvious that the mode of contact itself either was or could become an object of transfer. If the chancery evidence for that conclusion can be read as semiotic calque, it may be thought to reveal something of the mechanics but less of the motives underlying the adoption of a particular linguistic strategy. Emergence to status as *lingua franca* of any expression, whether dialect, pidgin or creole requires input from several sources, of which very few could be defined according to strictly linguistic criteria. And yet, simply because the material transfer is language, its altered status has ultimately to be analysed in terms compatible with linguistic structure. These terms, and their accompanying methodologies, have been much amplified in recent years, perhaps most generously in the field now called *contact linguistics,* where data tend to be outnumbered by hypotheses for their interpretation. Of the latter few are altogether worthless, and the advantage of most is their sociolinguistic bias. For it is from that posture that the emergence of lingue franche can best be illuminated, even when we are less well informed than we should wish about conditions likely to induce behavioural change, technical innovation and, eventually, social reorganization. Since it is those phenomena, whose conjuncture is probably never, or seldom, an accident, which would signal/accompany adoption of a lingua franca, information about the circumstances of decision-making (e.g. a shift in material needs, awareness of alternative courses of action, experience in selecting one or more of these) is obviously crucial. Contact linguistics, like all branches of that art, is still

147

predominantly theoretical, methodologically useful but historically exiguous.

The attempt here to chart the areas of earlier contact and to analyse a specific context of acculturation was intended to generate a framework within which could be assessed language transmission, selection, genesis and change. Whatever else might be thought of that framework, it has the advantage of ancient and not so often interrupted witness. Its disadvantage is expression in a single register, which could make *style* a more important factor than is normally the case in linguistic description. If not quite monolithic, chancery language does tend to crystallise in phrasal patterns and lexical collocation that would no doubt be unusual in most other contexts. On the other hand, it is precise, often concise, and makes do with generally transparent imagery. Based upon a jussive or imperative syntax and a lexicon of juridical and commercial origin, its grammar facilitates emulation and the search, where appropriate, for translational equivalents. Now, the latter was appropriate in circumstances of linguistic impasse, but also in situations requiring clarification, courtesy and compromise. I have referred to Qalqashandī's terse depiction of treaty negotiations between Egyptian officials and the Crusader settlements in Syria.[1] An archetype of Mediterranean dialogue, that particular mode of discourse (Arabic : Latin/French/Italian) would persist for several centuries, to embrace the very period conventionally supposed to have produced *the* Lingua Franca (Sabir).[2] Definitions of the *type* as well as conjecture about its putative *origins* have so stunningly proliferated in recent scholarship that no single version is likely to attract unqualified assent. My analysis of the chancery datum is intended to provide a longer chronological perspective and, perhaps, a variant methodology for interpreting this kind of evidence.

The material evidence for Sabir has been several times set out, and occasionally employed in support of hypotheses about the genesis and diffusion of the entire category of linguistic expression it is thought to represent.[3] Vague reference to contact language(s) is of course ancient, and can be inferred even where not quite explicit. Reports of pilgrims blessed with the gift of tongues, of itinerant and polyglot merchants, of expeditionary forces and overseas garrisons and the like are plentiful, but before 1600 (Fray Diego de Haedo) seldom yield what might pass as linguistic description. The anticipated precursors to Sabir have not in fact, or at least not yet, appeared. Gleanings from poetry (Encina), theatre (Molière), and talisman (?lorica) are admittedly tantalising, but not quite witness to the circumstances of actual language contact. That, I submit, is accessible in the kind of documentation assembled above (Chapter 2), though inevitably distorted by the very fact of written transmission. While, on the one hand, writing does convey register and format in a way that speech would not, it is, on the other hand, not only inadequate to the accurate rendering of phonetic values but also inappropriate to the recording of spontaneous utterance. It is, after all, only very recently that such informal registers as dialect, pidgin and creole have achieved satisfactory representation in script. The tendency to "improve", "correct" and assimilate to an acknowledged standard is both well-known and deep-rooted. It must be conceded, of course, that the characteristically analytic grammar of a pidgin or creole *can* be indicated in writing, but seldom was if perceived as the "corruption" of some acceptable alternative (e.g. the "standard" language). Exceptions were provoked by a wish to amuse or ridicule, like Molière (Le bourgeois gentilhomme, c. 1670) or the bizarre and probably apocryphal report found in a single edition (1943!) of Al-Bakrī (K. al-Masālik wal-Mamālik, c. 1070).[4] Context for the latter is a favourite Arabic genre, the travelogue, and a hypercritical view of linguistic solecism (lahn). Use of the Arabic script for foreign and sub-classical (dialectal) expression compounds the eccentricity of such renderings.[5] Those few lines, badly inscribed, could hardly have been the whole tale (Aesop: The Miller and his son and their ass): in favour of reading the text as a specimen pidgin are (1) uninflected verbal nouns (rwh/'d/'wl); (2) lack of definite/indefinite article; (3) the preverbal durative marker dy. Against that reading would be the "dual" suffix -ny (pronominal and verbal!) and the curious word-order (SOV). I suspect that kyk = kll (with palatalised velar stop), i.e. "everyone"; that by mhl = "in one place", i.e. "together"; that dy is the relative pronoun; that -ny is an adverbial particle, etc. The lexicon, however, is unmistakably Arabic, the word-order not quite, and the orthography something of a puzzle. The scribe had a sharp ear for the glottal stop (final as well as initial!) and, save for the last word in his report, i.e. mhy, which can hardly be mhmm, must have understood what he wrote. A text such as this, consisting mostly of stock phrases, would not do to illustrate a useful pidgin, but does attest to rudimentary language acquisition. Incidentally, Qalqashandī lists Mar'idī (sic) as a major city ('āṣima) of the Ethiopians (Ḥabasha).[6]

Now, Sabir was a pidgin. A lingua franca may, but need not be. It will, however, and regardless of type, provenance and transmission history, share with every pidgin the same *functional* role, namely, interlingual communication. For a pidgin the sole function, this might be only one of many for a lingua franca, which could in other contexts serve as literary standard or cultural emblem. If these roles could be neatly separated, the task of linguistic description would be immeasurably facilitated. Since they cannot, all the now familiar factors of contact must be considered: e.g. interference (borrowing and shift/ substrate phenomena), selection (register, diglossia, code-switching), strategy (context, assertion, ambiguity), and status (speaker, perception, allegiance). As always, it is a matter of degree: while most languages will exhibit some impingement of these factors, function as lingua franca implies simultaneous exposure to all of them. The evolutionary consequence may be a change of direction (e.g. shift) or acceleration of an innate trend (e.g. simplification). In recent and current study contact-induced change has come to be analysed under the cumbrous but expressive rubrics: *pidginization* and *creolization,* intended to evoke respectively reduction/restriction and expansion/ extension in both the structure and use of language.[7] An advantage of the suffix is attention to *process rather than product,* and to the distinct possibility that neither trend need issue in an actual pidgin or creole. It has also been proposed that any linguistic change be related to one or other of the two processes, effacing thus a traditional distinction between the phenomena of contact and genetic transmission. Perhaps not quite effaced, but at least attenuated, by resort to such notions as "drift" (structural adjustment), "wave" (areal diffusion), and "cycle" (regular alternation of subsystems). All this exhibits considerable refinement of analytical procedure, at the expense, to be sure, of clear-cut categories, sharp boundaries and unassailable constraints. The gain, if any, may be calculated by reference to a broader perception of language as a social paradigm.

The baseline would be "communicative competence": a set of universals to describe linguistic variation as constant beyond the impingement of ad hoc factors upon performance.[8] The distinction is difficult, as much a matter of terminology as of interpretation, and is a major theme in current dispute about identification respectively of universals and substrate phenomena.[9] The ever increasing abundance of data on pidgins and creoles has produced so extensive a range of "contact situations" that some stand in these matters has seemed desirable, if indeed not imperative. Diametrical positions are exhibited in monogenesis with (subsequent) relexification (Whinnom) and the bioprogram (Bickerton), with several intermediate and more plausible options. In the arguments for universals an element of determinism might seem to assist prediction, in the event diluted by the operation of too many variables.[10] For quite some time it has been clear that calculation of these demands historical reconstruction of contact: in terms of demographic ratio, social policy, economic aim and political plan, in short all those factors that have attracted the attention of historians of colonialism. Always heterogeneous, the mix is never quite predictable, even in areas for which historical documentation is plentiful. The contact is of course not always "colonial", though the best documented happen to be. For the period of Mediterranean history examined here the empirical data are not really comparable to the materials employed in current analysis of language contact. While archives cannot be interrogated in quite the way that informants can, it may be confidently assumed that the fact of contact is comparable, and hence patient of orderly description.[11]

Prior to attempting some of this, I should like to recall three statements, from scholars of quite different formation and interests, relevant to the nature of contact, in terms respectively of *fusion, fission,* and *interference*:

> "Given free rein, a language has only dialects, none of which has the advantage over the others, and for this reason it habitually splinters. But as communications improve with a growing civilization, one of the existing dialects is chosen by a tacit convention of some sort to

be the vehicle of everything that affects the nation as a whole. The reasons for the choice differ widely."

(F. de Saussure)[12]

"The view is widely held today that there is a natural universal form underlying all languages, a form to be taken as part of the description of each language. Departures from the natural universal form, requiring to be stated in individual descriptions, represent 'costs'. What current linguistic theory seeks to characterize and use as explanation is the natural universal form. The fact that all languages depart from that form, and pay such costs, is left unexplained. Closeness to or distance from such an underlying universal form, and 'payment' as it were of 'costs' for departure, may depend in part on the role a language or language-variety has played in maintenance of social boundary and communicative distance."

(D. Hymes)[13]

"Car on ne peut objectiver son propre langage avec sa forme interne, sa vision du monde originale, son habitus linguistique spécifique, qu'à la lumière d'un langage autre, étranger mais presque aussi 'sien' que son langage propre... l'hellenisme créa pour tous les peuples barbares que lui étaient rattachés une puissante instance de langues étrangères qui fut fatale aux formes directes nationales du discours littéraire."

(M. Bakhtine)[14]

If this juxtaposition appears bizarre, it does at least invoke the contexts in which linguistic expression is likely to develop: as *bond,* as *boundary,* and as *compromise.* Each of these may be reckoned a parameter in the assessment of structural change, which can only be observed as the result of actual use. Segments of that will range from deliberate to involuntary, from formal to casual, and from creative to prosaic, but seldom without some trace of invention/improvisation, whether inspired or desperate. To extract this range from the written record is not impossible but arduous, owing largely to the constraints of orthography and punctuation as well as facile (but often unconscious) resort to formulae. Of this some at least of the evidence

adduced in Chapter 2 will have been neither facile nor unconscious, but the result of considerable lucubration and search for
equivalence. It was/is the *experiment* characteristic of administration seeking means to express authority: one consequence
was elevation of a local idiom to the status of lingua franca.
Now, another term for that product is *koine,* which, however,
I have regularly (intentionally but perhaps ill-advisedly) employed in reference to the *infrastructure* (procedural, juridical,
formal, cultural) that enables and informs composition of a
lingua franca.[15] For the documentation of contact its utility may
be thought similar to that of an "international style" of artifact,
which could indicate diffusion or emulation or, admittedly,
merely local solution to similar problems.[16] In linguistic scholarship koine mostly (!) refers to a standard language expanded
by input from several dialectal sources with concomitant level-
ing of morphological and syntactic differences and adoption of
a general and possibly restricted lexicon, the consequence of
wider use than any of its original components might have
experienced.[17] The term has not traditionally been applied to
pidgins and creoles, which are of course types of lingua franca.
While "origin as local idiom" would be appropriate to any form
of language, not so many achieve the status of lingua franca, and
for reasons that are seldom purely linguistic. A pidgin is by
definition a lingua franca and nativised creoles often remain
such. Modern examples of lingua franca, like Arabic and
English, French, Russian and Spanish, are not normally classi-
fied as pidgin or creole, but have generated these and may well
themselves have been subject to some of the process.

Detection is difficult: English and Arabic have been
investigated to that end, with negative or ambivalent results.[18]
The problems encountered in this sort of exercise can be ascribed
to a massive documentation, a transmission history so dense as
to obscure separate strands of input. Arabic, for example, is
attested simultaneously (!) in several registers, in the possession
of many groups of non-native speakers, and across a territory
with quite different substrate languages. These phenomena,
overlaid by its cultural dominance as a literary standard, merge
in a composite analysable for the most part only in peripheral
areas, e.g. Central Asia, Africa and the Iberian peninsula. More
of that in due course. Evidence of prior creolization, whether or
not of pidgin origin, has been assembled for now standard

languages of restricted territorial scope, e.g. Marathi.[19] There the case for Aryan-Dravidian interpenetration is complicated (perhaps also supported) by the presence of diglossia (Sanskrit-Prakrit) exhibited in social cleavage and an overall literary standard (Sanskrit). In that respect the situation is a parallel of Arabic, but for Marathi Southworth is able to demonstrate Dravidian substrate phenomena (phonological and morphological), functional similarity of morphemes, and some basic vocabulary replacement, in considerable excess of their incidence in Hindi. This is clearly a case of language shift (Dravidian-Indic) and, depending upon the time scale involved, creolization. The diachronic dimension is difficult to establish, since Marathi is first attested in the 10th century, when all of these features were in place. A pre-existent pidgin stage is speculative, but in the light of South Asian language distribution, hardly impossible.

The conventional arguments for pidginization, then, include pace of change, multilingual contact, and absence of a target language. The latter point might seem to follow from the second (i.e. not bi- but multi-lingualism), but could also arise from native speaker strategies to facilitate or even hinder acquisition (e.g. "foreigner talk", "baby talk").[20] This factor, systematic simplification, has been interpreted by Ferguson and others as a universal of pidgin structure, at least in respect of copula suppression in equational clauses.[21] That such must originate not with the learner but with the native speaker (teacher?) was mooted, with regard to inflexion (general use of infinitive for finite verb forms) by Schuchardt in 1909 and by Spitaler and Wehr (general use of accusative for all nominal declension in Arabic) in 1952/53.[22] All of this belongs properly to the specific mode of *language acquisition,* reconstruction of which can only be extrapolated from the very material being assessed, at least for historical periods. Studies of contemporary language learning distinguish between acquisition of language (enculturation) and of a language (acculturation): difference of pace (child vs adult), of ability to abstract, combine and generalise, to recognise and fill (or delete) grammatical and lexical slots, between greater or less regard for established categories ("proper" usage), and the absence/presence of a substrate.[23] There is also a *difference of function* : a second language may be acquired for a specific, not a general purpose.

That would apply to every pidgin and to most lingue franche when secondarily acquired. In the case of the latter, bilingualism may seldom or never be achieved.

As important as the effect upon learner is that upon the language learned. Perpetuation by native speakers of "errors" generated by imperfect learning of a target language is a distinctive feature of shift and creolization.[24] This phenomenon may be limited to certain registers or concentrated only at the leading edge of interlingual contact. Other ("core") manifestations of the language, e.g. in literature or as employed by monolingual users among themselves, would be unaffected. Thus, and not surprisingly, contact creates a spectrum of usage of which varieties could be virtually described as idiolects. While that is undoubtedly the historical reality, the premiss of scientific description is synthesis, that is, propositions of general validity. As is well-known, these can be formulated in several ways. Because it accounts for the entire spectrum without prognosis of the eventual result (e.g. pidgin, creole or neither), Whinnom's *hybridization* has to be complex but is also very useful.[25] Calculated on a scale of "barriers" to complete merger: ecological (degree of contact), ethological (speakers' attitudes), mechanical (language structures), and conceptual (speakers' perceptions of reality), the hybrid may never crystallise but is nonetheless witness to contact. Since contact is always somewhere present, the category hybrid might be applied to accommodation of any structurally intrusive element, even a lexical item, e.g. a German finite verb (managen) from "manage" or an Arabic internal plural (aflām) from "film". In both instances the semantic slot was created, not merely filled, by the loan.

It is of course the extent of intrusion that enables one to speak of hybrid formation. All four of Whinnom's barriers can be occasionally breached without seriously distorting the trajectory of a language. Morphological reinterpretation of the sort just cited attests the capacity of a given language (here German or Arabic) to assimilate alien elements at the cost of only mild distortion (here phonological). For any lingua franca this is standard, and even pidgins and creoles, once formed, may undergo what is called "normal transmission". But, unless the product of bilingualism, even extensive lexical borrowing will not generate "interference" beyond the immediate phonetic context of the loan (e.g. how does a German speaker *read* "er hat gemanagt"?). However difficult to measure, there would be an important difference in reception of a loan respectively through spoken and written contact. In the latter, non-assimilation of loans to native orthography would make especially conspicuous their alien origin. For the kind of material investigated in this study, preserved exclusively in writing, phonology is likely to be elusive. In particular the role of script as cultural emblem must seem to attenuate the impact of at least lexical loans. That caveat would extend to the formulaic evidence assembled to illustrate chancery style (Chapter 2), for which I have argued a dominantly visual role. In a picto/logographic script interference from loans can hardly be a problem, since the imagery is interlingually transferable, impeded only by the use of complements and determinatives, whose phonetic/semantic values would be local. In a syllabic/alphabetic script this feature is a general constraint, so that any loan is likely to be visually intrusive but would constitute "interference" only in a language of morphological density. In an analytical language, where the grammatical value of components is expressed in syntax, a loan can be accommodated without dislocation. The cleavage is, however, less than tidy: in Semitic alphabets desinential (case) inflexion is not regularly indicated, so that in practice meaning must be inferred from syntax. Hybrid formations are inevitable in any case of language contact. An interference curve, ranging from loans to substrate phenomena, can be calculated in terms of *salience,* both quantitative (frequency) and qualitative (distribution).[26]

Collection of the pertinent data will inevitably elicit some sort of exegesis, which may indeed have determined the collection itself. An aim common to all such is detection of regularity (repeated occurrence) to an extent that could be labeled systemic.[27] Since this has never proved especially difficult, it remained merely to provide regularity with a diachronic dimension (continuum), along which linguistic change could be plotted as "normal" (genetic) or "imperfect" (multiple ancestry). This tableau, the traditional context of historical linguistics, will generate useful, if necessarily speculative, answers to a predetermined set of questions. Useful, in that every language may be presumed to have a history, but not exhaustive, since its reconstruction can never be other than conjectural. The history of a language is the cumulative conduct of its speakers/writers.

I have referred to the "glossing" technique employed by West Semitic scribes in the composition of letters in Akkadian at Ugarit and elsewhere.[28] When apposition is marked by a special configuration of wedge(s) (Glossenkeil), only in the case of Canaanite insertions can one speak of a substrate phenomenon. The same device may signal Akkadian interpretations of Sumerian logographs or closer specifications of Akkadian terms. It may also indicate a non-Akkadian word which is not a gloss but simply a component of the narrative. All these can also be employed without the marker, which is to say that "glossing" is an inherent feature of peripheral Akkadian.[29] In what can only be described as a Mischsprache, that would not constitute intrusion, but certainly interference in relation to its Middle Babylonian model. In other words, the perspective varies according to the baseline selected.

Like the chancery format itself, the gloss exhibits a *meta-language*. Its actual content is almost less significant than the exegetical need for it. An orthography like Akkadian cuneiform or, for that matter, the Semitic alphabets, that requires supplementary information (e.g. complements, determinatives, matres lectionis) to eliminate ambiguity is by nature subject to "glossing" for the deduction of specific semantic values. Since without that information no sequence of signs is unequivocal, the meta-language is essential but also flexible: any of several possible readings may be selected. Such an arrangement might be thought to produce the ideal lingua franca, that is, a *slot structure* with infinitely variable tokens. The variety is of course not infinite, since the linear order of components (syntax) is itself a limiting factor. Another is the reasonable expectation that the meta-language, once identified, will exhibit lexical consistency. This, however, is uncertain: while Canaanite glosses appear in contexts otherwise characterised by West Semitic features (e.g. stative afformatives, preterite preformatives, mixtures thereof), that is hardly so for Hittite and Hurrian lexica.[30] At Ugarit use of the Glossenkeil in conveyancing deeds to specify locations (i.e. proper names) suggests formulaic composition with "blanks" to be filled in as appropriate.[31] That would not be lexical glossing, but rather, a bureaucratic procedure to ensure juridical uniformity, and corresponds nicely with the underlying concept of chancery format.

The formula is an *arbitrary constraint,* in some circumstances self-imposed, but in others recommended, even required, by the particular task at hand. In this matter chancery scribes are seldom free agents: there would be a degree of predictability in the product of their labour. Since the task is likely to involve communicative clarity, one aim must be to facilitate (aural/visual) perception. A lingua franca must by definition serve that purpose, and it might thus be supposed that ease of production could be coordinated with ease of perception. The obvious strategy is recourse to a paradigm as free as possible of idiosyncrasy, e.g. inflexion and other bound morphemes, polysemy, and clause subordination requiring complex rules for word order. Such paradigms have regularly evolved in the history of language, mostly but not always the result of contact, seldom but occasionally the product of design. Agency tends to be anonymous, save in well documented and controversial cases such as Modern Hebrew, but can be assumed to account for certain specific devices like script innovation, punctuation, and loan translation (calque). These have to be conscious acts, solutions to identifiable problems, whatever their subsequent and probably unintended diffusion. Once in place and their practical value perceived, they provide a paradigm for further evolution that makes the trajectory appear inevitable. Constraints to complete merger in a single lingua franca are not linguistic, but social, political and cultural (see above: Hymes).

Descriptions of peripheral Akkadian as Mischsprache and as lingua franca are linguistically and historically verifiable. Linking the epithets is also plausible, indeed conventional, as the simplest explanation of the interference phenomena there. This is possible, as I have mentioned, owing to the evidence of a contemporary standard (Middle Babylonian) by which variation can be measured. Assessment of peripheral Arabic, also a Mischsprache and lingua franca, is achieved in exactly the same way (see below). Similarly, descriptions of Koine Greek and Vulgar Latin. Other likely specimens, such as Mycenean Greek, Ugaritic, Phoenician, and Aramaic (a rather special case) are, though not all for the same reasons, less patient of this analysis. It is partly a question of evidence: absence of standard or of variant(s); partly of the method itself, which is simplistic and liable to severe distortion across time, space, register and

context. That can be eliminated or at least reduced by acknowledgement of the "polyglossic spectrum" which accommodates
nicely the coexistence of functional variants.[32] The significance
of this focus is its inclusion of individual speakers/writers as
well as language communities. The concomitant possibility of
defining the spectrum as a gradation of idiolects is not likely to
affect the documentation I have selected for study. What does
matter of course is perception of the variants as subsystems of
a single language, rather than as convergence of two or more.
That is also the baseline of Hodge's *linguistic cycle* in which
morphological and syntactic density (sM vs Sm) alternate as
characteristics of one linguistic continuum.[33] A deceptive tidiness in both methods permits their enlistment in favour of
arguments for genetic transmission, in which contact phenomena are reinterpreted as merely confirming natural development. The circularity in all this is well- known to linguists.
Hodge's thesis was elicited from his examination of ancient
Egyptian which has a recorded history of some 4000 years, did
not become a lingua franca, and was also not, according to him,
a Mischsprache.[34] Or at least not necessarily: the latter posture
was provoked by the perennial problem of Afroasiatic and
specific links between Egyptian and Semitic. The Egyptian data
have been differently dissected by Greenberg who, on the basis
of shifting regional centres proposed a series of dialectal coag-
ulates = "koines" that would account for variation as well as the
prestige dominance of an administrative standard.[35] The argument is "polyglossic" and its terminology apt, avoiding the
implications of both Mischsprache and lingua franca. The fairly
explicit sense of self-containment is probably derived from a
general impression of Egyptian history which tends to be perceived as isolationist. No such exegesis would do for Mesopotamia and Akkadian, whatever the strictly linguistic data might
suggest.

Now, a period of four millennia, were it even more generously recorded than the Egyptian one, is almost bound to
exhibit a flattened curve of language change. In addition to the
regressive effect of a widened base, time-depth will obscure a
multiplicity of factors contributing to change in favour of some
such general notion as "wave" or "drift", i.e. areal and structural trends perceived (with comfortable hindsight!) to explain the
phenomenon, and mostly as internally induced. Dispute about

this is celebrated (e.g. Boas/Sapir/Kroeber) and once turned upon the legitimacy of taxonomic allocation in the study of culture and of language.[36] Despite the acknowledged impossibility of achieving biological/botanical precision, taxonomy has not expired: witness Whinnom's "hybridisation" (above). The primary yield of that exercise was a not altogether felicitous vocabulary of linguistic description (e.g. "genetic" = single parentage). Terminology has since improved: use of such as "systemic", "salience", "interference" etc. reflect a view of cultural/linguistic expression in flux, inconsistent, hardly predictable but nonetheless identifiable as a momentary distillate (in time, in space) of an ongoing and general process. Recognition of these moments tends of course to isolate them, analysis to confirm their similarity or at least comparability, and synthesis to restore their essential continuity. If the diachronic concern of historical linguistics is in particular addressed to tasks of reconstruction, continuity can also be spatially and synchronically perceived. That has been the issue of pidgin/creole studies, where arguments for *lateral homogeneity* are more persuasive than ones for earlier stages and putative proto-languages. The image is of blurred boundaries and multiple fusion, the now familiar legacy of Weinreich.[37] Although the focal point of that study was the bilingual speaker, the "mechanisms of interference" are set out in a manner that comprehends easily both multilingualism and polyglossia, however these might be located in the spectrum of speech-acts. If the findings there must be qualified, it would be precisely because the evidence is aural: "interference" is heard rather than seen. The harvest is thus more abundant, richer and unencumbered by the levelling effect of graphic systems. Its deposit in written language is reduced, distorted, and also likely to be transmitted by monolinguals as a natural part of the native stock.[38] The context of use and degree of assimilation are thus quite different, with resistance often outweighing stimulus and a conservative tendency to block or at least to conceal innovation. The "resistance factor" is itself a compound: of self-image (nativism/purism), allegiance ("language loyalty"), literacy (standardisation) and the like, difficult both to disaggregate and to calculate.[39] All this is worth recalling, if only to stress that in diachronic description variables exceed by far the supply of reliable constants.

The latter ought in theory to include all the modes of "interlingual identification" (Weinreich) which, however manifested and wherever located, should share certain features. To this topic an enormous literature has been addressed, liberally distributed across the subdivisions of language study and notably, sociolinguistics and psycholinguistics. For reasons that require no elaboration, overlap in their respective areas is modest despite the similarity of raw material. While it would be reckless to identify language contact with language acquisition, there is some common ground between catalyst and process. Partaking of both, Selinker's coinage *interlanguage* is convenient since its psychological locus can only be illustrated by surface structures.[40] Convenient also because it lends some (admittedly nebulous) substance to what I have called the "meta-language" of glossing, formulaic phrase, and compositional paradigm. Though I should wish to assert that these are acquired properties, the means by which that is achieved may well be the effect of a "latent acquisition structure" (Selinker). The behavioural evidence is anyway aural/visual. In other words, the possibilities of interlingual identification are many, but not infinite, and can be fairly accommodated by a few rules of congruity. These are simpler and less liable to transgression in writing than in speech.

I have mentioned the Italian version of an Arabic letter written from Tunis to Pisa in 1366.[41] Containing an offer of safeconduct for Italian traders, its message was public. Composed in the *Maghribī script,* it might seem to have been addressed to a very limited readership indeed. But that is not certain: Italian translations in *Italian script* of Arabic commercial documents exhibit an eccentric form of that language. An example is a letter from Cairo to Venice dated 877/1473.[42] Interference is primarily lexical: the first two paragraphs, consisting respectively of inscriptio/salutatio and intitulatio/devotio (in that order: see above Chapter 2), are so closely calqued on Arabic phraseology as to be unintelligible to a monolingual speaker of Italian (even of the Venetian dialect). Thereafter, the translation is patchy (lengthy omissions), ungrammatical (defective concordance, inconsistent verbal inflexion, e.g. indicative for subjunctive) and embellished by an Arabic loan (xagalado from Ar. zaghala = debase) to render Arabic maghshūsh (debased). In the penultimate paragraph, an inventory of gifts from the Egyptian ruler, the vocabulary is drawn almost entirely from the commercial lexicon of the medieval Mediterranean, being a mixture of Italian, Arabic, South Asian and Far Eastern commodity designations, as can be found in Pegolotti's Pratica della Mercatura (14th century), e.g. candi (Ar. qand = cane sugar), zibetto (Ar. zabad = foam : musk), sesse (Ar. shāsh = muslin) etc. Those are standard cultural loans, with minor morphological adaptation and no structural significance. It is unlikely that native lexica were displaced. But without the requisite expertise (experience) this text could not be understood. Its relation to the Arabic version is skewed: detailed attention is given only to the titles of recipient and originator (the latter missing from the Arabic) and the gift list (an enclosure in the Arabic, also lost); a Venetian envoy, anonymous in the Arabic, is named, permitting a connexion to be made with other state papers pertinent to this transaction; the actual message is merely cued in Italian, without the specific detail of the Arabic. Finally, the location of the Italian version in the memoranda of the Libri Commemoriali would suggest its archival retention as an aide-mémoire (regesto) for diplomatic proprieties (titulature and gift exchange). It is thus not a translation but rather, a business record prepared in Venice on receipt of incoming correspondence, unlike the above-mentioned Tunisian text inscribed for the benefit of Pisan merchants on the quayside.

In fact, for this period of intense commercial and diplomatic exchange, actual *"translations"* are rare. The copious residue consists of *"versions"*: Levantine and Maghribī Arabic, Ottoman Turkish, Greek, Venetian and Ligurian, Castilian, Catalan and French. As I have occasionally and elsewhere proposed, the traditional view of the European texts as dependent upon/ secondary to the Oriental ones could at least be modified if not uniformly rejected.[43] Historically, they may be arranged in sets: *vertically,* by repeated renewal over decades, even centuries, of the same agreements between the same states; *horizontally,* by diffusion of standard models to new powers entering into the orbits of Mediterranean commerce. A histogram would come very close to a square, since both vectors contain the same components, namely, the sum of factors upon which trade was based. It is possible to trace most of these, say the lex naufragi or collective responsibility abolition, in depth from 1254-1517 for Venice-Egypt and laterally after 1292 for Aragon-Egypt. The most explicit specimen of lateral diffusion was Florentine adoption of a Venetian model for their transactions with Egypt beginning in 1485.[44] As was earlier indicated, the clauses (fuṣūl = capitoli) of these texts are instructions (directives) to Egyptian administrators. While that may in part account for an Arabic version, the primary reason for the latter were the accompanying marks of authentication (signature, titles and date) which would only be valid in approved chancery format. For such stereotype material as the clauses of a commercial licence, that could be achieved by filling in the appropriate details on a chancery "blank", a procedure especially revealing in the text of 902/1497 which bears the signature of a sultan six months deceased.[45] Now, the wording of that document is a nearly verbatim rendering of a licence issued in favour of Venetian merchants 55 years earlier and extant only in Italian. It is of course impossible to assert that there never was an Arabic version of the 846/1442 document, but important to recall that one of the two extant Italian versions is located in the archivio di stato at Florence, whence it was retrieved to produce the Arabic document of 902/1497. A comparison of the two may strengthen this supposition.

The irony in reference (lines 11-12) to the Florentine government as both Senate (mashāyikh) and Doge (dūj), at that of all times (!), merits remark, but cannot really be adduced as witness to an Italian Vorlage. It was Egyptian chancery custom, born of long transaction with Venice. Reference in both texts to "the days of former kings" (ayyām al-mulūk al-sālifa = el tempo di Soldani passadi) is frequent; quite rare in Egyptian chancery practice is the enumeration of such: here, in article XX of the Arabic (lines 180-89) a selection is given, almost identical to that in article XXII of the Italian (p. 492). Since both articles address the same issue, namely, provisions for merchants underway, the list of names, probably those Egyptian rulers best known to European merchants, might suggest dependence of the Arabic upon the Italian. Similarly, the unique reference to "Turkoman" pirates (tarakmīn/turkumān (sic) = Turchomani) in article XII of each version (lines 119-24; p. 490) must, in the light of another article (XXXI = lines 284-93) dealing with corsairs (qurṣān), but only in the Arabic version (!), be read as a borrowing. The actual referent is not quite clear : Türcoman ought to be Türkmen, a specific ethnicity not common in the role of Levantine seamen. From the eccentric Arabic orthography, one might infer an Italian coinage, but that is audacious, since in Italian "turco" and "turcomanno" are not synonymous. Moreover, Qalqashandī also knew the difference and provides some data on the dispersion of Turcoman tribal units in Syria.[46] One might suppose that by 1497, and with some semantic slippage, the reference was to non-Ottoman Turks in southwestern Anatolia engaged in para-military activity of various kinds, amongst which service as marines (ajnād baḥriyya) could be included, though that is not piracy. The evidence of orthography is perhaps more reliable in the case of arabūn (Arabic version line 34) = "deposit". The Semitic root is lost there and a loan from Greek/Latin is at least conceivable.[47] Whether in this instance it was borrowed is complicated by caparo in the Italian version (p. 487 Article I), the standard rendering but admittedly not a phonetic source of arabūn. However, both words belong to the lingua franca of Mediterranean commerce and not to the respective vocabularies of jurisprudence (Italian pegno = Arabic rahn). The argument for a common source is almost persuasive.

A variant mode of lexical loan is exhibited in Italian zemechia (Article XIII, p. 490) = "(consular) stipend", rendered ma'lūm in the Arabic version (line 126). The translation is unexceptionable but also unnecessary, since zemechia is itself a transcription of the Egyptian term jāmakiyya (from Persian via Turkish).[48] Because Arabic ma'lūm is generic and jāmakiyya specific, this process is an inversion of the glossing technique defined above. But since jāmakiyya is the customary term in this very context, ma'lūm may be read as an intentional gloss, and would be so even unprovoked by the Italian Vorlage. The motive could only be style, perhaps(?) elegant variation. Now, chancery style is often elegant, but rarely in texts such as these. Here it is prosaic, indeed pedestrian, repetitive and above all, formulaic, in aid presumably of clarity, ensured by the frequent occurrence of as few words as possible. Thus, the two compo-nents (petitio/dispositio) of each article are introduced by approximately the same formulae: respectively dhakara anna = anchora ha recorda che ("he has recalled that") and PN (title) yataqaddam amrahu = perche nui comandemo ("he/we has/ have ordered") in the manner of iterum/itidem. The décalage in the dispositio is arbitrary: perche nui comandemo = wa-rasamnā bihi, also standard chancery usage and familiar enough in both Venice and Florence. Into that framework insertion of the regulatory material demanded little syntactic skill: it was largely a question of technical terminology in easily analysable sequence (parataxis).

By "technical terminology" I mean the lexica that designated authority, activity and procedure in the varied but not limitless world of commerce and diplomacy. Such were qurṣān, arabūn and jāmakiyya. Like the two latter, qurṣān is also pan-Mediterranean: ultimately from Latin cursus/corso (voyage/route"), its forms include qurṣār, qurṣāl, kursāl, kursālī and by the 12th century appears to have displaced earlier Greek peiratēs (Latin pirata; Hebrew pīraṭa) and Arabic ḥarāmī ("brigand") as generic designation of corsair.[49] Documentation is admittedly not explanation of the process. Perhaps a better example is consolo = qunṣul (Italian articles IX and XIII, pp. 489-90; Arabic lines 98, 102, 126, 129), since the office itself of consul, unlike the corsair, was an Italian innovation, even if its juridical functions may have owed something to Islamic law.[50] The loan into Arabic would thus be acknowledgement of perceived difference. To call the resident foreign consul nā'ib ("delegate") would undoubtedly have confused. Conversely, certain Egyptian administrative posts were not translated, but transcribed in Italian, e.g. chaschi = khāṣṣakī ("page"), beredi = barīdī ("courier"), azebo = ḥājib ("chamberlain"), naibo = nā'ib ("deputy/delegate"), and with some modification: luelli = mutawallī ("superintendant") and bassirini = mubāshirūn ("officials").[51] Though the technique was effortless and the local reference unambiguous, these were not loans but rather, a kind of *shorthand* for immediate and practical purpose. A broader impact upon the lexicon of Italian is not attested, unlike, for example, the productive derivations from amīr ("commander") which generated the term admiral in all European languages and was occasionally borrowed back into Arabic as a foreign lexeme.[52] While armiraio is of frequent occurrence in the Italian version of the treaty under discussion, its referent is not "admiral" but one or all of the administrative postholders mentioned above. Since these belonged to the civil service, absence of amīr from the Arabic version is hardly surprising, and would not diminish the likelihood of an Italian Vorlage.

By far the best evidence for that probability is the sequence of articles (p.486: tabulation), almost parallel in both versions and with no structural reasons for being so. The arrangement of material in documents such as these is, save for introduction and conclusion, more or less arbitrary: the only semblance of order is the standard coverage of the Mamluk dominions, i.e. Egypt-Palestine-Syria, and that is followed here in both texts. From juxtaposition of the two versions it must seem that the determinant factor in their issue was *not language but format*. Viewed in that light linguistic overlap, indeed "interference", is inevitable. But this is not merely, or even chiefly, structural. In neither version do the lexemes so far noticed affect an anyway loose and rambling syntax; they do however serve to distinguish both from their respective standard languages. In terms of "communicative competence" chancery format exhibits a code (verbal repertoire), a genre (linguistic routine) and dedicated application (language domain).[53] Successful employment requires training and adherence to the rules. On the other hand, a framework and many of the working parts *are supplied* . Within that system certain expressions are not merely possible but feasible and, above all, appropriate, as it is unlikely that they would be uttered in any other form. For some time now these contextual parameters have been recognised and increasingly refined. Like domain allocation, register selection is a creative act: chancery language was devised for a specific purpose. It is not of course an ex nihilo creation. The language of each version belongs to a recognisable type of Arabic and Italian, indeed shares with those broader categories certain structures, turns of phrase and vocabulary.[54] Each exhibits, nonetheless, a jargon (Fachsprache) that needs to be acquired for use. While that could be said of any jargon, the varieties considered here happen also to be contact languages. Multiple input was bound to generate a hybrid, but one in which every participant had some advantage. If that was not an original aim of chancery rhetoric, it was a consequence of chancery practice: language actually performed and presumably found acceptable, if the diffusion of such texts can be read as index of their intelligibility. Their proliferation in this particular mode (Italian/Arabic) dates from the late 12th century and lasts until well into the 16th.[55] Earlier modes show *different ingredients* in the *same configuration.*

Before turning to those, I should like to address the epithet "marginal" in respect of chancery language. Reinecke distinguished trade jargons, which remained secondary, from plantation and settler creoles, which became primary.[56] Now more or less axiomatic in the study of contact languages, that cleavage is relevant to code, genre and domain only insofar as these terms can never represent the range of communicative competence. All these suggest restricted function, perhaps better a "voluntary dedication" and in that sense marginal in relation to total competence. As recoded, chancery language is no-one's mother tongue, hardly a discovery but nevertheless worth recalling, since most specimens contain traces of more than one standard language. It might be argued that a jargon is peculiarly susceptible to intrusive elements, and that because a special effect is consciously sought. The aim would be *referential accuracy,* as with the transcription of Egyptian administrative nomenclature (see above) in Italian texts, or, for example, of muda there (Article IV, p. 495) to indicate "shipping season" (from Arabic mudda = "period/time" : tempo de galie), a gesture to local parlance.[57] Such are indeed marginal phenomena and could hardly occur in any other context. Occasionally this contact might generate a bizarre, or at least not quite perspicuous, coinage, as in the equivalence pelegrini = jurjān (Italian Article XVI, p. 491; Arabic lines 143, 146, 149) in what must be a collective designation of Christian pilgrims to Jerusalem. Evidence for this reading, elsewhere assembled, is fairly substantial, but I have not yet identified the source of the Arabic appellative.[58] Since standard Arabic ḥājj (pl. ḥujjāj) may be so used in this context (i.e. with reference to other than Meccan pilgrims), and since a transcription blgy (=pellegrino) is also attested (apud Ibn Jubayr c. 1180),[59] one is inclined to seek an eponym. The most obvious is the Genoese presence in Cyprus and Palestine: the agency of the Banca di San Giorgio from the early 15th century in respect of transport and establishment of consuls precisely for the protection of pilgrims to the Holy Sepulchre and elsehwere.[60] Combined with the local legend of

St. George (Jaffa-Lydda-Jerusalem-Bethlehem: the pilgrim route), the source would be at least plausible, but admittedly conjectural. If in Italian the linguistic analogy is romeo ("pilgrim to Rome"), the Arabic morphology of jurjān is less clear, though the form in context can only be a plural. The rendering may have been playful: even in chancery documents the Church of the Resurrection (Arabic qiyāma) was punned as "rubbish heap" (qumāma).[61] The notion of marginality might thus extend to the domain of in-jokes and local lore, not so far after all from Reinecke's depiction of mariners' argot. But it is unnecessary, and probably unwise, to pursue further that simile.

Chiefly because the attitude of chancery scribes to their product was not one of contempt or disregard. Quite the opposite, though beyond the flourish of rhetorical formulae there was a distinct element of practicality. Studies of technical styles and of business language have accumulated in recent years, and a number of typical features detected.[62] These include automation (fixed phraseology), impersonality (passive verbal constructions), and dissimulation (concealment of agency), all in aid of an instantly recognisable, if emphatically flat, prose style. The fact (and I think it is one) that this style can be achieved in any language must facilitate interlingual communication. The poetic register is notoriously "untranslatable", owing to metrical constraint, cultural allusion and frequently unique collocation, while the styles of journalism, advertising and commercial correspondence are easily transferred from one medium to another. This phenomenon, familiar in the modern world, is also attested for the ancient. In either context the crucial linkage is not vertical and genetic, but lateral and typological. Style does of course evolve, but stylistic *homogeneity* is just as, if not more, easily perceived in areal diffusion and across language borders. On the other hand, unless it is closely related to historically verifiable data, a typology of style is likely to be impressionistic. While, for example, the remuneration clause in conveyancing deeds exhibits a fixed collocation ("satisfied. . . heart") from Middle Babylonian to medieval Arabic, the grammar fluctuates between third, second, and first person ("his/your/my heart") in accordance with local paradigms.[63] And a feature like concealment of agency may be expressed in various ways, e.g. "it is felt", "one feels", "they feel", etc. Choice would be ad hoc or idiomatically conditioned: cf. "English spoken", "on parle francais", and "si parla italiano". An identical impulse may surely be discerned, but with due respect to local conventions. Now, these paradigms and conventions make borrowing less easy to detect than in cases where interference can be established. Of the examples just adduced, the remuneration clause is a loan; the device for concealment of agency (or simply impersonality) is probably not.

The *continuum* I have sought throughout this study to identify is thus typological, in support of which were adduced the familiar diffusions of ceramic design and writing.[64] A corresponding diachronic continuum ought, on the abundant evidence of historical contact, to be a not unreasonable postulate. But the essential control, witness to intragenetic evolution, is admittedly patchy, so that within the typology every contact phenomenon would be identical only with itself. Escape from that circularity may be possible for languages with long continuous histories, such as Akkadian and Arabic, and with careful scrutiny of other than the chancery register.[65] Of course no typology is entirely immune to chronological décalage, and I have mentioned the snares (e.g. archaising and local initiative) in attempting to establish script and pottery sequences. As it happens, the earliest securely dated materials for a history of Arabic are chancery documents.[66] In the considered judgment of their most recent analyst, these papyri (mostly of Egyptian provenance) exhibit a language quite distant from the literary standard (Classical Arabic) but also (!) without interference from either Aramaic or Greek.[67] Both assertions may be thought controversial: the first owing to dominance of the literary register in traditional (indigenous and other) analysis of Arabic grammar, the second due to the indisputable presence of lexical loans (largely Greek and Latin) and the very fact of a chancery format that had to be borrowed from somewhere.[68] If there is a danger of confusing language with style (and I have been so accused), it is surely less grave than neglect of context (purpose, readership and, hence, register selection) in linguistic description. The loans themselves, e.g. pakton = baqṭ and sigillion = sijill, represent coinage that can hardly have been whimsical. More significant are the sequence of components and admission of the independent juridical validity of documentary evidence.[69] The effect of these factors upon development of specialised discourse at least, and more often than not of the recipient language as a whole, ought not to be underestimated.

Of contact language Arabic might be expected to exhibit an ideal type. From the baseline just adduced its propagation would depend upon considerable flexibility and receptivity to innovation, characteristics inherent in the version of its grammar published by Hopkins. These matters have since been taken further, but from a diametrical point of departure, by Versteegh.[70] Here, those characteristics are read as the *product* of diffusion rather than as its *agents.* In terms of the relevant scholarship, that exegesis would be retrogressive, were it not for the new technology applied to the ancient problem. To depict the structural differences between "old" and "new" Arabic (admittedly not quite identical with Classical and Middle) as consonant with pidgin/creole phenomena has the merit of direct attention to the social context of linguistic change. That makes it a terminologically sophisticated version of the old "conquest: foreign learner: koine" syndrome manifesting a sharp descent from purity to corruption. The starting point is of course *not* the elevated style (or styles) of scripture and pre-Islamic poetry, but the pliable idiom of the papyri: *already* a product of contact and patient of further adjustment.[71] It may also be recalled that the Arab diaspora dates from a millennium and a half *before* Islam. While reconstruction of their language(s) during that period would be almost fanciful, the Arabic version cannot have been insulated from the normal effects of a polyglot environment (e.g. Akkadian, several forms of Aramaic, possibly Egyptian, and certainly Thamūdic, Liḥyānite and Ṣafāitic, as well as Greek and Latin).[72] That kaleidoscopic image, eventually enhanced by the addition of Persian, Coptic and Berber, is of course no substitute for the demographic data necessary to establish ratios of migration and miscegenation, of isolation and assimilation in respect of native speakers. Such data have been, and I reckon will remain, elusive or at best conjectural.[73] The only reliable, or for that matter possible, resort is to what was actually written by way of communication between speakers of the several languages adduced above.

It may, on the other hand, be conceded that the aural evidence of Arabic dialects and pidgins *does* reflect tendencies, trends and types of linguistic behaviour that must have contributed to its historical development. If all, or most, of these can be subsumed under reduction of redundancy and replacement of synthetic by analytic constructions, approximation to the pidgin-creole paradigm is achieved. This procedure is most persuasive when its starting point is the highly synthetic and densely inflected (as well as lexically exotic) literary standard. If that should not be so (and I have yet to be convinced), the trajectory of Arabic would be both lengthened and flattened to accommodate its historical role as lingua franca punctuated by occasional (and with Islam, persistent) elevation to other registers. To adduce these as the origins from which diachronic change can be calculated is, in my view, to misperceive the synchronic status of different styles for special purposes. Should one such be chancery production, a degree of rhetorical input may be expected, at least for certain elements, e.g. the arenga.[74] But mostly it is the sequence of components and adherence to formulae that determine the embellishment of these texts which otherwise exhibit a common business style. Comparison with the development of Latin in the Roman empire *is* thus instructive: functional cleavage between sermo plebeius and sermo urbanus with a documented spectrum of mixture and uncertainty. That this exegesis was the insight of the creolist Hugo Schuchardt has felicitous bearing on the present discussion.[75] The prescriptive effect of a literary register upon *any* written form may be assumed, of course, but the actual degree of "interference" (as it were) only evaluated from case to case. For chancery instruments, as I have sought repeatedly to show, the effect can be neatly marginalised as routine format. The operative "grammar" of the scribe reveals a practical concern for clarity (Mitteilungsbedürfnis) despite the pressure of an aesthetic ideal (Bildungsprinzip). There was, however, at least one sociological difference between the diffusion of Latin and of Arabic: conversion of the empire to Christianity aided the consolidation of sermo plebeius, while conversion to Islam strengthened the position of al-lugha al-fuṣḥā.

Whether that difference could have affected the strategies of language acquisition is another matter. One suspects that the mechanisms for learning are universal (cf. Selinker's "interlanguage"), but must acknowledge that the circumstances of learning are of considerable variety. For the marketplace, the plantation, the garrison and the school, uniform input seems unlikely. Anyone attempting insertion of loanwords into an utterance is familiar with the phonological effect upon the loan or the immediate environment or both. In writing the same act can generate uncertainty (festschrifts : Festschriften) or plainly repellent coinage (lingua francas), but without making the message unintelligible. Frequent recourse to such will, however, have that effect. This may be induced by habit, carelessness, affection or (see above) a genuine desire for accuracy. However analysed, e.g. as borrowing, as code-switching, as ad hoc memorised lexical items, the practice applied to a segment of length will produce a recognisable style. Description of the product as rule-governed (if x then also y) may achieve a kind of harmony between learning strategy and surface structure.[76] The isolated loan, calque or "lapse" would not then be significant. Here again, the quest is for a continuum that will both comprehend the data and permit a theoretical postulate or more.

For either end of the time-scale selected I think this is possible: Akkadian and Arabic exhibit many of the same phenomena in response to their diffusion as lingue franche (!), hardly the result of direct contact. The linkage is literally "circumstantial": the increasing corpus of grammars of peripheral Akkadian draw largely, if not exclusively, upon chancery documents and business correspondence.[77] On the evidence of scribal repositories and accurately recorded findspots, it has even been deemed possible to identify idiolects, individual spelling habits, and defective or at least uneven training. Of course these can be found anywhere, but become interesting when they can be traced to substrate causes. A fastidious specimen of such analysis is now available in S.Izre'el's study of RS 20.33 (UGAR V 20). The tablet, a letter from a not quite identified officer posted in Amurru (between Byblos and Ugarit) to an unnamed ruler ("the king my lord"), was discovered in the archives of Rap'anu, a well-known scribe/administrator at Ugarit.[78] While the occasion is explicit (impending assault on the Syrian coast by the ruler of Egypt), date and destination are not, a situation not unusual in cuneiform sources.[79] But from examination of, particularly, orthography and morphology it was possible to assign the text to the 14th century BCE, an operation enabled of course only by an extant corpus of Amurru

Akkadian.[80] Other evidence, e.g. consonantal gemination, regular alternation of sibilants (ś: s), and a certain employment of "Akkadograms" (reflecting "absolute" nominal inflexion) suggest, if not conclusively demonstrate, a Hittite-Akkadian influence, though the first of these appears to be differently conditioned from the Boghazköy phenomenon.[81] Nonetheless, a Hittite destination (Hattusa or, perhaps, Carchemish?) can be mooted, which does not, however, explain the findspot. As entrepôt, diplomatic relay, or even translation bureau (Akkadian to Hittite?), Ugarit is more than merely plausible.[82] On the other hand, this particular letter may not, for a variety of reasons, have progressed any further. But here, as elsewhere in the reconstruction of history from cuneiform materials, one is confronted with intolerable lacunae, rather straining the role of conjecture. What can be captured from texts like the above is epistolary style: the Amurru letter is hardly formulaic, fairly lively and may have been dictated in the field.[83] Though produced by a scribe (i.e. messenger formula: umma + genitive; prostration formula), the mode of discourse is informal, repetitive and emotive, and the conclusion abrupt (clearly not a consequence of the medial break). It is tempting to see here a draft, of the sort mentioned by Qalqashandī some 3000 years later, and intended for chancery engrossment, perhaps at Ugarit.

Of comparable origin and style is the Ugaritic text RS 16.402 (PRU 2 12). Here, the author of the letter, apparently a military officer, is posted to the north of the capital, near Mukiś / Alalaḫ, and the enemy would not be Egypt, but Hatti (?).[84] A 14th century BCE date is possible, but hardly agreed. The addressee is a title ("the queen my lady"), a "king" is referred to eight times, and the Hurrian (?) name of the originator, iw / rrṭrm, is almost legible.[85] Like the Amurru text (RS 20.33) this is a battlefield report with but a trace of chancery etiquette (messenger and prostration formulae). For such spontaneous and quite possibly urgent expression, the choice of language may seem arbitrary. The Ugaritic tablet was found not in the property of Rap'anu but in the central archive collection, which might suggest a local destination rather than stage in transit. Identification of the addressee is crucial but far from clear : Aḫatmilki is conceivable but Puduḫepa not in my opinion impossible.[86] Either would accommodate recourse to Ugaritic and neither require further processing, at least not translation. The availability of this choice reflects no law of diffusion but merely geography and convention. For Akkadian, as later for Arabic, the spread of findspots is probably a reliable index to usage. For Ugaritic, as I have now so often intimated, boundaries are blurred by a *Canaanite complex* which extends, spatially and chronologically, to include Phoenician.[87] While an overlap in script is hardly surprising, linguistic analysis is impeded by the variety of extant materials. It is the familiar problem of discourse (genre, register and style) selected from a wider competence to achieve immediate and specific ends.

Expectation of continuity, if not identity, is amply attested in historical scholarship.[88]   Strict adherence to an isogloss principle provides some justification for this view, e.g. the consonantal inventory of the "reduced" cuneiform alphabet nearly coincides with that of Phoenician, the feminine morpheme is /t/, there is an oblique form for independent pronouns, absence of nominal inflexion, of a definite article, of mimation, etc. Because of the *quite different residue* for each language, syntactic (e.g. verbal inflexion: tense or aspect?) and lexical (e.g. ytn = "give", ḥrṣ = "gold") materials are difficult to assign exclusively, that is, without reference to similar or parallel phenomena in Hebrew or Moabite. The predominantly contextual criteria for semantic values have produced a greater overlap, for example, between Ugaritic and Hebrew than between Ugaritic and Phoenician.[89] That imbalance would no doubt be redressed by a corpus of Phoenician poetry. In the absence also of Phoenician chancery documents, an expected perpetuation of Canaanite administrative usage cannot be demonstrated. Recently proposed, however, is a much earlier date for Phoenician offshore activity than has been hitherto acknowledged. On the basis of both stratification and paleography, the two artifacts (respectively silver and bronze inscribed cups) found at Hala Sultan Tekke (Cyprus) and Tekke Knossos (Crete) have been dated to the 13th and 11th centuries BCE.[90] While the linguistic value of the inscriptions (designating maker/owner) is minimal, the fact that one (Cyprus) is in cuneiform and the other (Crete) in a primitive version of linear might be thought to document a Canaanite continuum. The variant spelling of "cup" (ks/kṣ) could well indicate orthographic uncertainty during a period of transition from one script to another, but that is conjecture. Not yet discovered is a form of Phoenician that would illustrate the paperwork underlying commercial expansion of the sort attested by archaeology and which is abundant at Ugarit. At least the supposition of continuity is reasonable. As preserved, the Phoenician lexicon could not perform that service.[91]

For Ugaritic itself, some evidence of register selection, even of a putative diglossia, can be elicited from the much wider range of verbal expression. As in Arabic, a poetic register can be identified by theme, imagery, and prosody.[92] The corpus is small, almost perspicuous and much edited.[93] There are also cultic (mrzh = symposium), ritual (sacrificial offerings), incantation (snakebite), omen (teratology) and medical (hippiatry) treatises, each characterised by generous use of technical terms.[94] But by far the most extensively represented category is administrative and epistolary prose. Apart from its formulaic quality (occasionally lapsed), the register exhibits a range of free morphemes, indeclinable particles, and a fixed word order (SVO), features generally typical of analytic syntax. A mild propensity to regard this language as later than, even as a debased form of, that employed in the poetic register has no real basis in chronology, and is somehow reminiscent of arguments about the same phenomena in Arabic (see above).[95] A case for Ugaritic as lingua franca would of course rest upon the evidence of prose style. I have asserted that literacy in Ugaritic could have extended as far south as Bet Shemesh and west as far as Cyprus (Alaśiya), but also that "Canaanite" until c. 1200 BCE was recorded only in cuneiform.[96] If that date were seen as primarily *graphemic* watershed, it would follow that the *linguistic* evidence either side must be identical or at least very similar. Neither genre nor lexicon is of much help here: the commemorative and votive inscriptions that constitute the Phoenician corpus reflect indeed a nearly homogeneous style, but not that of commerce and diplomacy.

However, from the fact itself of alphabetic writing, marked word divisions, and absence of matres lectionis, certain orthographic/phonological isoglosses may be discernible. Some, like loss of the phonemes /g̱h/, /ḥ/ and /ṯ/, are attested in both scripts, events not precisely datable since the "reduced" cuneiform alphabet may have continued in use after 1200 BCE.[97] As might be expected, it is the Byblos linear inscriptions, being closest in time and place to the Ugaritic materials, that support an argument for continuity: the use of word-dividers, a verbal reflexive theme Gt, the relative pronoun z = d, the preposition b - = "from", all features absent from later Phoenician.[98] Incipient but hardly developed phenomena, such as waw conversive and the definite article, are also exhibited in Byblos and Ugarit.[99] Less easily interpreted is the incidence of enclitic m/n and deictic -t, since in both prepositions and demonstratives they may be free variants.[100] Whether any or all of these could be invoked in aid of a case for "Canaanite" as lingua franca is not of course an exclusively linguistic problem. The diffusion of "standard Phoenician" (Sidon-Tyre) in the first millennium BCE must qualify as an at least archaeological datum, and thus invite historical exegesis, which it has not failed to do. Conventional resort is to dialect geography, and therefore to stress divergence.[101] Given the distribution of inscribed artifacts, as well as an exasperatingly discrete time scale, that analysis is certainly feasible. One consequence would be to make the early Byblos material (12th-10th centuries BCE) a local vernacular rather than earliest linear Canaanite. It might, on the other hand, be both, appearing as "dialectal" residue only in 3rd century Cyprus (Lapethos).[102] That in my view would be the preferred version, since it ascribes change to substrate phenomena, a reasonable tactic in description of a contact language.

An example is 'z, the Cypriot form of the demonstrative z, generated (according to some) by prosthetic resolution of an initial consonant cluster.[103] The relative 'š, which appears in Zenjirli (Kilamuwa 9th century BCE), would require another interpretation, but from which substrate is not necessarily excluded.[104] Specifically local variants are easy enough to chart, and the trajectory of Punic provides abundant evidence.[105] There it seems likely that the process was one of language shift (Berber speakers to Phoenician), probably imperfect acquisition, and perpetuation of "errors" (by Phoenician speakers). Such input ought eventually to produce a creole. Demographic composition, type of colonial settlement, replenishment from the Levant, maintenance of the target language, etc. are factors not calculable for the first centuries of expansion. And from the inscriptional residue it is difficult to extrapolate substantial interference, lexical or grammatical. It may be hazardous, but is nonetheless tempting to compare the contact situation with that of Arabic in the same area 1500 years later. By that time the substrate included Coptic and Greek (Egypt), Berber and Latin (North Africa and Spain), but little or none of this is evident in the *earliest* Arabic documentation (see above): some lexical loans and a familiar (because ancient) chancery format. The language as such exhibits an unembellished prose style consonant with earlier inscriptional materials, but composed for another (and quite different) purpose. Evidence of creolization is not found there, but in the regional vernaculars, recorded many centuries later. The comparison with Punic is thus skewed: by the distribution of data and continued availability of the target language (written Arabic). Essentially, the difference is one of *scale* : the sheer quantity of Arabic data, the evidence of diglossia and of multiple domains, of the possible range of expression in that language, which diminish the need to explain in terms of substrate or borrowing. The limited Phoenician corpus, even associated with the longer and more varied Canaanite tradition, could not have issued in Punic without borrowing or shift.[106] A further difference, of course, was the *nature* of contact: Phoenician colonisation was commercial, industrial and probably agricultural; the later Arab version, though it entailed all these activities, was also a military occupation. A settlement pattern based on garrisons, cadastral registers, capitation levy, customs and excise could not but affect the pace of language diffusion. It would also affect the perception of a particular language and its acquisition as useful, prestigious or necessary. But assessment of these processes is statistical: any approximation to reliability depends upon size of sample as, indeed, is so far strictly linguistic data.

The quantitative bias is thus both empirical and methodological. Put simply: the larger the corpus the easier it becomes to dismiss external motivation for linguistic change.[107] But when that line is consistently pursued, its corollary must be that every historically attested contact situation can be characterised as fully bilingual and each user of both languages eternally vigilant: not to blend, confuse or otherwise transgress. I set out the reductio ad absurdum merely to recall that the *simpler* assumption is in fact interference, in such context virtually certain. Detection, however, can be difficult. For the chancery materials investigated here, the primary borrowing mode, when not merely transcription, is calque (loan translation). An example was the Sicilian (Judaeo) Arabic sijill maftūḥ = litterae patentes, combining a much earlier Greek loan (sigillion = any document bearing a seal) with a rendering of Latin patentes/ apertae ("open") different from but synonymous with the standard Arabic chancery term manshūr (i.e. sijill manshūr).[108] While there could hardly be doubt as to the meaning, its innovative character is discernible by reference to the technical terminology of Roman, Byzantine and Islamic chancery practice. In the formulaic lexicon of that register the phrase constitutes interference, unexpected but traceable. A similar operation could be performed on most of its components, e.g. in the messenger formula Akkadian umma + genitive = Ugaritic thm PN, where the grammatical dislocation appears to lie in the former.[109] An (uncommon) Ottoman Turkish devotio formula Allāhun 'ināyeti ile, ben.... = "By the grace of God, I...." is another example.[110] Now, all these are identifiable precisely *because* the context is Arabic, Akkadian, or Turkish, inverting thus the quantitative bias in favour of internally motivated change. It may be argued of course that these innovations were hardly productive beyond the chancery register, a point I have more than once conceded.[111] As it happens, the Ugaritic locution "message of..." (thm PN) occurs also in the poetic corpus, with reference to intercourse between the gods (Baal, Yam, Mot) but also mortals (Keret).[112] The declamatory image, familiar enough in mythology and epic, has a likely origin in court protocol.

I have mentioned Cyprus as a distinctive stage in the diffusion of Phoenician. Its features are largely orthographic/ phonetic and lexical.[113] A verdict on whether or not substrate would require rather more information than is at present available on the linguistic history of the island. Employed were Akkadian (certainly: Amarna) and Ugaritic (probably: see above, Chapter 2), but the so-called Cypro-Minoan syllabaries (three?) exhibit phenomena not yet allocated to either Akkadian or Canaanite. An Aegean script whose values are certainly not those of Linear B is inscribed on artifacts found at Enkomi, Kalavassos, Kition, Hala Sultan Tekke, Kourion and several other sites, but also Ugarit.[114] Several collations (with Linear A) and decipherments, in which a disputed Hurrian element is salient, have further corroborated contact between island and mainland, as well as an impression of intensive experiment in recording speech.[115] In this Middle and Late Bronze corpus of *c.* 400 inscriptions some 125 signs have been distinguished, a sum which could represent the syllabary of a single language but, owing to the dispersion of findspots, has been reckoned to include at least lexical items from two others. Admittedly untidy, that hypothesis fits the notion of "experiment" for a period of uncertainty about the match of script to language. But if the two other languages are in fact Hurrian and Canaanite, means of recording them were available, in Akkadian and Ugaritic cuneiform. In any case, interpretation of CM II as Hurrian and CM III as Canaanite would not clarify CM I which, if it is not Cretan-Minoan, must be the native language of Cyprus, upon which analysis of external evidence (Akkadian, Egyptian and Ugaritic) has so far shed no light.[116] Nor from the Iron Age (Archaic and Classical) Cypriot syllabary employed (mostly) to render Greek has significant aid been extrapolated.[117] For identification of substrate phenomena in local alphabetic (!) Phoenician the phonological yield of any of these syllabaries is meagre, and generates a problem analogous to that involved in reconstructing Ugaritic phonology on the basis of Akkadian sign values.[118]

Now, the Classical syllabary persisted in use for some six centuries after the introduction of alphabetic script by Canaanite and Greek immigrants, a curious décalage in respect of the contemporary trend. For that a strictly linguistic reason is not immediately obvious, nor for the failure of the earlier Cypro-Minoan script to gain serious adoption on the Asian mainland. A pivotal role for Cyprus is conceivable: the point beyond which neither Akkadian nor Ugaritic cuneiform spread further west, beyond which the Aegean scripts (hardly) spread further east, and where the alphabet only after long co-existence with a local syllabary was eventually established. But for a "pivot" the time-scale is inordinately generous, approximately twelve centuries (1500-300 BCE). Abundant Mycenean pottery in Cyprus, but no trace of Linear B, might indicate an inverse carrying trade: Cypriot merchants/sailors fetched their own wares in the Aegean, and with their own (Cypro-Minoan) syllabary had no need of another script. The plausible derivation of that syllabary from Cretan Linear A would encapsulate completely the "Mycenean effect" in Cyprus, which is merely to recall that ceramic residue may be only tangential to local cultural development. To my knowledge, no one has yet proposed that Linear A was derived from Cypro-Minoan.

The technology transfer exhibited in adoption/adaptation of script to language must imply enhancement or diminution of cultural identity. Any such action imposed or taken under duress would produce the latter, as in acceptance of the Arabic script from Spain to the Malay peninsula for those languages eventually designated Muslim. Islands of obstinacy could survive, as in the retention of Hebrew script for Jewish languages. The overlap is well-known and instructive: a Persian Jew in North Africa would write Arabic with Hebrew letters, combining thus a lingua franca and a social code. A millennium earlier a Cypriot could achieve the same effect by writing Greek with a local syllabary. But such self-cancelling techniques are exceptional. The value of a lingua franca lies in the absence of constraints and involves some sacrifice of specific identities. Apart from certain formal properties, the difference between Hebrew and Arabic scripts is merely the role of Arabic as lingua franca. The formal properties themselves might seem, at least with hindsight, to have been devised for precisely such a role: a small number of basic shapes, provided with multiple values by a tidy system of pointing, and in an easily learned sequence, to which was added efficient phonemic vowel notation. The distance from Aramaic writing was considerable.[119] Although this efficiency was undoubtedly a factor in propagation of the script, diffusion of the language was enabled by identification with the *koine*: the matrix of intelligibility, authority and, above all, practicality to which I have so often alluded.[120] Essential were an agreed lexicon of administrative and juridical terms/ concepts, acknowledged procedural uniformity, and an emblematic format to convey these. The Aegean materials cannot be accommodated in this matrix, and Phoenician only if read as the legacy of Ugarit. Phoenician was of course employed by non-native (Neo-Hittite) speakers, e.g. at Zenjirli, Karatepe, and by Arameans, e.g. at Arslan Tash.[121] And its script, with none of the neat symmetry of the later Arabic one, was easily applied to Hebrew, Aramaic and Greek.[122] With these transfers the gradual effacement of cuneiform and Aegean notation began, not because of some intrinsic inadequacy, but certainly facilitated by a different set of writing materials, unfortunately and ironically not evident in the residue of lapidary inscriptions.

It might be wondered whether diffusion of a single script in the Mediterranean did not of itself generate a kind of unity. The point of departure was *c.* 1200 BCE and the westward trajectory punctuated by many modifications, e.g. Greek, Etruscan, Latin, Punic, Iberian, but none so severe as to disfigure entirely the original model. A semantic advantage of the alphabet was elimination of logographs, but that would hardly induce erosion of language boundaries. Rather the opposite. Phonology fared differently: the shape of Greek, for example, as recorded in Linear B, Classical Cypriot and its version of the Phoenician alphabet exhibits a remarkable evolution. No syllabary based on CV units, even with separate signs for five vowels (V), can render the consonant clusters (CC/CCC) characteristic of Greek, e.g. a-to-ro-po-se = anthropos. Explanation may resort, diachronically, to the time span between Mycenean and Ionian or Attic Greek, or synchronically to a very complex set of spelling rules for Linear B.[123] Since the difficulties of the latter are so neatly resolved by the adapted alphabet, it is tempting to conclude that the variable here is not phonetic structure but the means of depicting it in script. After all, a dominant CV pattern, were it actually a feature of Greek, could also have been alphabetically rendered. While retention of purely consonantal script for Phoenician/Punic may seem unnecessarily arduous, at least from the learner's point of view, it may be recalled that there no syllable begins with, or consists only of, a vowel. Insertion of these is morphologically predictable, though admittedly dependent upon context, e.g. pā'al (perfect) vs pā'il (participle). The question would be whether a common mode of depicting sound segments (at least CV/CC) did or did not facilitate inter-lingual intelligibility. That possibility, if it is one, need anyway not be critical: lingua franca, at least at the point of contact, is a transactional device and its diffusion as much a matter of formulaic "expectation" as of acoustic perception. As I have more than once suggested, the linguistic exercise is a search for *equivalence* and "translation" merely a general term for its several products.

These could be called *homologies,* of which gradual accumulation (mostly painstaking, but occasionally and felicitously accidental) enabled intelligible contact across natural language boundaries.   The simplest, and crudest, was transcription. Since some phonetic accommodation is always discernible (e.g. zemechia = jāmakiyya, armiraio = amīr), this term is preferable to "transliteration" which, however, was probably the literate borrower's intention. On the other hand, many instances of such transfer would be not of sign but sound, and the result only approximate. Here the critical factor is literacy, certainly, but also bilingualism. It might seem that fluency in both source and target languages would diminish, if indeed not entirely eliminate, recourse to transcription. That this is not so is of course attested by the profusion of loanwords in any language not demonstrably isolated by terrain. From the modes of transfer can be gleaned a scale of the effort and/or sophistication involved.[124] Assignment of transcription to the lower end does indicate least effort, possibly failure to find equivalence, and hence compromise. But, as already proposed, an advantage to this device is its *referential accuracy,* an immediacy of practical value and especially in the context of chancery language, where a creative translation could confuse, or deflect the aim of bureaucratic convention (thus: not nā'ib but qunṣul = console/ consul). It may be, then, that transcription was deliberately selected despite awareness of a translational equivalent. Thus also baqṭ = pakton, not owing to the lack of Arabic terms for "lease" or "commercial treaty", but because the loan identified more readily the Egyptian deed of conveyance and/or the established terms of Nubian trade.[125]

More demanding is the loan translation (calque), along the lines of a quite unnecessary "overview" (Uberblick) = survey or seriously misleading "oversight" (Ubersicht) = supervision. An example given above (sijill maftūḥ = letters patent) was intelligible but also unnecessary, unless coined in ignorance of the standard Arabic term. Rather better, because the lacuna was real, is "barmherzig" = misericors (via OHG armahërz), where the etymology is clearer than in "merciful" = merces/merx (but employed in Christian usage as misericors).[126] While lexical items created in this manner are not always trivial, the role of calque is more easily perceived in broader spans of expression. These are phrases, which become formulaic by repeated use and calques by the very act of recycling in another language. Save possibly the arenga, few components of the chancery format cannot be so described. In the cuneiform version, for instance, both messenger and prostration formulae exhibit respectively identical syntax in Ugaritic and Akkadian, e.g. status construc- tus in the former and verb final in the latter.[127] Grammatically, Akkadian umma + genitive ("Herewith (message) of PN") and Ugaritic final qlt ("...I fall") represent mild dislocation at first encounter, but are easily assimilated in a formulaic framework. In the post-Roman materials consistent inclusion of such items as corroboratio, recognitio and apprecatio is itself a calque, but unobtrusive in a tradition being formed by that very inclu- sion.[128] Such matters as address, signature, date, and witness would be expected in any epistolary/contractual format: only their relative positioning might indicate the effect of a Vorlage.

Straightforward translation is less obviously mimetic than calque. By that I mean merely that "dictionary" collocation will often do, especially for the non-technical language that fills the interstices of a chancery document. But the proportion of "ordinary discourse" in this format is comparatively small: mostly prepositions, conjunctions, a few finite verbs, and even fewer substantives without special or technical referents. The "field despatches" of the two officers mentioned above repre- sent the limits of informality in this genre. Neither is a transla- tion, and it may be doubted that either was intended to be translated. But if they were, then an exercise rather different from marking and filling the slots of a formulary destined for official or public sight would be required. The manifold chal- lenge faced by the translator of literature has been often de- scribed and occasionally understood.[129] Not only conventional syntax and restricted lexicon, but also a need to avoid ambiva- lence, nuance and semantic association, ought to make the chancery text an easier object of transfer. Since these constraints attend the original composition, and often in a polyglot context, the search for interlingual equivalents could easily *accompany* the drafting process. At least some of the documents adduced in the foregoing pages will have come into being in precisely that way, namely, as the product of bilingual scribes. Thus envisaged, "translation" is not simply a passage between forms (though it can be that as well) but rather, an element in the selection of format and even style. It was some such notion that provoked Bakhtine's description of the "Hellenistic effect" as a permanent feature of second language acquisition.[130] Whatev- er, for example, the functions (!) of the date formula, its shape reflects a multilingual input (cf. prepositions: Akk. ištu, Ugar. 1, Aram. men, Arab. fī) based on a juridical equivalent.[131] Choice of phrase was not quite arbitrary.

The fourth mode was transposition, e.g. replacement in the invocatio/blessing formula of a local pantheon by the named deity of monotheism. Rather more subtle perhaps is substitution of a performative aspect (thus PN says) for the imperative (say!) in the messenger formulas, reflecting different circumstances of delivery.[132] The transfer is cultural, not simply linguistic, though a rigorous distinction can probably not be sustained. However, the homology is identifiable. Now, all these contribute to enhanced accessibility of the chancery idiom and constitute, as it were, the "interlanguage" strategies (see above) of its diffusion. It may be they would not qualify as universals of language acquisition, but it can hardly be doubted that this particular style was from the outset determined by precisely such factors of equivalence. Whether "translation" took the form of metaphrase (literal) or paraphrase (free), its fidelity to the "original" was guaranteed by a fixed and predictable context (format), and intelligibility by reference to the *public domain.*

In his analysis of literary translation Steiner adduced the concept of "cultural topology" to depict the spectrum of permissible metamorphosis in interlingual discourse.[133] Applied to the more obvious transformations necessitated by a switch of medium (say, literature to music, to painting, to cinema) the notion is felicitous, but the case can be (and is) made for the quite remarkable options open to the translator concerned exclusively in getting from one language to another. It is well-known that this is easier said than done: the fact that Strindberg, Kafka and Borges belong to world literature and not (merely) to a local environment has of course something to do with their own talents, but not only. The centrifugal motion (Steiner called it hermeneutic) by which a monolingual origin is transcended is a technical achievement quite separate from the original talent. For the language of diplomacy and commerce, anonymously composed and bound to no single culture, the topological argument is at best marginal. Barriers to acquisition and hence diffusion are far outnumbered by the homologies I have sought to exemplify. These are admittedly formal: substantive transfer does of course involve a hermeneutic act.

The substance is neither intractable nor, despite being language, exclusively linguistic. Saussure's naïve description of a national language selected "by tacit convention" from a family of dialects has at least the merit of recalling that the choice is arbitrary.[134] Whatever else informs that convention (hardly "tacit" in the case of Modern Hebrew or Standard Arabic!), its product will not be selection of one and elimination of other contenders. The standard term is "koine", a blend of several varieties and no-one's native "dialect". As already indicated, I have used "koine" differently in this study but concede its value in reference to composite phenomena. One of these, but only one, is the lingua franca. That represents fusion of a sort, and certainly more than one convention, discrete perhaps but mostly explicit, as in the many formulaic transfers so far adduced. While these illustrate the *breach* of national language boundaries, the *amalgamating process* is approximately the same, but never complete. Chancery language is (mostly) compelled to co-exist with a range of other varieties retained or devised for other purposes. Much has been made of the costs entailed by such apparent squandering of resource. In his sally at the "natural universal form" thought by some to underly all language Hymes proposed a countercurrent for the "maintenance of social boundary and communicative distance."[135] Implicit is a tribal instinct to preserve patrimony, identity, self-esteem, privacy etc., some at least of those barriers to hybridisation (Whinnom) or crystallisation (Weinreich) in the formation of new languages.[136] Conservatism (the "resistance factor") is an ambivalent mechanism of description: if it could be seen to impede formation of a lingua franca, it may also explain retention of specific forms *in* a lingua franca over a long period of time, e.g. the remuneration clause in conveyancing deeds.[137] But the point about co-existence is, I think, important. This idiom is widespread but functionally limited: it would erode social boundary and reduce communicative distance in only one domain = transaction of business. That is the minimal, but also normal, role of a lingua franca in respect of its non-native speakers/writers/hearers/readers. Other functions may of course accrue (e.g. creoles).

While the proposal of diffusion by homology is intended to include a great deal more than translation, it is admittedly best perceived in specimens of bilingual contiguity. From these "versions" (see above), available in a number of combinations but in very uneven quantity, emerges nicely the art of semantic juxtaposition. One set, hitherto unmentioned because hardly Mediterranean, consists of Akkadian texts with Aramaic epigraphs (7th century BCE: Neo-Assyrian).[138] But the data are instructive: for deeds of conveyance (property, persons) Fales has shown that the Aramaic, inscribed on otherwise blank margins (edges) and corresponding in layout to the standard sequence of Akkadian legal texts, is a post facto phenomenon, semiotically transferred for archival registration. With such formulae and their purpose I have dealt at some length (Chapter 2). For contracts (loans, pledges), on the other hand, the Aramaic may appear as summarisation of the Akkadian (as in the conveyance documents), or as verbatim rendering of the Akkadian on an equally prominent face of the tablet, or as sole (i.e. monolingual) witness to the transaction. In this category Aramaic is not ancillary to Akkadian but, as can be seen from its application to sealings, of equal juridical weight. Thus not ex post facto but simultaneous in formulation of the legal record. The polyglot chancery was by then hardly an innovation: of interest, as always, are the mechanics of a process that leads to composition of "original" documents in more than one language, that is, from a practice of archival annotation (dockets) to complete linguistic symbiosis.[139] Here, as elsewhere (e.g. Arabic and Italian), though it provokes some confusion as to what exactly can be designated a loanword, transcription is a significant channel. More important, because perceptible over longer stretches of discourse, is calque: e.g. l'm ḥṭ'm tḥm = "on the basis of the boundary he rendered a decision".[140] It is of course the unitary task, a legal transaction, as well as physical contiguity from which symbiosis may be inferred. Whether this presumption can be generally extended to other registers (genres) of the two languages is far from assured, but also not quite unreasonable.

Now, it is precisely that question which inevitably surfaces in any discussion of lingua franca. The very image of a "contact language" presupposes communities whose initial encounter is casual and informal, e.g. merchants on the quayside, garrison troops outside working hours, tourists, even border populations whose contact may be constant but ad hoc. With time contact either lapses or is regularised to a point enabling serious acquisition and diffusion of one or more of the participant languages. It is then that such factors as incentive, interaction, innovation stimulus/receptivity and the like can be discerned and measured, eventually allocated to the standard investigative categories: maintenance/shift, elaboration/attrition, death/revival, etc. The emergence/adoption/imposition of a lingua franca may involve a politico-economic decision but is also demographic: lapse, survival, or diffusion is a product of the number of non-native speakers recruited.[141] Calvet's coinage "langue véhiculaire" evokes nicely the image of agency and commodity transfer.[142]

It must seem that the language of commerce and diplomacy is, if nothing else, "vehicular". For such specimens as Akkadian, Greek, Latin and Arabic, it exhibits a slightly depressed register in relation to the literary productions in those languages. In the comparatively humble origins of Aramaic, however, it reflects perfectly the ancillary role of a language whose earliest records consist of archival dockets (see above), bilingual inscriptions, and the administrative correspondence of an imperial power whose native tongue it was not. The eastward diffusion of its writing system may be reckoned additional proof of its perceived practicality.[143] The Canaanite corpus is more difficult to evaluate. A trajectory from Ugaritic to Neo-Punic would have to depict 1500 years and 2500 miles, a task not made easier by severe lacunae and a curiously alien perspective. I have alluded to both: the first is an approximately average profile of archaeological achievement, the second an absence of *internal* witness to form(s) of government and administrative structure(s). It is thus difficult to envisage the context of decisions that would account for such remarkable dissemination of the language. For Ugaritic the initially ancillary role, that is, within an Akkadian format, is an obvious interpretation and one that would anticipate the later origins of Mesopotamian Aramaic. In support, there is some evidence of the "docket" practice, though very little of bilingual renderings. For active (as well as passive) use of the language beyond Ugarit I have tried to make a case.[144] It is admittedly not a strong one, and would benefit immeasurably from explicit reference to a colonial policy, such as Aristotle's comment many centuries later on the economy of Carthage. By then of course Phoenician had been for some time *the* vehicular mode and its alphabet a

Mediterranean property. Though analogy might justify postulating a Carthaginian solution to, say, problems of overpopula-
tion or surplus production at Ugarit, Sidon or Tyre, I sought to
explain diffusion by cumulative technology ("stockpiling"),
particularly in the areas of marine transport and administrative
resources.[145] From the evidence of cultural artifact (as far west
as Huelva and Mogador) it may be inferred that agency was also
Phoenician: that language, script and other techniques (e.g.
metallurgy, architecture, ornament) were initially Levantine
exports. But from the archaeological context it is difficult to
extrapolate a demographic dimension. A language diffusion
curve showing the rate of non-native accretion must rely upon
the sporadic data of "interference" (Cypriot Phoenician was an
example), and would thus be of little statistical value.

    In keeping with the orbital presentation of my argument,
I ought to confirm that the object of diffusion here is not a single
language, but a *sub-system* of several. It may be that "object"
is misleading, since I consider the chancery register to be as
much agent as product in dissemination of the cultural koine
which generated international law. Its agential role is discernible as homology and as format, a meta-language that dictates
arrangement of parts and identifies equivalents. These, the
parts and equivalents, are the product, realised in a variety of
lexical and grammatical shapes in numerous versions of the
same meta-language. If all this does constitute an argument, it
might be asked how a sub-system so specialised is insinuated
into a general communication network, pre-existent and com-
prehending several sectors of discourse. The conventional
reply is reference to a functional slot not yet or only inadequate-
ly filled, perhaps even conspicuous for disabling an otherwise
efficient structure. In modern language planning the syndrome
is common and the remedy assiduous production of neolo-
gisms, which may be reanalysis of ancient or moribund usage,
possibly inventive derivation from familiar roots, but more
likely than not calque from other languages.[146] Though here
concerned with what I reckon to be the very origins of chancery
language, I admit that those procedures (or some very similar)
must have figured in the creation of this idiom. However, I
suspect also that the "slot" was not perceived (as vacant) but
was itself created, accessory perhaps to completion of the first

orbit. Now, that statement is hardly appropriate to a serious
historical investigation. Let me say, rather, "to the cumulative
effect of several completed orbits", when the need or wish to
perpetuate the motion became an acknowledged goal. Whatever the numerical value of "several", it is the figure that signals
density of communication sufficient to stimulate regular response, records thereof, and a system of notation for both. An
orbit might be generated by attraction of centre to periphery (or
vice versa), but also within a polynuclear framework (without
a centre). Examples of the former: Neo-Assyrian, Roman, and
Islamic empires;[147] of the latter: Canaanite colonies and Italian
maritime republics.[148] But calculation from the baseline of
interaction models (i.e. isolation/inertia) may distort by tele-
scoping the perspective: an unrecorded segment of false starts,
broken journeys and intersecting routes cannot be included.
The "cumulative effect" has got to be a matter of *record,* a
conjuncture of space, time and memory.

In my analysis that record is a semiotic sub-system, a mode
of storage and retrieval, but also a collection of formulae. The
designation "lingua franca" is a reference to its general and
utilitarian character, and not to a putative Arabic etymology
lisān al-firanj ("Frankish tongue").[149] The materials assembled
here are thus quite different from those in the Kahane-Tietze
study of Levantine Lingua Franca: "Turkish nautical terms of
Italian and Greek origin".[150] And yet that remarkable glossary
(878 items), limited to a single lexical field and unidirectional
loans (i.e. into Turkish), reflects the piecemeal accumulation (*c.*
1450-1800) of a jargon and such familiar modes of transfer as
syntactic reanalysis and calque.[151] But even heavy lexical borrowing does not make a lingua franca, though Turkish did
(together with Arabic) serve as such in Ottoman chanceries
from Baghdad to Algiers. There the operative vocabulary was
not nautical but juridical, and derived from its Arabic and
Persian models in chancery usage.[152] The nautical lexicon
exhibits of course a borrowed technology whose agents were
(mostly) identifiable Greek and Italian mariners/engineers recruited to Ottoman service, a common enough phenomenon of
imperial administration. The jargon facilitated naval projects,
whether ship-building or warfare, and occasionally found metaphorical application in other registers.[153] In comparison with

Arabic and Persian elements, the "Frankish" impact upon the structure of Ottoman Turkish was negligible. Nonetheless, an orbital trace may be discerned.

As a model, the *circulation of goods* is mildly treacherous. While raw materials seldom return to source, manufactures may: with different function (e.g. containers as ornaments) or in different form (e.g. garments from textiles), apart of course from the risk of being returned unsold, or, indeed, lost at sea. Language as artifact might be thought susceptible to all these, but in practice only to functional and formal alteration. As vehicle it must be negotiable, but like any currency may be debased. Preservation of real value is dependent upon a number of market factors, none of which is linguistic. Nominal (= "face") value, on the other hand, can be sustained by convention, much of which is linguistic. I have depicted that as format, in terms of the model: an acceptable rate of exchange. The routine questions of the sociolinguist: "who speaks what to whom, when/where/how/why ..." presuppose as reply a context of some sort. Its minimal linguistic ingredients will include such as topic, comment, focus and perspective; its non-linguistic ones at least status, competence, domain and intention. I think it is not too much to assert that both sets may be read from a chancery document, in fact as explicit signals. The communicative task is achieved by acceptance of convention, a transaction incidentally not limited to this particular style.

The (admittedly crude) economic imagery just adduced would make of language a commodity: expression of labour and of consumption. Fashioned for and addressed to a specific market, its production ought to exhibit *optimal design*. While for most utterance that is clearly not so, it happens that the creators of chancery style have at least aspired to that condition.[154] Guidelines, still impressive, may be found in the handbooks of rhetoric. But from those prescriptions it is some distance to the residue of texts composed, authenticated and despatched or otherwise promulgated. If elegance is rarely salient, at least the skeletal structure is in place and intelligible, by enabling recognition of a consignment even before perusal. Reception is, as it were, prefigured and expectation fulfilled. Now, the economic model is in fact more complex.[155] Not only are the raw materials of language (words) in constant circulation, its manufactures (utterances) have different values related to use (intention) and to exchange (acceptance). Linguistic "capital" then, is inexhaustible and its products never finally consumed, though they may be rejected, debased, recycled, etc. The difference between capital and currency is thus not great (e.g. we "coin" a phrase), nor indeed between production and consumption (e.g. we can "talk" to ourselves). But for diffusion of the kind here considered (i.e. across natural language boundaries), there is an "added value" (Marx: Mehrwert) in the very act of commodity transfer. There is also a corresponding "cost" in the conversion of one currency to another, for which the conventional Mediterranean term "agio" seems more than merely appropriate. In exchange transactions that charge has always got to be met, but may be compensated, even exceeded, by the added value of extended circulation. In this process the commodity has not been altered. It has however moved, been repackaged (possibly) and repriced (certainly). The input is *labour,* which I have identified as administrative rationalisation or adoption of standard bureaucratic procedures.

At this point a proper ergometric analysis would be useful. But a time and motion study even for the medieval chancery cannot be simulated, for lack of data as well as a strong possibility that the same parameters did not obtain. Without addressing this particular issue, Rossi-Landi has juxtaposed mechanism/syllogism as procedures for production respectively of non-verbal and verbal artifacts (e.g. utensils = sentences).[156] His programme is not historical but typological: to demonstrate the homologous generation of both classes of artifact as components of one or more sign-systems. So exposed the link between language and economy is perspicuous. Though effort is not quantified, a tidy schema (p.107) of "product levels" illustrates progressive labour input. The schema is also "artificial" (sic) since the levels are not in unavoidable sequence, but nonetheless a co-ordinated range of goods is exemplified. Also exemplified is the cumulative character of this labour: the uninterrupted accessibility of raw materials as well as of artifacts means that ab initio starts would be optional, and probably not often elected. Turning to the available pattern would save time and thought. Perpetuation of a chancery format must seem both easy and prudent. To "flood the market" with innovations would, on the other hand, be costly and confusing.

It is the occasion for exchange that makes of a product a commodity. A message, of whatever composition, is bound to be that, but its semiotic value is likely to exceed the mere fact of exchange. Having alluded ad nauseam to this quality of the chancery style, I need hardly insist upon its inclusion within a sign-system of much wider significance than might at first sight be gleaned from its arid and formulaic expression. Because of several (in my view) salient properties, I have designated that sign-system a "juridical koine", but its insertion into the process of exchange makes it also "economic". The fact that so much of my evidence happens to be directed to the material economy (commercial treaties, contracts, deeds and the like) does account for a good deal of the technical terminology in this idiom, but is not the reason for now calling it economic. That resides in the nature of "transaction", where all ingredients are in some sense "contact languages". The economist's concern with commodity as stimulus, object and result of exchange is analogous to that of the linguist with sign as code, emblem and content of communication.[157] At the very beginning of this study I proposed that "trade" be taken to comprehend the processes of change as well as the procedures of exchange, on the grounds that diffusion left so little intact.[158] While the substance and shape of many material commodities can undoubtedly survive a long journey, the insertion of these into a new context is more than likely to generate change, if not in the commodity (by adaptation) then in the context itself (by reception, dislocation, etc.). For the verbal commodity (=message) a similar traverse cannot but produce change. The ways in which this occurs or must occur ought by now to be familiar (or are anyway familiar?). Admittedly, it would be helpful to know something of the *scale* of diffusion: whether confined to a class of scribes and circle of merchants (= micro) or widely distributed amongst the recipient population (= macro). Like bureaucratic jargon today, the style itself was probably limited to those whose professional duties required it. Unbound lexica and phraseology might find further employment. Lateral extension (to other scribes, merchants, bureaucrats, etc.) would be quite natural; vertical extension (to other registers, outsiders, etc.) would encounter incomprehension and, very likely, no little resistance. I have mentioned the eccentric Arabic and Italian of the medieval commercial documents: who, other than those directly concerned with business, might wish to use such language? If no-one, then what per cent of the Mediterranean population in the 15th century (*c.* 30 million?) would have been even marginally engaged in long distance trade? Even 1% would yield a substantial vehicle of contact and exchange, a conjectural figure but hardly exaggerated.

If one dare use the term, the sampling technique in this study has been deliberately selective. It was also governed by source availability, which becomes thus a variable in the measurement of diffusion. Not, however, an independent (control) variable, since its volume is itself the record of diffusion. If, then, the sample is merely coterminous with the phenomenon being analysed, description is a self-contained exercise, possibly of intrinsic worth but of little statistical value.[159] To alleviate, if not quite to circumvent that constraint, I have adduced such technologies as cartography, script and pottery in the expectation that diffusion based on similar traffic patterns would exhibit common features. From even rough conjunctures, like production of portolani and increased volume of chancery paperwork, a reciprocal impetus might be inferred.[160] There the assumption would be that quantitative change in different but related spheres may be read as directly proportional, a view of activity that I have several times conceded is just possibly tautological.

A plausible research design ought also to accommodate inversely proportional change, if only to illustrate reduced cost, efficiency gain, some trace of motive for departure from traditional paths. As direct proportion labour input would be expected to increase cost per unit, but beyond a certain threshold of production to reduce it. Whether that commodity formula can be applied to "lingua franca" as here defined is a question to which I should of course welcome an affirmative reply. The completion/repetition of orbits was intended to evoke an image of feedback, of which one product at least would be dialogue. Experiment with form(s) and eventual establishment of norm(s) comprise the standard approach to that task, and this is what I have sought to exemplify. Identification of a "threshold", the point at which unit cost is perceived to fall, is less easy than, say, for the production and distribution of silk.

Permeation of the market, indeed the "marketplace", is crucial, and I have acknowledged the paucity of demographic data. Certainly, by the 15th century the machinery was in place: it is unlikely that any transaction, commercial or diplomatic, foundered for want of a common idiom. For this as well as for the preceding period the primary index to labour input is volume of testimony, from which logically retrogression into comparative silence might be deduced. Somehow that must be thought both unsatisfactory and unrealistic. The alternative suggested here was to disaggregate the volume of archival data as an array of forms for a variety of purposes. But however differentiated (e.g. treaty, covenant, letter, invoice, receipt, credit transfer) these classes of document attest to a *contractual* perception of economic and social relations. Volume could thus be interpreted as refinement, not merely increase, of contact. By way of illustration (again): the difference between the Amarna correspondence (14th century BCE) and Venetian negotiations in Alexandria some three millennia later.[161] By then the levels of discourse had proliferated in response to multilateral participation in commerce and lawsuit alike. Mode of formal utterance was fixed, recourse to it vastly expanded. A diffusion curve would exhibit more copiously documented transactions of greater value, but also a greater number of transactions per party. Both can be attributed to reduction of cost per transaction, i.e. the paperwork was easier because it was largely formulaic. It would also take less time.

Certain imponderables affect this version of bureaucracy, e.g. ceremonial posture, fastidiousness, procrastination, dereliction, etc. Whether tasks are allocated time according to desert or until completed, whether graded according to importance or dealt with as they occur, whether assigned according to recipient's competence or randomly distributed, are factors that influence despatch of business but cannot be quantified. Measurement is in fact for this whole enterprise elusive: a framework, some content, but little by way of dimension. Possibly somewhat arbitrary, the framework has the merit of symmetry, beginning and ending with a central role for the "orbital polis".[162] Within its span a contraction of *time* is discernible, an impression provoked by the accumulation of data in a *spatial* continuum. I have mentioned this reciprocal action as a significant factor in the gradual emergence of a linear history.[163] The danger of an optical illusion must be acknowledged: contiguity in space and time is easily read as causality (post hoc ergo propter hoc). Density of contact in the Mediterranean space could also be simply the product of frequency (occasion) and distribution (point) scales: the sum of possible movement at any time without regard for a causal nexus. While that image of energy generated by proximity is undoubtedly valid, it evades the challenge of narrative description. Rather more useful was the imagery of electrical circuit or magnetic field, in which either variable input or non-contiguity could be reckoned, if not always and accurately measured.[164]

A persistent element of fortuity would anyway inhibit application of a quantum model. In December 1507 Alvise Pizamano, captain of the Venetian galee di Barbaria, dropped anchor at the tiny Moroccan port of Bādis.[165] That harbour was not quite unknown in Venice, but figures in the shipping records only as an optional call. Nonetheless, on that occasion, which may well have been the first, a treaty was negotiated between the Waṭṭāsid commandant of the port and Pizamano, in the name of the Doge Leonardo Loredan. Of commerce there is hardly mention. Stipulation for emergency provisions, redemption of captives, and a safe haven: ad hoc relief from the hazards of a winter voyage, to this day something of a risk in the Mediterranean.

Notes

CHAPTER 1

1. J. Wansbrough, 'The safe-conduct in Muslim chancery practice', BSOAS XXXIV, 1, 1971, pp. 20-35; Idem, Encyclopaedia of Islam, second edition, vol. III, pp. 1178-9 s.v. Imtiyāzāt; and see below, Ch.2, pp. 132-6.

2. C. Renfrew and J.Dixon, 'Obsidian in western Asia: a review', in G. Sieveking (ed), Problems in Economic and Social Anthropology, London, 1976, pp. 137-50; N. Yoffee, Explaining Trade in ancient Western Asia, Monographs on the Ancient Near East 2/2, Malibu, 1981, pp. 14-15; cf. G.Wright, 'Archaeology and Trade, An Addison-Wesley Module' in Anthropology, No.49, 1974, pp. 12-17 (distribution analysis).

3. D. Collon, 'Ivory', in J.D. Hawkins (ed), Trade in the Ancient Near East, IRAQ XXXIX, 1977, pp. 219-22; G.Herrmann, 'Lapis lazuli: the early phases of its trade', IRAQ XXX, 1968, pp. 21-57; J.Crowfoot Payne, 'Lapis lazuli in early Egypt', ibid, pp. 58-61.

4. J. Wansbrough, BSOAS L, 2, 1987, pp. 361-2 ad M. Silver, Economic Structures of the Ancient Near East, London 1985.

5. C. Renfrew and K. Cooke (edd), Transformations: mathematical approaches to culture change, New York, 1979.

6. Cf. M. Powell, 'Three problems in the history of cuneiform writing: origins, direction of script, literacy', in M. Powell, Aspects of Cuneiform Writing, Visible Language XV, 4, 1981, pp. 419-40, esp. 431-8; and see below, Ch.2, pp.181-7.

7. M. Schiffer, 'A preliminary consideration of behavioral change', in Renfrew and Cooke, Transformations, pp. 358-68.

8. F. Braudel, The Mediterranean and the Mediterranean World in the Age of Philip II, London 1975, vol. I, pp. 168-230 (boundaries) ; cf. J. Hexter, Journal of Modern History 44, 1972, pp. 480-539.

9. Braudel, op. cit. I, pp. 371-9.

10. J. Wansbrough, 'A Mamluk ambassador to Venice in 913/1507', BSOAS XXVI, 3, 1963, pp. 503-30.

11. J. Wansbrough, 'A Mamlūk commercial treaty concluded with the Republic of Florence 894/1489', in S. Stern (ed), Documents from Islamic Chanceries, Oriental Studies III, Oxford, 1965, pp. 39-79, esp. 44-5.

12. A Millard, 'Cartography in the Ancient Near East', in J. Harley and D.

Woodward (edd), The History of Cartography, vol. I, University of Chicago Press, 1987, pp. 107-16; and see below, nn. 45-47.

13. W. Leemans, 'The trade relations of Babylonia and the question of relations with Egypt in the Old Babylonian period', JESHO 3, 1960, pp. 21-37; D. Edzard, 'Die Beziehungen Babyloniens and Ägyptens in der Mittelbabylonischen Zeit und das Gold', ibid, pp. 38-55.

14. F. Plog, 'Alternative models of prehistoric change', in Renfrew and Cooke, Transformations, pp. 221-36.

15. J. Wansbrough, 'Res ipsa loquitur: history and mimesis', Albert Einstein Memorial Lecture, Israel Academy of Sciences and Humanities, Jerusalem 1987 (delivered 16 March 1986), pp. 6-11.

16. S. Skilliter, William Harborne and the Trade with Turkey 1578-1582, London 1977, pp. 39-40, 44-5; and see below, Ch. 2, pp. 77-78.

17. E. Ashtor, Levant Trade in the Later Middle Ages, Princeton University Press, 1983, pp. 385-8; the "northern tier" was apparently an ancient preference, see G. Bunnens, 'Tyr et la mer', in E. Gubel (ed), Studia Phoenicia I-II, Orientalia Lovaniensia Analecta 15, Leuven 1983, pp. 7-21, esp. 16-17; but cf. L. Casson, Ships and Seamanship in the Ancient World, Princeton University Press, 1971, pp. 270-99.

18. Braudel, Mediterranean, pp. 355-79, esp. 362: Sardella's tabulation of data from Marino Sanudo; cf. Ashtor, op. cit., p. 380 and n. 76 (ref. F. Melis).

19. J. Munn-Rankin, 'Diplomacy in western Asia in the early second millennium B.C.' IRAQ XVIII, 1956, pp. 68-110, esp. 99-108.

20. A. Goetze, 'An Old Babylonian itinerary', JCS VII, 1953, pp. 51-72, esp. 64-7; W. Pitard, Ancient Damascus, Winona Lake, Indiana, 1987, pp. 39-48; similarly, the toponym Muṣur: see M. Elat, 'The economic relations of the Neo-Assyrian empire with Egypt', JAOS 98, 1978, pp. 20-34, esp. 21-2 n. 8.

21. M. Astour, 'Ugarit and the great powers', in G. Yung (ed), Ugarit in Retrospect, Winona Lake, Indiana, 1981, pp. 3-29, esp. 13-14; cf. Y. Aharoni, 'The land of 'Amqi', IEJ 3, 1953, pp. 153-61.

22. Pitard, op. cit., pp. 55-72; cf. Wansbrough, BSOAS LI, 3, 1988, pp. 543-4.

23. M. Liverani, 'Contrasti e confluenze di concezioni politiche nell'età di El-Amarna', RA LXI, 1, 1967, pp. 1-18; Idem, 'Le lettere del Faraone a Rib-Adda', OA X, 1971, pp. 253-68; Idem, 'Memorandum on the approach to historiographic texts', Or. 42, 1973, pp. 178-94.

24. Y. Holmes, 'Egypt and Cyprus: late Bronze Age trade and diplomacy', in H. Hoffner (ed), Orient and Occident = AOAT 22, 1973, Neukirchen-Vluyn, pp. 91-8; Idem, 'The messengers of the Amarna letters', JAOS 95, 1975, pp. 376-81.

25. Astour, art. cit., pp. 8-9 map; J. Nougayrol, PRU IV, Paris, 1956, pp. 10-18, 63-78.

26. S. Frankenstein, 'The Phoenicians in the Far West: a function of Neo-Assyrian imperialism', in M. Larsen (ed), Power and Propaganda: a symposium on ancient empires, Copenhagen Studies in Assyriology, vol. 7, Copenhagen, 1979, pp. 263-94, esp. 287-9; P. Wathelet, 'Les Phéniciens et la tradition homérique', in E. Gubel, Studia Phoenicia I-II, pp. 235-43.

27. Frankenstein, art. cit., pp. 273-83; B. Mazar, 'The Philistines and the rise of Israel and Tyre', PIASH I, 1967, pp. 1-22; Bunnens, art. cit., esp. p. 9 no.4; and see below, n.44.

28. G. Bass, 'Cape Gelidonya: a Bronze Age shipwreck', Transactions of the American Philosophical Society, vol. 57, part 8, Philadelphia, December, 1967; Idem, 'Cape Gelidonya and Bronze Age maritime trade', in H. Hoffner (ed), Orient and Occident = AOAT 22, 1973, pp. 29-38; Idem, 'A Bronze Age shipwreck at Ulu Burun (Kas) : 1984 campaign', AJA 90, 1986, pp. 269-97.

29. R. Barnett, 'Early shipping in the Near East', Antiquity XXXII, 1958, pp. 220-30, esp. 226ff.; M.De Graeve, The Ships of the Ancient Near East (c. 2000-500 B.C.), Orientalia Lovaniensia Analecta 7, Leuven, 1981, esp. pp. 123-43; cf. Casson, op. cit., pp. 94-6.

30. E. Linder, 'Ugarit: a Canaanite thalassocracy', in G. Young (ed), Ugarit in Retrospect, 1981, pp. 31-42; P. Xella, 'Die Ausrüstung eines kanaanäischen Schiffes (KTU 4.689)', WO 13, 1982, pp. 31-5; and see below, nn. 178-88.

31. J. Nougayrol, PRU III, Paris, 1955, pp. 107-8 (RS 16.238); for kabturu/kptr= Kaphtor=Crete (?) : M. Astour, 'Ugarit and the Aegean', in H. Hoffner (ed), Orient and Occident = AOAT 22, 1973, pp. 17-27, esp. 19, 25-6; and see below, n. 97.

32. Casson, op. cit., pp. 43-96.

33. M. Larsen, 'The tradition of empire in Mesopotamia'; S. Frankenstein, art. cit.; M. Liverani, 'The ideology of the Assyrian Empire'; all in M. Larsen (ed), Power and Propaganda, Copenhagen, 1979, pp. 75-103, 263-94, 297-317, resp.

34. R. Revere,' "No man's coast": ports of trade in the eastern Mediterranean', in K. Polanyi, C. Arensberg and H. Pearson (edd), Trade and Market in the Early Empires, Glencoe, Illinois, 1957, pp. 38-63, esp. 51-5; cf. Yoffee, op. cit., pp. 11-12; Wright, op. cit., pp. 36-7.

35. Larsen, art. cit., pp. 100-02; Frankenstein, art. cit., pp. 271-3; Elat, art. cit., pp. 26-8; cf. G. Bunnens, art. cit. and/or G. Kestemont, 'Tyr et les Assyriens', in E. Gubel (ed), Studia Phoenicia I-II, pp. 7-21 and 53-78, resp.

36. Elat, art. cit., pp. 28-30; cf. I. Eph'al, The Ancient Arabs, Jerusalem, 1984, pp. 12-17, 138-41, 241 map.

37. Eph'al, op. cit., pp. 101-11; Idem, 'On warfare and military control in the ancient near Eastern empires: a research outline', in H. Tadmor and M. Weinfeld (edd), History, Historiography and Interpretation: studies in biblical and cuneiform literatures, Jerusalem, 1983, pp. 88-106.

38. A. Oppenheim, 'Essay on overland trade in the first millennium B.C.', JCS XXI, 1967, pp. 236-54, esp. 239, 253-4.

39. E.g. Adummatu = Dumat al-Jandal (Jawf) and [A]dummu = Edom (?): Eph'al, op. cit., pp. 119-21, 185-8.

40. G. Bowersock, Roman Arabia, Harvard University Press, 1983, pp. 111-47; M. Rostovtzeff, Caravan Cities, Oxford, 1932; and see below, nn. 168-72.

41. A. Grayson, Or. 49, 1980, pp. 140-94, esp. 150-5, 164-5, 170-1; L. Levine, 'Preliminary remarks on the historical inscriptions of Sennacherib', in H.

Tadmor and M. Weinfeld (edd), History, Historiography and Interpretation, pp. 58-75; D. Edzard and G. Frantz-Szabó, Itinerare, RLA V, pp. 216-20.

42.   Goetze, art. cit.; Idem, 'Remarks on the Old Babylonian itinerary', JCS XVIII, 1964, pp. 114-19; W. Hallo, 'The road to Emar', ibid, pp. 57-88.

43.   J. Levy, 'Studies in the historic geography of the Ancient Near East', Or. 21, 1952, pp. 1-12, 265-92, 393-425; Goetze, art. cit. (1953), pp. 64-70, 72 map; Hallo, art. cit., p. 87 map.

44.   J. Muhly, 'Phoenicia and the Phoenicians', in Biblical Archaeology Today, Israel Exploration Society, Jerusalem, 1985, pp. 177-91; Idem, 'Homer and the Phoenicians', Berytus 19, 1970, pp. 19-64; J. Coldstream, 'Greeks and Phoenicians in the Aegean', in H. Niemeyer (ed), Phönizier in Westen, Mainz, 1982, pp. 261-75.

45.   A. Millard, art. cit.; A. Shore, 'Egyptian cartography', also in J. Harley and D. Woodward (edd), The History of Cartography, vol. I, 117-29; W. Röllig, Landkarten, RLA VI, pp. 464-7; L. Le Breton, 'De l 'état de notre connaissance des itinéraires antiques', RA LII, 1958, pp. 110-16; P. Garelli, 'La notion de route dans les textes', ibid, pp. 117-27.

46.   Harley and Woodward, op. cit., pp. 1-5, 45-9, 132-47, 148-76; by "map" I intend not an iconic version of secular, sacred or mythical space, but rather, a deliberately conceived representation of terrestrial surface.

47.   E.g. the Massaliote Periplus (500 BCE?) possibly known to Pytheas: Harley and Woodward, op. cit., p. 150 n. 16.

48.   C. Lamberg-Karlovsky, 'Trade mechanisms in Indus-Mesopotamian interrelations', JAOS 92, 1972, pp. 222-9, more instructive than the earlier studies of M. Mallowan, 'The mechanics of ancient trade in western Asia', IRAN 3, 1965, pp. 1-7, and of A. Oppenheim, 'The seafaring merchants of Ur', JAOS 74, 1954, pp. 6-17; on the latter cf. J. Oates et alii, 'Seafaring merchants of Ur?', Antiquity LI, 1977, pp. 221-34 and the reply thereto of A. Masry, Antiquity LII, 1978, pp. 46-7.

49.   E.g. P. Kohl, 'The balance of trade in southwestern Asia in the mid-third millennium B.C.', Current Anthropology 19, 3, 1978, pp. 463-92, esp. 469-75.

50.   Cf. Kohl, art. cit., p. 474, and the comments of H. Claessen (p. 476), J. Oates (p. 481), D. Potts (p. 482), H. Sankalia (p. 482) and J. Shaffer (p. 483).

51.   Yoffee, op. cit., pp. 25-6; Wansbrough, 'Res ipsa loquitur' (cited above, n. 15).

52.   Wright, op. cit., pp. 3-4, 38-9 (boundaries), 9 (symbiotic region), 10-11 (ports of trade); and see below, nn. 176-7.

53.   Cf. W. Smith, Interconnections in the Ancient Near East: a study of the relationships between the arts of Egypt, the Aegean, and Western Asia, Yale University Press, 1965, and thereto : J. Muhly, JAOS 90, 1970, pp. 305-9; Astour, 'Ugarit and the Aegean', p. 27; J. Sasson, 'A sketch of North Syrian economic relations in the Middle Bronze Age', JESHO IX, 1966, pp. 161-81.

54.   Y. Portugali and A. Knapp, 'Cyprus and the Aegean: a spatial analysis of interaction in the seventeenth to fourteenth centuries B.C.', in A. Knapp and T. Stech (edd), Prehistoric Production and Exchange: the Aegean and Eastern Mediterranean, Institute of Archaeology, Monograph XXV, University of California, Los Angeles, 1985, pp. 44-69, esp. 46, 50-53; for interaction

models, see p. 68 n. 3, and T.Earle and J.Ericson (edd), Exchange Systems in Prehistory, New York 1977, esp. Part III.

55. Portugali and Knapp, art. cit., pp. 60-64; (a postulate supported by textual evidence from the Late Bronze Age, e.g. Amarna, Hatti, Ugarit).

56. A. Knapp, 'Production and Exchange in the Aegean and Eastern Mediterranean: an overview', in Knapp and Stech, op. cit., pp. 1-11, esp. 8-9.

57. E.g. the monograph of M. Silver (cited above, n.4); S. Humphreys, 'History, economics, and anthropology: the work of Karl Polanyi', History and Theory 8, 1969, pp. 165-212; cf. G.Dalton, 'Karl Polanyi's analysis of long-distance trade and his wider paradigm', in J. Sabloff and C. Lamberg-Karlovsky, Ancient Civilization and Trade, University of New Mexico Press, 1975, pp. 63-132; J. Gledhill and M. Larsen, 'The Polanyi paradigm and a dynamic analysis of archaic states', in C. Renfrew et alii, Theory and Explanation in Archaeology, New York, 1982, pp. 197-229; J. Renger, 'Patterns of non-institutional trade and non-commercial exchange in ancient Mesopotamia at the beginning of the second millennium B.C.', in A.Archi (ed), Circulation of Goods in Non-Palatial Context in the Ancient Near East, Instituto per gli studi Micenei ed Egeo-Anatolici, Rome, 1984, pp. 31-123, and thereto P. Vargyas, 'The problems of private economy in the Ancient Near East', BO XLIV, 3/4, 1987, pp. 376-86.

58. Cf. R.Adams, 'Anthropological perspectives on ancient trade', Current Anthropology 15, 3, 1974, pp. 239-58, esp. 243 ad settlement nuclei and communication foci (B. Hodder 1965); C. Renfrew, 'Trade as action at a distance', in Idem, Approaches to Social Archaeology, Harvard University Press, 1984, pp. 86-134.

59. Adams, art. cit., pp. 246-8; M. Larsen, 'Partnerships in the Old Assyrian trade', in J.D. Hawkins (ed), Trade in the Ancient Near East, IRAQ XXXIX, 1977, pp. 119-45; K. Veenhof, 'Some social effects of Old Assyrian trade', ibid, pp. 109-18; cf. Yoffee, op. cit., pp. 9-12.

60. A. Falkenstein, The Sumerian Temple City, Monographs in History: Ancient Near East 1/1, Malibu, 1974; J. Renger, 'Interaction of temple, palace, and "private enterprise" in the Old Babylonian economy', in E. Lipinski (ed), State and Temple Economy in the Ancient Near East, Leuven, 1979, I, pp.249-56; H. Limet, 'Le rôle du palais dans l 'économie néo-sumérienne', ibid, I, pp. 235-48; D. Edzard, 'Die Archive von Suruppag (Fara) : Umfang und Grenzen der Auswertbarkeit', ibid, I. pp. 153-69; W. Hallo, 'God, king, and man at Yale', ibid, I, pp. 99-111; even more recently, J. Makkay, 'The origins of the "temple-economy" as seen in the light of prehistoric evidence', IRAQ XLV, 1983, pp. 1-6.

61. Silver, Economic Structures, pp. 7-31.

62. Silver, op. cit., pp. 39-41, 101-02, 140; cf. I. Gelb, 'Household and family in early Mesopotamia', in E. Lipinski (ed), State and Temple Economy in the Ancient Near East, I, pp. 1-97, esp. 25-8, 56-68, 81-91; but also M. Powell, 'Economy of the extended family according to Sumerian sources', Oikumene 5, Budapest, 1986, pp. 9-14; W. Leemans, 'The family in the economic life of the Old Babylonian period', ibid, pp. 15-22; H. Klengel, 'The economy of the Hittite household (E)', ibid, pp. 23-31; N. Jankowska, 'The role of the ex-

tended family in the economic life of the Kingdom of Arraphe', ibid, pp. 33-42; J. Zabocka, 'Der Haushalt der Neuassyrischen Familie', ibid, pp. 43-9; M. Dandamayev, 'Economy of Tabiya, a Babylonian of the sixth century B.C.', ibid, pp. 51-3.

63. J. Wansbrough, BSOAS XLIX, 3, 1986, pp. 573-4 ad E.Ashtor, Levant Trade (cited above, n. 17).

64. Ibid, and BSOAS XXXI, 3, 1968, pp. 619-22, XXXVI, 3, 1973, pp.648-50, LII, 2, 1989, pp. 337-8 ad S.D. Goitein, A Mediterranean Society: the Jewish communities of the Arab world as portrayed in the documents of the Cairo Geniza, University of California Press, 1967-88 (Vols I-V); see also Larsen, 'Partnerships', IRAQ XXXIX, 1977, pp. 121, 123; cf. Wansbrough, BSOAS LI, 2, 1988, pp. 320-1 ad J. Israel, European Jewry in the Age of Mercantilism, 1550-1750, Clarendon Press, Oxford, 1985.

65. I have employed this imagery elsewhere for the development of a linguistic canon: see Quranic Studies: sources and methods of scriptural interpretation, Oxford University Press, 1977, pp. 85-118, esp. 89.

66. Cf. C. Renfrew, The Emergence of Civilization, London, 1972, chapters 15-21: on interaction, threshold and multiplier effect; Renfrew and Cooke, Transformations (cited above, n. 5), chapters 14 and 21: model simulation and systems collapse.

67. Transformations, pp. 339-47, 487-99: zero growth, catastrophe, anastrophe.

68. D. Ayalon, Gunpowder and Firearms in the Mamluk Kingdom, London, 1956, esp. pp. 46-111.

69. Cf. M. Brett, 'Morocco and the Ottomans: the sixteenth century in North Africa', JAH 25, 1984, pp. 331-41; H. Fisher and V. Rowland, 'Firearms in the Central Sudan', JAH 12, 1971, pp. 215-39.

70. See above, n. 47; T. Campbell, 'Portulan charts from the late thirteenth century to 1500', in Harley and Woodward, op. cit., pp. 371-463, esp. 380-86, 428-35.

71. Ibid, p. 381; Casson, Ships and Seamanship, pp. 245-6; Idrīsī's cartography was derivatively Ptolemaic; the earlier schematic maps of Balkhī, Istakhrī and Muqaddasī can hardly be related to development of the portolan: cf. plates in A. Fahmy, Muslim Sea-Power in the Eastern Mediterranean, London, 1950, pp. 33, 57, 67, 89, 93 (from K. Miller, Mappae Arabicae, Stuttgart, 1926-31, vols. I-V); cf. J. Kramers, Analecta Orientalia I, Leiden, 1954, pp. 145-222 (Geography).

72. Cf. Campbell, art. cit., pp. 386-8, 438-45; Casson, op. cit., pp. 270-99.

73. Casson, op. cit., pp. 97-154.

74. See below, Ch. 2, pp. 130-33. .

75. Above, n.64: Goitein, op. cit., I. pp. 273-352; Idem, Letters of Medieval Jewish Traders, Princeton University Press, 1973, pp. 305-39, and thereto Wansbrough, BSOAS XXXVIII, 3, 1975, p. 442; A. Udovitch, 'Time, the sea and society: duration of commercial voyages on the southern shores of the Mediterranean during the High Middle Ages', in Settimane di studio del Centro italiano di studi sull'alto medioevo, XXV, La Navigazione Mediterranea Nell 'Alto Medioevo, Spoleto, 1978, pp. 503-63; R. Duncan-

Jones, Structure and Scale in the Roman Economy, Cambridge University Press, 1990, pp. 7-29; on the southern and northern routes, cf. above, n. 17.

76. B. Kreutz, in Udovitch, art. cit., pp. 559-61, and 'Ships, shipping, and the implications of change in the early medieval Mediterranean', Viator 7, 1976, pp. 79-109; R. Unger, The Ship in the Medieval Economy 600-1600, London, 1980, esp. chs. 3 and 4.

77. E.g. P. Hübinger (ed), Bedeutung and Rolle des Islam beim Ubergang vom Altertum zum Mittelalter, Wege der Forschung CCII, Darmstadt, 1986: esp. R. Lopez, 'Mohammed and Charlemagne: a revision' (1943), pp. 65-104; D. Dennett, 'Pirenne and Muhammad' (1948), pp. 120-59; A. Riising, 'The fate of Henri Pirenne's thesis on the consequences of the Islamic expansion' (1951), pp. 178-222; cf. A. Havighurst (ed), The Pirenne Thesis: Problems in European Civilization, Boston, 1958; R. Hodges and D. Whitehouse, Mohammed, Charlemagne and the Origins of Europe, London, 1983.

78. Dennett, art. cit., pp. 125-34; an earlier collection of data in W. Heyd, Histoire du commerce du Levant au Moyen-Age, Leipzig, 1885-86 (repr. Amsterdam, 1959), I, pp. 1-128.

79. See above, n. 71: Fahmy, op. cit.

80. Cf. S. Bolin, 'Mohammed, Charlemagne and Ruric' (1953), in Hübinger, op. cit., pp. 223-65; Hodges and Whitehouse, op. cit., pp. 88-101, 111-22, 158-68; M. Brett, 'Ifriqiya as a market for Saharan trade from the tenth to the twelfth century A.D.', JAH X, 3, 1969, pp. 347-64 ad M. Lombard, 'L' or musulman du VIIe au XIe siècles', Annales, Economies, Sociétés, Civilisations II, 1947, pp. 143-60.

81. M. Brett, 'Morocco and the Ottomans', (cited above, n. 69) ad A. Hess, The Forgotten Frontier: a history of the sixteenth-century Ibero-African frontier, Chicago University Press, 1978; cf. M. García-Arenal and M.Viguera (edd), Relaciones de la Peninsula Ibérica con el Magreb (siglos XIII-XVI), Madrid, 1988.

82. Braudel, Mediterranean, pp. 776-802; cf. Brett, art. cit., p. 333; see above, n. 52, and below, n. 177.

83. G. Von Grunebaum, Medieval Islam, University of Chicago Press, 1953; J. Wansbrough, The Sectarian Milieu, Oxford University Press, 1978; J. Koren and Y. Nevo, 'Methodological approaches to Islamic studies', Der Islam 68, 1, 1991, pp. 87-107.

84. Israel, European Jewry, pp. 5-52; See about n. 64.

85. D. Miller, Artefacts as Categories: a study of ceramic variability in Central India, Cambridge University Press, 1985, esp. pp. 197-205; Y. Garlan, 'Greek amphorae and trade', in P. Garnsey et alii, Trade in the Ancient Economy, London, 1983, pp. 27-35; G. Pucci, 'Pottery and trade in the Roman period', ibid, pp. 105-17; A. Carandini, 'Pottery and the African economy', ibid, pp. 145-62; M. Finley, The Use and Abuse of History, London, 1975, pp. 87-101 'Archaeology and history'; W. Dever, Recent Archaeological Discoveries and Biblical Research, Washington University Press, 1990, pp. 1-36 'Artifacts, ecofacts, and textual facts'.

86. See above, n. 6: M. Powell, art. cit.; G. Driver, Semitic Writing: from pictograph to alphabet, revised edition S. Hopkins, Oxford University Press, 1976;

J. Hawkins, 'The origin and dissemination of writing in Western Asia', in P. Moorey (ed), The Origins of Civilization, Clarendon Press, Oxford, 1979, pp. 128-66; J. Oates (ed), Early Writing Systems, World Archaeology, vol. 17, 3, Institute of Archaeology, London, 1986; C. Renfrew, Emergence (cited above, n.66), chapter 19 (homo symbolicus).

87.   W. Haas, 'Writing: the basic options', in W. Haas (ed), Writing Without Letters, Mont Follick Series, Vol. Four, Manchester University Press, 1976, pp. 131-208, esp. 200.

88.   J. Goody and I. Watt, 'The consequences of literacy', in J. Goody (ed), Literacy in Traditional Societies, Cambridge University Press, 1978, pp. 27-68, esp. 38; Idem, The Logic of Writing and the Organization of Society, Cambridge University Press, 1986, esp. pp. 45-86.

89.   See below, Chapter 2, pp. 88-96.

90.   Ibid, pp. 51-3: I am aware of the problems inherent in this formulation.

91.   W. Watt, 'The Byblos matrix', JNES 46, 1987, pp. 1-14; cf. J. Justeson, 'Universals of language and universals of writing', in A. Juilland et alii (edd), Linguistic Studies . . . . Joseph Greenberg, Saratoga, California, 1977, Vol. 1, pp. 57-94.

92.   Driver, op. cit., pp. 91-4; Hawkins, art. cit., pp. 158-61; M. Sznycer, 'Les inscriptions pseudo-hiéroglyphiques de Byblos', in J. Leclant, Le Déchiffrement des Ecritures et des Langues, Paris, 1975, pp. 75-84; G. Garbini, Storia e Problemi dell 'Epigrafia Semitica, Naples, 1979, pp. 83-5; G. Mendenhall, The Syllabic Inscriptions from Byblos, American University of Bairut, 1985.

93.   E.g. F. Cross, 'Newly found inscriptions in Old Canaanite and Early Phoenician scripts', BASOR 238, 1980, pp. 1-20; J. Naveh, Early History of the Alphabet: an introduction to West Semitic epigraphy ånd paleography, Jerusalem, 1982; cf. M. Bernal, 'On the transmission of the alphabet to the Aegean before 1400 B.C.', BASOR 267, 1987, pp. 1-19.

94.   S. Kaufman, 'The pitfalls of typology: on the early history of the alphabet', HUCA 57, 1986, pp. 1-14 (and refs. p. 8, n. 17: Tell Fekherye); on different data, cf. also F. Fales, Aramaic Epigraphs on Clay Tablets of the Neo-Assyrian Period, Rome, 1986, pp. 106-26.

95.   E.g. Astour, 'Ugarit and the Aegean' (cited above, n. 31); J. Sasson, 'Canaanite maritime involvement in the second millennium B.C.', JAOS 86, 1966, pp. 126-38; Idem, art. cit. (above, n. 53).

96.   Astour, 'Ugarit and the great powers' (cited above, n.21); Idem, 'Place Names', in L. Fisher, Ras Shamra Parallels, vol. II, Rome, 1975, pp. 249-369, and further geographical-topographical studies: e.g. JNES 22, 1963, pp. 220-41, Or. 38, 1969, pp. 381-414, Or. 46, 1977, pp. 51-64.

97.   E.g. L. Hellbing, Alasia Problems, Studies in Mediterranean Archaeology, vol. LVII, Göteborg, 1979; J. Strange, Caphtor/Keftiu: a new investigation, Acta Theologica Danica, vol. XIV, Leiden, 1980.

98.   Cf. M. Artzy et alii, 'Alaśiya of the Amarna letters', JNES 35, 1976, pp. 171-82.

99. C. Schaeffer, 'Une écriture chypriote particulière à Ugarit?', UGAR III, Paris, 1956, pp. 227-32, Pls. VIII-IX; O. Masson, 'Documents chypro-minoens de Ras Shamra', ibid, pp. 233-50; and UGAR VI, Paris, 1969, pp. 379-92; and see below, n. 201, Chapter 2, n. 261, and Chapter 3, pp. 177-8.

100. E.g. M. Lejeune, 'Problèmes de lecture du vénète'; R. Lafon, 'Les écritures ibériques'; A. Tovar, 'Les écritures de l'ancienne Hispania'; R. Bloch, 'Le déchiffrement de la langue étrusque', all in Lecant, op. cit. (above, n. 92), pp. 9-28; and cf. I. Gelb, 'New evidence in favour of the syllabic character of West Semitic writing', BO XV, 1/2, 1958, pp. 2-7, esp. 4-5.

101. I. Gelb, 'Ebla and the Kish civilization', in L. Cagni (ed), La Lingua di Ebla, Naples, 1981, pp. 9-73, esp. 11-18; W. Lambert, 'The language of Ebla and Akkadian', ibid, pp. 155-60; Idem, 'Notes on a work of the most ancient Semitic literature', JCS XLI, 1989, pp. 1-32; A. Archi, 'Ebla and Eblaite', in C. Gordon et alii (edd), Eblaitica: essays on the Ebla archives and Eblaite language, vol. I, Winona Lake, Indiana, 1987, pp. 7-17; Idem, 'More on Ebla and Kish', ibid, pp. 125-40; cf. W. Lambert in BSOAS LII, 1, 1989, pp. 115-16; M. Civil, 'Bilingualism in logographically written languages: Sumerian in Ebla', in L. Cagni (ed), Il Bilinguismo a Ebla, Naples, 1984, pp. 75-97.

102. As above, n. 65.

103. J. Blau, Studies in Middle Arabic and its Judaeo-Arabic Variety, Jerusalem, 1988; Idem, A Grammar of Christian Arabic, based mainly on south-Palestinian texts from the first millennium, CSCO vols. 267, 279, Louvain, 1966-67, and thereto J. Wansbrough, BSOAS XXXII, 3, 1968, pp. 610-13; and see below, Ch. 3, pp. 168-70.

104. Bowersock, op. cit. (above, n.40), pp. 28-89.

105. J. Bellamy, 'A new reading of the Namarah inscription', JAOS 105, 1985, pp. 31-48, Pls. I-III.

106. M. O 'Connor, 'The Arabic loanwords in Nabatean Aramaic', JNES 45, 1986, pp. 213-29, esp. 222 n. 47 (Ḥijr) and 229 n. 98 ('Avdat), for which see now A. Negev, J. Naveh and S. Shaked, 'Obodas the God', IEJ 36, 1986, pp. 56-60, Pl. 11; D. Graf and M. O'Connor, 'The origin of the term Saracen and the Rawwafa inscriptions', Byzantine Studies 4, 1977, pp. 52-66; M. O'Connor, 'The etymology of Saracen in Aramaic and pre-Islamic Arabic contexts', BAR International Series 297, 1986, pp. 603-32; W. Diem, 'Die nabatäischen Inschriften und die Frage der Kasusflexion im Altarabischen', ZDMG 123, 1973, pp. 227-37.

107. Fales, op. cit. (above, n. 94); J. Greenfield, 'Aramaic in the Achaemenian Empire', Cambridge History of Iran, vol. II, 1985, pp. 698-713; for bibliographical orientation: K. Beyer, The Aramaic Language: its distribution and subdivisions, Göttingen, 1986.

108. A. Klugkist, 'The importance of the Palmyrene script for our knowledge of the development of the Late Aramaic scripts', in M. Sokoloff (ed), Arameans, Aramaic and the Aramaic Literary Tradition, Bar-Ilan University Press, 1983, pp. 57-74.

109. E.g. N. Abbott, The Rise of the North Arabic Script, OIP vol. I, University of Chicago Press, 1939, pp. 4-16, Pls. I-V.

110.   A. Grohmann, Einführung und Chrestomathie zur Arabischen Papyruskunde, Prague, 1954; Idem, Arabic Papyri from Hirbet El-Mird, Bibliothèque du Muséon, vol. 52, Louvain, 1963; Y. Nevo, Sde Boqer and the Central Negev: 7th-8th century AD, 3rd International Colloquium: From Jahiliyya to Islam, The Hebrew University of Jerusalem, 1985; Idem, 'A new Negev Arabic inscription', BSOAS LII, 1, 1989, pp. 18-23 and Plate; C. Kessler, 'Abd al-Malik's inscription in the Dome of the Rock: a reconsideration', JRAS, 1970, pp. 2-14, Pls. I-III.

111.   D. Pardee et alii, 'A Phoenician letter', in Handbook of Ancient Hebrew Letters, Society of Biblical Literature, Scholars Press, Chico, California, 1982, pp. 165-68 = KAI 50, and further bibliography; see below, Ch. 2, n. 107.

112.   J. Wansbrough, 'Diplomatica Siciliana', BSOAS XLVII, 1, 1984, pp. 10-21, esp. 17 nn. 25-6 ad studies of Curtius and von Grunebaum; see below, Ch.2, pp. 101-2 on the arenga.

113.   E.g. H. Vanstiphout, 'How did they learn Sumerian?", JCS XXXI, 1979, pp. 118-26; C. Gadd, Teachers and Students in the Oldest Schools, SOAS, London, 1956, pp. 3-45; and see below, Ch. 2, pp. 83-4.

114.   Cf. above, refs in n. 93.

115.   J. Redfield, 'The development of the market in Archaic Greece', in B. Anderson and J. Latham (edd), The Market in History, London, 1986, pp. 29-58; and see above, refs in n. 44.

116.   Bunnens, art. cit. (above, n. 17), pp. 18-19; Wathelet, art. cit. (above, n. 26), pp. 235-6; C. Bonnet-Tzavellas, 'La légende de Phoinix à Tyre', also in Gubel (ed), Studia Phoenicia I-II, pp. 113-23; M. Astour, 'The origin of the terms "Canaan", "Phoenician", and "Purple" ', JNES 24, 1965, pp. 346-50; Idem, art. cit. (above, n. 31), p. 24 (ad Linear B po-ni-ki-yo); they were also called "Sidonians"/ "Tyrians".

117.   Cf. the synopses (not very persuasive) of Y. Tsirkin in Lipinski, op. cit. (above, n. 60), II, pp. 547-64 'Economy of the Phoenician settlements in Spain', and in Oikumene 5, 1986 (cited above, n. 62), pp. 163-71 'The Greeks and Tartessos'.

118.   J. Gibson, Textbook of Syrian Semitic Inscriptions, vol. III, Phoenician Inscriptions, Clarendon Press, Oxford, 1982, nos. 4, 25, 13, 15, 27, 28, 36, resp. = KAI 1, 10, 24, 26, 13, 14, 43; M. Fuentes Estanol, 'Corpus de las inscriptiones fenicias en Espana', Aula Orientalis 4, Barcelona, 1986, pp. 5-30; W. Röllig, 'Contribución de las inscripciones fenicio-púnicas al estudio de la protohistoria de Espana', ibid, pp. 51-8; Cf. Z. Harris, A Grammar of the Phoenician Language, New Haven, Connecticut, 1936, pp. 157-61; S. Segert, A Grammar of Phoenician and Punic, Munich, 1976, pp. 33-45, 325-30.

119.   E.g. J. Greenfield, 'Scripture and inscription: the literary and rhetorical element in some early Phoenician inscriptions', in H. Goedicke (ed), Near Eastern Studies in Honor of W.F. Albright, Baltimore, 1971, pp. 253-68 (Ahiram, Tabnit, Eshmunazor, Karatepe); T. Collins, 'The Kilomuwa inscription - a Phoenician poem', WO 6, 1970/71, pp. 183-8; M. O'Connor, 'The rhetoric of the Kilamuwa inscription', BASOR 226, 1977, pp. 15-29; Y. Avishur, 'Word pairs common to Phoenician and Biblical Hebrew', UF 7, 1975, pp. 13-47; Idem, 'Studies of stylistic features common to the Phoènician inscriptions and the Bible', UF 8, 1976, pp. 1-22.

120. G. Bunnens, L'Expansion phénicienne en Méditerranée: essai d'interprétation fondé sur une analyse des traditions littéraires, Brussels and Rome, 1979; ad Philo (and Sanchunyaton) transmitted in Eusebius (c. 325 CE) via Porphyrius, see A. Baumgarten, The Phoenician History of Philo of Byblos: a commentary, Leiden, 1981, pp. 94-139 (whatever was intended, perhaps a late Phoenician riposte to Hellenic arrogance (?), that farrago is certainly not a history of the Phoenicians); ad Josephus, via Dios and Menander (3rd/2nd centuries BCE), see H. Katzenstein, The History of Tyre, Jerusalem, 1973, pp. 77-128: Antiquitates, chs. 8-9, Contra Apionem, chs. 1-2.

121. See above, refs in nn. 33-38.

122. G. Bass, 'Cape Gelidonya and Bronze Age maritime trade' (cited above, n.28) vs inter alios J. Muhly, 'Homer and the Phoenicians' (cited above, n. 44).

123. J. Wansbrough, 'Paul Wittek and Richard Hakluyt: a tale of two empires', Journal of Ottoman Studies VII-VIII (Special Issue presented to J.R. Walsh, edd I. Erünsal et alii), Istanbul, 1988, pp. 55-70, esp. 55-62 on Elizabethan literature of exploration.

124. S. Bolin, art. cit. (above, n. 80), pp. 249 n. 24 and 261 n. 41 (refs to G. Jacob); cf. E. Perroy, 'Encore Mahomet et Charlemagne', also in Hübinger, op. cit. (above, n. 77), pp. 266-75: not commerce but piracy and booty; R. Unger, op. cit. (above, n. 76), ch. 2; R. Hennig, 'Der mittelalterliche arabische Handelsverkehr in Osteuropa', Der Islam XXII, 1935, pp. 239-65.

125. Frankenstein, art. cit. (above, n. 26), esp. pp. 280-82.

126. Cf. M. Dubuisson, 'L' Image du Carthaginois dans la littérature latine', in Gubel, Studia Phoenicia I-II, pp. 159-67.

127. R. Duncan-Jones, The Economy of the Roman Empire: quantitative studies, Cambridge University Press, 1982, esp. pp. 63-119 and App. 8-18 = pp. 345-72.

128. O. Dilke, in Harley and Woodward, op. cit. (above, n. 12), pp. 209-33.

129. Ibid, pp. 201-9, 234-5.

130. See above, nn. 72-76.

131. E.g. Hübinger's collection of essays cited above, n. 77; A.Lewis, Naval Power and Trade in the Mediterranean A.D. 500-1100, Princeton University Press, 1951; F. Ganshof, Le Moyen Age, in P. Renouvin, Histoire des Relations Internationales, vol. I, Paris, 1953, esp. pp. 36-54, 119-56, 263-302.

132. K. Veenhof, 'Cuneiform archives: an introduction', in K. Veenhof (ed), Cuneiform Archives and Libraries, Nederlands Historisch-Archaeologisch Institute Te Istanbul, vol. LVII, 1986, pp. 1-36; E. Posner, Archives in the Ancient World, Harvard University Press, Cambridge, Mass., 1972; H. Bresslau, Handbuch der Urkundenlehre, Berlin, 1958, I, pp. 149-84; and see below, Ch. 2, pp. 83-6

133. G. Sabine, A History of Political Theory, New York, 1937, pp. 141-273; cf. G. Driver and J. Miles, The Babylonian Laws, Clarendon Press, Oxford, 1952, vol. I, pp.5-26, esp. 19 n. 8.

134. Duncan-Jones, op. cit., App. 17: Diocletian's price edict (301 CE).

135. Ibid, pp. 17-32.

136. See above, n. 57; Silver, Economic Structures, pp. 73-117, 118-44 ad Polanyi and Finley.

137.   Ibid, pp. 80, 107 ad Humphreys and Hopkins.

138.   Ibid, pp. 118-21.

139.   See above, n. 58: foci vs nuclei.

140.   See above, n. 18: Sardella on Venice; and n. 75: time and distance.

141.   Ashtor, Levant Trade (cited above, n. 17), pp-373-6: Goitein, Mediterranean Society (cited above, n. 64), I, pp. 313-52.

142.   A. Bridbury, 'Markets and freedom in the Middle Ages', in Anderson and Latham, op. cit. (above, n. 115), pp. 79-119; P. Sawyer, 'Early fairs and markets in England and Scandinavia', ibid, pp. 59-77; Idem, 'Kings and merchants', in Sawyer and I. Wood (edd), Early Medieval Kingship, University of Leeds (School of History), 1977, pp. 139-58; H. Pirenne, Histoire Economique de l'Occident Médiéval, Bruges, 1951, pp. 244-50, 535-41 (les foires de Champagne).

143.   W. Röllig,' Der altmesopotamische Markt', WO 8, 1976, pp. 285-95; B. Landsberger, 'Akkadisch-Hebräische Wortgleichungen', Festschrift W. Baumgartner, SVT 16, 1967, pp. 176-90.

144.   An example (but unrelated to the present discussion) of the possibilities: J. Wansbrough, 'Antonomasia: the case for Semitic 'tm', in M. Mindlin, M. Geller and J. Wansbrough (edd), Figurative Language in the Ancient Near East, SOAS, University of London, 1987, pp. 103-16; see also (more to the point) K. Veenhof, ' "Dying tablets"and "hungry silver" : elements of figurative language in Akkadian commercial terminology', ibid, pp. 41-75.

145.   W. von Soden, AHw, pp. 451-2 (s.v. kāru), pp. 583-4 (s.v. maḫīru) ; CAD K pp. 231-9 (s.v. kāru), M pp. 92-9 (s.v. maḫīru).

146.   E.g. W. Leemans, Foreign Trade in the Old Babylonian Period, Leiden, 1960; M. Larsen, The Old Assyrian City-State and its Colonies, Copenhagen, 1976; K. Veenhof, Aspects of Old Assyrian Trade and its terminology, Leiden, 1972.

147.   See above, refs in nn. 35-37; on Aramaeans, cf. Pitard, Ancient Damascus (cited above, n. 20), pp.81-9; H. Sader, Les Etats araméens de Syrie, Beirut, 1987, pp. 271-86; and Wansbrough, BSOAS LI, 3, 1988, pp. 543-4.

148.   P. Parr, 'Aspects of the archaeology of North-West Arabia in the first millennium BC', in T. Fahd (ed), L'Arabie préislamique et son environment historique et culturel, Université de Strasbourg, Colloque 24-27 juin 1987, pp. 39-66, esp. 52-63; F. Winnett and W. Reed, Ancient Records from North Arabia, Toronto, 1970, pp. 89-120.

149.   I. Eph'al, Ancient Arabs (cited above, n. 36), pp. 14-16, 182-5 (Jebel Ghunaym); Parr, art. cit., pp. 56-63.

150.   RS 20.123 = UGAR V, Paris, 1968, pp. 420-23 and 240-43 (no. 137); M. Astour, 'Ma'hadu the harbor of Ugarit', JESHO 13, 1970, pp. 113-27; but cf. R. Stieglitz, 'Ugaritic Mhd - the harbor of Yabne-Yam?', JAOS 94, 1974, pp. 137-8; S. Kaufman, The Akkadian Influence on Aramaic, AS 19, University of Chicago Press, 1974, p. 68 (s.v. mahazu); R. Borger, 'Hebräisch MḤWZ (Psalm 107, 30)', UF 1, 1969, pp. 1-3.

151.   Ad M. Heltzer, Goods, Prices and the Organization of Trade in Ugarit, Wiesbaden, 1978, see D. Pardee, 'Ugaritic', AfO XXVIII, 1981/1982, pp. 270-

72; and P. Vargyas, 'Trade and prices in Ugarit', Oikumene 5, 1986, pp. 103-16; Idem, ad Archi, cited above, n. 57; J. Wansbrough, 'Ugarit: a Bronze Age Hansa?', in K. Haellquist (ed), Asian Trade Routes: continental and maritime, Curzon Press, 1991, pp. 21-26, 253-54, 278-81.

152. M. Heltzer, 'The metal trade of Ugarit and the problem of transportation of commercial goods', in Trade in Ancient Near East (cited above, nn. 3, 59), pp. 203-11; R. Stieglitz, 'Commodity prices at Ugarit', JAOS 99, 1979, pp. 15=23.

153. E. Linder, art. cit. (above, n. 30); R. Yaron, 'Foreign merchants at Ugarit', ILR 4, 1969, pp. 70-79.

154. On "kings" and "royal" imagery, cf. B. Peckham, 'Phoenicia and the religion of Israel: the epigraphic evidence', in P. Miller et alii, Ancient Israelite Religion (Essays in honor of Frank Moore Cross), Philadelphia, 1987, pp. 79-99, and thereto J. Wansbrough, BSOAS LII, 2, 1989, pp. 334-35.

155. Wansbrough, art. cit. (above, n. 15).

156. See above, n. 74.

157. K. Pagel, Die Hanse, ed F. Naab, Braunschweig, 1983, pp. 123-37 (Schriftlichkeit/Verträge), 164-71 (Kanzlei); P. Dollinger, The German Hansa, London, 1970, pp. 85-115 (organisation), 379-98 (treaties).

158. See above, refs in nn. 76-80, 131.

159. F. Dölger, Byzantinische Diplomatik, Ettal, 1956, esp. pp. 225-44 'Der Vertrag des Sultans Qalā'ūn von Agypten mit dem Kaiser Michael VIII Palaiologos (1281)'.

160. Ashtor, Levant Trade (cited above, n. 17), pp. 460-512; Heyd, Histoire du commerce (cited above, n. 78), II, pp. 555-711.

161. J. Gottmann, 'Orbits: the Ancient Mediterranean tradition of urban networks', J.L. Myres Memorial Lecture, London, 1984 (delivered 3 May 1983); cf. Idem, The Significance of Territory, Charlottesville, Virginia, 1973, pp. 11-52, esp. 11-27; see also Idem (ed), Center and Periphery: spatial variation in politics, Beverly Hills, California - London, 1980, pp. 220-21; and below, nn. 176-77; Renfrew, 'Trade as action' (cited above, n. 58).

162. Ad "orbits" see above, pp. 7, 11, 20-3, 26, 31-2, 46-7, 53.

163. Gottmann, art. cit., pp. 4-7.

164. That is, between municipalities, not states: "at least eleven" would be safer, since archival allusions are occasionally ambiguous; M. De Mas Latrie, Traités de paix et de commerce: les relations des Chrétiens avec les Arabes de l'Afrique Septentrionale au Moyen Age, Paris 1866 (repr. Burt Franklin Research & Source Works Series #63, New York, n.d.), II, pp. 22, 23-6, 109-13, 367-72, 222-28; M. Amari, I Diplomi Arabi di R. Archivio Fiorentino, Florence, 1863, pp. 239-40, 1-6 & 255-6, 14-16 & 273, 36-7; A. Silvestre de Sacy, Notices et extraits des manuscrits de la Bibliothèque du Roi et autres, XI, Paris, 1827, pp. 3-6, 26-32; ASV, Libri Commemoriali, IX # 183; J. Wansbrough, 'A Moroccan amir's commercial treaty with Venice of the year 913/1508', BSOAS XXV, 3, 1962, pp. 449-71; S. Bono,' Le relazioni commerciali fra i paesi del Maghreb e l'Italia nel medioevo', Quaderni dell'Istituto Italiano di Cultura di Tripoli, 4, Tripoli, 1967, pp. 1-20.

165.   E. Ashtor, 'Républiques urbaines dans le Proche-Orient à l'époque des croisades?' Cahiers de Civilisation Médiévale XVIII, Université de Poitiers, 1975, pp. 117-31.

166.   P. Holt, 'The treaties of the early Mamluk sultans with the Frankish states', BSOAS XLIII, 1, 1980, pp. 67-76.

167.   See above, nn.9-11: much of this exegesis had an earlier formulation in my doctoral thesis (unpublished) for the University of London (1961): "Documents for the History of Commercial Relations between Egypt and Venice 1442-1512".

168.   P. Crone, Meccan Trade and the Rise of Islam, Oxford, 1987; R. Simon, Meccan Trade and Islam: problems of origin and structure, Budapest, 1989; thereto J. Wansbrough, BSOAS LII, 2, 1989, pp. 339-40 and LIII, 3, 1990, pp. 510-11, resp.; see also, U. Rubin, 'Meccan trade and Qur'anic exegesis (Qur'an 2:198)', BSOAS LIII, 3, 1990,pp. 421-8; R.Serjeant, ad Crone, op. cit., in JAOS 110, 1990, pp. 472-86.

169.   Crone, op. cit., pp. 134-8, 161-99; Simon, op. cit., pp. 75-95, resp.; on the transfer of cultic phenomena and sanctuary motifs, see now Y. Nevo and J. Koren, 'The origins of the Muslim descriptions of the Jahili Meccan sanctuary', JNES 49, 1990, pp. 23-44; for the "port of trade" syndrome, see above, refs in nn. 34, 57-58.

170.   E.g. J. Wellhausen, 'Muhammads Gemeindeordnung von Medina', Skizzen und Vorarbeiten, vol. IV, Berlin, 1889, pp. 65-83; R. Serjeant, 'The Sunnah Jāmi'ah, pacts with the Yathrib Jews, and the taḥrīm of Yathrib: analysis and translation of the documents comprised in the so-called "Constitution of Medina", BSOAS XLI, 1, 1978, pp. 1-42; M.Gil, 'The constitution of Medina: a reconsideration', IOS 4, 1974, pp. 44-66; U. Rubin, 'The "Constitution of Medina": some notes', SI LXII, 1985, pp. 5-23.

171.   M. Kister, 'Al-Ḥīra: some notes on its relations with Arabia', Arabica XV, 1968, pp. 143-69; Idem, 'On the wife of the goldsmith from Fadak and her progeny', Le Muséon 92, 1979, pp. 321-30.

172.   M. Lecker, The Banu Sulaym: a contribution to the study of early Islam, Jerusalem, 1989, and thereto G. Hawting, BSOAS LIV, 2, 1991, pp. 359-62.

173.   C. Renfrew, Emergence (cited above, n. 66), pp. 440-504.

174.   C. Renfrew and K.Cooke (edd), Transformations (cited above, n. 5), pp. 481-505.

175.   J. Wansbrough, 'Res ipsa loquitur' (cited above, n. 15), pp. 24 n. 25, 26.

176.   O. Lattimore, 'The periphery as locus of innovation', in J. Gottmann (ed), Centre and Periphery (cited above, n.166), pp. 105-08.

177.   R. Strassoldo, 'Centre-periphery and system-boundary: culturological perspectives', ibid, pp. 27-61; and see above, nn. 52, 58, 82.

178.   L. Casson, Ships and Seamanship (cited above, n. 17), pp. 201-13, 243-5, 277; B. Kreutz, art cit. (above, n. 76), pp. 80-86, 104-09; cf. L. Basch, 'The lateener from Thasos', MM 57, 1971, pp. 329-30.

179.   L. Basch, 'Phoenician oared ships', MM 55, 1969, pp. 139-62, Pls. 6-9, and 227-45, Pls. 10-11, esp. 144-52 (Luli, to which see also MM 57, 1971, pp. 326-9, P1.

9), 230-34 (Necho); cf. Casson, op. cit., pp. 94-6; De Graeve, op. cit. (above, n. 29), pp. 123-43.

180. Basch, art. cit., pp. 142-3 and fig. 2 (Byblos); Casson, op. cit., pp. 36-8 and fig. 61 (Medinet Habu).

181. Casson, op. cit., pp. 202-03 and esp. addendum p. 447: refs to Basch, IJNA 1, 1972, pp. 1-58 and Christensen, IJNA 2,1973, pp. 137-45; see also G. Boss, art. cit. (above, n. 28) on Ulu burun=AJA 90, 1986, p. 275 (mortise and tenon construction).

182. Casson, op. cit., pp. 297-99; Idem, 'The role of the state in Rome's grain trade', in J. D'Arms and E. Kopff, The Seaborne Commerce of Ancient Rome: studies in archaeology and history, American Academy in Rome, Memoirs XXXVI, Rome, 1980, pp. 21-34; G. Rickman, 'The grain trade under the Roman Empire', ibid, pp. 261-76; for other bulk shipping, see R. Meiggs, 'Sea-borne timber supplies to Rome', ibid, pp. 185-96; J.Ward-Perkins, 'The marble trade and its organization: evidence from Nicomedia', ibid, pp. 325- ; A. Snodgrass, 'Heavy freight in Archaic Greece', in P. Garnsey et alii, Trade in the Ancient Economy (cited above, n. 85), pp. 16-26; Garnsey , 'Grain for Rome', ibid, pp. 118-30.

183. See above, refs in nn. 30, 150, and p. 48; and below, n. 213; UT refs = C. Gordon, Ugaritic Textbook, Analecta Orientalia 38, Rome, 1965; RS refs = P. Bordreuil and D. Pardee, La Trouvaille epigraphique de l'Ougarit, 1. Concordance, Paris, 1989; the key text RS 20.008 = KTU 4.689, in Xella, art. cit. (above, n. 30), for which see also M. Heltzer, The Internal Organization of the Kingdom of Ugarit, Wiesḫaden, 1982, pp. 188-91.

184. G. Bass, arts. cit. (above, n. 28), esp. AJA 90, 1986, pp. 291-2; C. Schaeffer, 'Remarques sur les ancres en pierre d'Ugarit', UGAR VII, Paris, 1978, pp. 371-81; H. Frost, 'The stone anchors of Ugarit', UGAR VI, Paris, 1969, pp. 235-45, and refs in Heltzer, op. cit. (above, n. 183), p. 188 nn. 4-5; H. Frost, 'Anchors sacred and profane', in M.Yon (ed), Arts et industries de la pierre, Ras Shamra-Ougarit VI, Paris, 1991, pp. 355-410.

185. Bass, art. cit., TAPA 57, 1967, p. 45; Basch, art. cit., MM 55, 1969, p.160.

186. Heltzer, op. cit. (above, n. 151), pp. 153-5: RS 20.212 (!) = UGAR V, N 33; cf. J. Sasson, art. cit. (above, n. 95), p. 132.

187. See above, n. 152: Stieglitz, art. cit., pp. 127, 18, 22; Heltzer, art. cit., pp. 204-5, that is, at least of Gelidonya size, whose chief cargo was copper! Cf. Bass, AOAT 22, 1973 (cited above, n. 28), p. 34.

188. Cf. D. Sperber, Nautica Talmudica, Bar-Ilan University Press, 1986, pp. 21-2: Heb. masōṭ = "oar", tōrēn = "mast"; ibid, pp. 107-09: Heb. meṣūpīt = "sighting tube", but a Piel of Ṣ.P.H also = "cover" and cf. also Heltzer, op. cit. (above, n. 183), p. 189 n. 10 : Akkad. muṣiptu = "garment/textile". The text RS 20.008 really ought to include "sail"; ad Sperber, cf. Wansbrough. BSOAS LII, 2, 1989, pp. 336-7.

189. Casson, op. cit., pp. 30-42; W. Taylour, Mycenaean Pottery in Italy and Adjacent Areas, Cambridge University Press, 1958, pp. 1-6, 54-79 (Sicily), 181-90.

190. See above, n. 31.

191.   B. Blance, 'Early Bronze Age colonists in Iberia', Antiquity XXXV, 1969, pp. 192-202, Pls. XXIV-XXV.

192.   Casson, loc. cit., esp. 36-9 and addendum p. 442: ref S. Wachsmann, IJNA 10, 1981, pp. 187-220; 11, 1982, pp. 297-304 (Aegean origins).

193.   Casson, op. cit., pp. 110-15, 147, 151.

194.   Fahmy, Muslim Sea-Power (cited above, n. 71), pp. 115-37, 149-66.

195.   J. Wansbrough, art. cit. (above, n. 164), p. 451 n. 8; Kreutz, art. cit. (above, n. 76) pp. 99-100; with specific application of "tarida" to cavalry transport, design and dimensions become available (13th century): J. Pryor, 'The transportation of horses by sea during the era of the Crusades', MM 68, 1982, pp. 9-27, 103-25, esp. 105-08 (Genoese construction).

196.   R. Serjeant, The Portuguese off the South Arabian Coast: Hadrami chronicles, The Clarendon Press, Oxford, 1963, pp. 132-37; cf. L. Casson, The Periplus Maris Erythraei, Princeton University Press, 1989, pp. 283-91.

197.   See above, pp. 22-3.

198.   See above, pp. 31-4, and below, Ch. 3, pp. 170-1.

199.   E. Grumach, 'The Cretan scripts and the Greek alphabet', in W. Haas (ed), op. cit., (above, n. 87), pp. 45-70.

200.   W. Brice, 'The principles of non-phonetic writing', ibid, pp. 29-44.

201.   See above, refs in n. 99.

202.   M. Sznycer, art. cit. (above, n. 92); Mendenhall, op. cit. (above, n. 92).

203.   H. Cazelles, 'Les textes de Deir Alla', in J. Leclant, op. cit. (above, n. 92), pp. 95-99; cf. the decipherment controversy: H. Franken, VT 14, 1964, pp. 377-9, Pl. 1; A. Van Den Branden, VT 15, 1955, pp. 129-50; H. Franken, ibid, pp. 150-52; A. Van Den Branden, ibid, pp. 532-5; H. Franken, ibid, pp. 535-6.

204.   M. Sznycer, 'Les inscriptions protosinaitiques', in Leclant, op. cit., pp. 85-93.

205.   But cf. M. Bernal, art. cit. (above, n. 93), esp. 3-6.

206.   Grumach, art. cit., p. 65.

207.   See above, p. 35; and below, Ch. 2, pp. 133-7; H. Jensen, Die Schrift in Vergangenheit und Gegenwart, Berlin, 1969, pp. 572-81 (Lautschrift/ Kurzschrift).

208.   See above, n. 93: Cross, art. cit., pp. 15-17; Naveh, op. cit., pp. 40-41.

209.   R. Stieglitz, 'The Ugaritic cuneiform and Canaanite linear alphabets', JNES 30, 1971, pp. 135-39; cf. G. Windfuhr, 'The cuneiform signs of Ugarit', JNES 29, 1970, pp. 48-51; W. Helck, 'Zur Herkunft der sog. "Phönizischen" Schrift', UF 4, 1972, pp. 41-45; E. Puech, 'Origine de l'alphabet: documents en alphabet linéaire et cunéiform du IIe millénaire', RB 93, 1986, pp. 161-213, Pls. II-III; A. Lundin, 'Ugaritic writing and the origin of the Semitic consonantal alphabet', Aula Orientalis 5, 1987, pp. 91-99.

210.   Naveh, op. cit., pp. 19-20; Jensen, op. cit., pp. 130-38; and above, refs in n. 99.

211.   Bass, AJA 90, 1986 (cited above, n. 28), esp. pp. 293-96.

212.   E.g. the 1507 treaty between Venice and Egypt (cited above, n. 10); Ashtor, Levant Trade, pp. 465, 545-46.

213. See above, p. 48; P.Millett, 'Maritime loans and the structure of credit in fourth-century Athens', in Garnsey (ed), op. cit. (above, n. 85), pp. 36-52; ad RS 18.025 = PRU V, 1965, no. 106: J.Ziskind, 'Sea loans at Ugarit', JAOS 94, 1974, pp. 134-37; and D. Pardee, 'The Ugaritic text 2106: 10-18: a bottomry loan?', JAOS 95, 1975, pp. 612-19.

214. H. Pleket, 'Urban elites and business in the Greek part of the Roman Empire', in Garnsey (ed), op. cit., pp. 131-44; C. Whittaker, 'Late Roman trade and traders', ibid, pp. 163-80; Ashtor, Levant Trade, pp. 367-82.

215. E. Ashtor, 'Banking instruments between the Muslim East and the Christian West', JEEH 1, Rome, 1972, pp. 553-73; S.Labib, 'Geld und Kredit: Studien zur Wirtschaftsgeschichte Agyptens im Mittelalter', JESHO 2, 1959, pp. 225-46; Idem, Handelsgeschichte Agyptens im Spätmittelalter (1171-1517), Wiesbaden, 1965, pp. 261-85.

216. H. Idris, 'Commerce maritime et kirad en Berbérie Orientale', JESHO 4, 1961, pp. 225-39; A. Udovitch, 'At the origins of the western commenda: Islam, Israel, Byzantium?', Speculum XXXVII, 1962, pp. 198-207; Idem, Partnership and Profit in Medieval Islam, Princeton University Press, 1970, pp. 170-248; J. Pryor, 'The origins of the Commenda contract', Speculum LII, 1977, pp. 5-37.

217. See above, n. 1: Wansbrough, art. cit., esp. pp. 32-5.

218. M. Finley, The Ancient Economy, London, 1985, pp. 32-33 (citing A. Déléage 1945); cf. R. Duncan-Jones, Structure and Scale (cited above, n. 75), pp. 199-210.

219. Finley, op. cit., pp. 27-29: n. 39 (p. 214) is hardly adequate.

220. Ibid, pp. 141-49, esp. 47 bottom, 191-98.

221. Duncan-Jones, op. cit., pp. 7-29; see above, n. 18.

222. Ibid, pp. 30-47, 187-98.

223. Ibid, pp. 159-84.

224. K. Hopkins, 'Taxes and trade in the Roman Empire (200 B.C. -A.D. 400)', JRS 70, 1980, pp. 101-25; but cf. Duncan-Jones, loc. cit. (above, n. 222).

225. R. Duncan-Jones, Economy of the Roman Empire (cited above, n. 127), p. 9; Idem, Structure and Scale, p. 39.

226. Ibid, p. 42 appears to argue the opposite; cf. Finley, op. cit., pp. 141-43, 196-98; and cf. Millett, art. cit. (above, n. 213).

227. Duncan-Jones, Structure and Scale, pp. 48-58; and cf. above, n. 85: D. Miller, op. cit. on "ceramic signatures".

228. Finley, op. cit., pp. 17-34.

229. See above, pp. 7-8, 17, and esp. 41-2, 47-53.

230. Finley, op. cit., pp. 156-57, 204-7; some instructive analogies in H. Brunschvig, Mythes et réalités de l'impérialisme colonial français 1871-1914, Paris, 1960.

231. J. Boardman, The Greeks Overseas: their early colonies and trade, London, 1980, pp. 38-44 (Al Mina), 114-17 (Naukratis), 153-6 (Cyrene), 165-89 (Pithekoussai, Syracuse, etc.).

232. M. Liverani, art. cit. (above, n. 33).

233. See above, pp. 16, 43-6.

234. J. Redfield, art. cit. (above, n. 115), esp. pp. 43-4.

235. W. Heyd, Histoire du commerce (cited above, n. 78), II, pp. 296-302, 478-80, 487-90; documentation in M. Amari, I Diplomi Arabi (cited above, n. 164), nos. 2-5, 7-12, 38-42, 44-7, 58 = Pisa: 63-8, 71-84, App. nos. 6-7, 23-4, 26, 29, 32, 34 = Florence.

236. J. Wansbrough, 'Venice and Florence in the Mamluk commercial privileges', BSOAS XXVIII, 3, 1965, pp. 483-523; and studies cited above, nn. 10, 11, 112.

237. Idem, art. cit. (above, n. 11), p. 45 n. 23 and refs Thuasne and Babinger.

238. E. Ashtor, Levant Trade, pp. 138, 285-6, 349-54, 495-9.

239. Ibid, pp. 367-82; Idem, 'Levantine weights and standard parcels: a contribution to the metrology of the later Middle Ages', BSOAS XLV, 3, 1982, pp.471-88.

CHAPTER 2

1. S. Skilliter, William Harborne....1578-1582 (cited above, Ch. 1, n. 16); Idem, 'William Harborne, the first English ambassador 1583-1588', in W. Hale and A. Bagis (edd), Four Centuries of Turco-British Relations, Eothen Press, 1984, pp. 10-25, esp. 11 n. 2.

2. J. Wansbrough, BSOAS XLIX, 3, 1986, pp. 573-4, and art. cit. above, Ch. 1, n. 236.

3. P. Wittek, 'The Turkish documents in Hakluyt's "Voyages" ', Bulletin of the Institute of Historical Research, University of London, XIX/57, 1942 (1944), pp. 121-39; cf. Wansbrough, art. cit. above, Ch. 1, n. 123; Idem, 'Diplomatica Siciliana', (Cited above, ch.1, n. 112), p. 18 n. 28; BSOAS XLII, 1, 1979, pp. 152-3 and V. Ménage, 'The English capitulation of 1580: a review article', IJMES 12, 1980, pp. 373-83 (ad Skilliter, op. cit.).

4. Specimens in Amari and De Mas Latrie (cited above, Ch. 1, n. 164); for some of the Arabic loans, cf. G. Pellegrini, Gli Arabismi nelle Lingue Neolatine I-II, Brescia, 1972; G. Caracusi, Arabismi Medievali di Sicilia, Palermo, 1983.

5. See below, Ch. 3, pp. 153-60; cf. J. Blau, Studies in Middle Arabic (cited above, Ch. 1, n. 103); a medieval Greek analogy in Dölger, Byzantinische Diplomatik (cited above, Ch. 1, n. 159), p. 297; and E. Zachariadou, Trade and Crusade: Venetian Crete and the Emirates of Menteshe and Aydin (1300-1415), Venice, 1983, pp. 185-6.

6. A. al-Qalqashandī, Kitāb Ṣubḥ al-A'shā, Cairo, 1913-19 (vols. I-XIV), XIV, pp. 70-71; cf. BSOAS XLVII, 1, 1984, p. 17 n. 27; Holt, art. cit. (above, Ch. 1, n. 166), p. 68; a cuneiform analogy in J. Goody, Logic of Writing (cited above, Ch. 1, n. 88), pp. 97-8 (L. Woolley: Assyria-Esnuna).

7. See below, pp. 104-6, and Ch.3, p. 156-7; Wansbrough, in BSOAS XXV, 3, 1962, p. 466 n. 6; in S.Stern (ed), Documents from Islamic Chanceries, p. 47 n. 33; in BSOAS XXVIII, 3, 1965, pp. 486-7; in BSOAS XXIV, 1, 1971, pp. 30 n. 41, 32 n. 54; V. Ménage, 'On the constituent elements of certain sixteenth-century Ottoman documents', BSOAS XLVIII, 2, 1985, pp. 283-304, esp. 290 n. 35; Dölger, op. cit., pp. 277-80.

8. Qalqashandī, op. cit., VI, pp. 458-63; cf. A. Noth, 'Die arabischen Dokumente König Rogers II von Sizilien', in C. Brühl, Urkunden und Kanzlei König Rogers II. von Sizilien, Köln-Wein, 1978, pp. 217-61, esp. 252-3.

9. Wansbrough, 'Diplomatica Siciliana', pp. 16 nn. 18-20, 18 nn. 28-31; W. Björkman, Beiträge zur Geschichte der Staatskanzlei im islamischen Agypten, Hamburg, 1928, pp. 45-6, 90; H. Bresslau, Urkundenlehre (cited above, Ch. 1, n. 132), II, pp. 377-81.

10. Björkman, op. cit., pp. 73-86.

11. Ibid, pp. 1-55; R. Vessel, 'Zu den Quellen Al-Qalqashandī's Ṣubḥ al-A'shā'. Acta Universitatis Carolinae - Philologica 2, Prague, 1969, pp. 13-24.

12. Björkman, pp. 115-18 = Qalqashandī, VI, pp. 197-365 (mustanadāt).

13. Ibid, pp. 21-22 = Ibn al-Ṣayrafī, Qānūn Dīwān al-Rasā'il; ibid, p. 100 = Qalqashandī, IV, pp. 28ff (division of labour); ibid, p. 114 = Qalqashandī VI, pp. 189-96 (format).

14. Qalqashandī, VI, p. 197 (mustanadāt); IX, p. 273 (bay'āt); XIII, p.1 (waṣāyā dīniyya); XIII, p. 321 (amānat), XIV, p. 1 (hudan).

15. Björkman, pp. 82, 85 = Qalqashandī, III, p. 247! (Ptolemy), IV, p. 9 (Aristotle), V, pp. 236, 238, 381 (Orosius).

16. Qalqashandī III, pp. 1-222, esp. 1-18.

17. Wansbrough, Quranic Studies (cited above, Ch. 1, n. 65), pp. 103-4; C. Versteegh, Greek Elements in Arabic Linguistic Thinking, Leiden, 1977, pp. 162-77, and thereto Wansbrough, BSOAS XLI, 2, 1978, pp. 372-3.

18. See above, Ch. 1, pp. 29-37.

19. J. Goody, op. cit., pp. 55-82.

20. Ibid, p. 12.

21. Ibid, pp. 52-5.

22. Ibid, p. 22.

23. J. Wansbrough, 'Scrolls and Scribes', in G. Hawting (ed), Sacred Writings in Oriental and African Religions, Occasional Papers XII, SOAS (ES), 1986, pp. 5-6.

24. Idem, Quranic Studies, pp. 43-52; and Sectarian Milieu (cited above, Ch. 1, n. 83), pp. 55-9; J. Augapfel, 'Das "Kitāb" im Qur'ān', WZKM XXIX, 1915, pp. 384-93; F. Nötscher, 'Himmlische Bücher und Schicksalsglaube in Qumran', Revue de Qumran I, 1958-59, pp. 405-11; F. Altheim and R. Stiehl, Die Araber in der Alten Welt III, Berlin, 1966, pp. 419-35 'Buchreligionen'; G. Widengren, Religionsphänomenologie, Berlin, 1969, pp. 546-73 and 574-93.

25. A. Cavigneaux, Lexikalische Listen, RLA VI, pp. 609-41; J. Krecher, 'Schreiberschulung in Ugarit: die Tradition von Listen und sumerischen Texten', UF I, 1969, pp. 131-58; H. Nissen 'Bemerkungen zur Listenliteratur Vorderasiens im 3. Jahrtausend (gesehen von den Archaischen Texten von Uruk), in L. Cagni, Lingua di Ebla (cited above, Ch. 1, n. 101), pp. 99-108; Idem, 'The archaic texts from Uruk', in J. Oates, Early Writing Systems (cited above, Ch. 1, n. 86), pp. 317-34.

26. See above, Ch. 1, n. 87.

27.   M. Green, 'The construction and implementation of the cuneiform writing system', in M. Powell, Aspects of Cuneiform Writing (cited above, Ch. 1, n. 6), pp. 345-72.

28.   Ibid, esp. pp. 361-8.

29.   See above, Ch. 1, nn. 92, 110.

30.   I. Gelb, 'The word for Dragoman in the Ancient Near East', Glossa 2, 1, 1968, pp. 93-104; C. Gadd, Teachers and Students, cited above, Ch. 1, n. 113; R. Sack, 'The temple scribe in Chaldean Uruk', in M. Powell, op. cit., pp. 409-18.

31.   J. Olivier, 'Schools and Wisdom literature', JNWSL IV, 1975, pp. 49-60; cf. H. Vanstiphout, art. cit. (above, Ch. 1, n. 113).

32.   K. Galling, 'Tafel, Buch und Blatt', in H. Goedicke (ed), Near Eastern Studies in Honor of William Foxwell Albright, Baltimore, 1971, pp. 207-23; A. Millard, 'An assessment of the evidence for writing in Ancient Israel', in Biblical Archaeology Today (cited above, Ch. 1, n. 44), pp. 301-12.

33.   E.g. A. Oppenheim, 'A note on the scribes in Mesopotamia', AS 16 (Studies in Honor of Benno Landsberger), University of Chicago Press, 1965, pp. 253-6; G. Pettinato, The Archives of Ebla: an empire inscribed in clay, New York, 1981, pp. 230-42; A. Rainey, 'The scribe at Ugarit: his position and influence', PIASH III, 1969, pp. 126-46; M. Heltzer, op. cit. (above, Ch. 1, n. 183), pp. 157-61; W. Horwitz, 'The Ugaritic scribe', UF 11, 1979, pp. 389-94.

34.   M. Fishbane, Biblical Interpretation in Ancient Israel, Clarendon Press, Oxford, 1985, pp. 23-43, esp. 34, 36.

35.   See above, Ch. 1, refs in n. 132: K. Veenhof, E. Posner, H. Bresslau.

36.   E. Posner, op. cit., p. 24 n. 23.

37.   Ibid, pp. 95-7, 138f, 159.

38.   Ibid, pp. 125-7, 174-82, 186-7, 226, 74-86, 102-16, resp.

39.   Ibid, pp. 206-12; H. Bresslau, op. cit., I. pp. 185-90; Björkman, op. cit., pp. 96-104 = Qalqashandī, III p. 282, - IV p. 304.

40.   K. Veenhof, op. cit., pp. 12-14; P. Matthiae, 'The archives of the Royal Palace G of Ebla', ibid, pp. 53-71; A. Archi, 'The archives of Ebla', ibid, pp. 72-86.

41.   J. Reade, 'Archaeology and the Kuyunjik archives', ibid, pp. 213-222; S. Parpola, 'The royal archives of Nineveh', ibid, pp. 223-36.

42.   W. Van Soldt, 'The palace archives at Ugarit', ibid, pp. 196-204.

43.   J. Margueron, 'Quelques remarques concernant les archives retrouvées dans la palais de Mari', ibid, pp. 141-52; T. Palaima and J. Wright, 'Ins and outs of the archives rooms at Pylos: form and function in Mycenaean palace', AJA 89, 1985, pp. 251-62.

44.   K. Veenhof, op. cit., pp. 1-36 Introduction.

45.   Ibid, p. 2 n. 4a; Palaima and Wright, art. cit., pp. 251 n. 2, 260 n. 29.

46.   Veenhof, Introduction, pp. 7-11, 23-8; T. Kwasman, 'Neo-Assyrian legal archives in the Kouyunjik Collection', ibid, pp. 237-40.

47.   Pace Veenhof, pp. 23-4, but note p. 30: "Our main source of judiciary records is private archives."

48.   Bresslau, op. cit., I, pp. 377-8; Veenhof, p. 14 n. 56 (D. Charpin).

49. Krecher, art. cit. (above, n. 25); J. Nougayrol, 'L' Influence babylonienne à Ugarit, d'après les textes en cunéiformes classiques', Syria 39, 1962, pp. 28-35.

50. E.g. RS 17.230 (seal of Initesub on Carchemish-Ugarit agreement ad merchant exterritoriality): C.Schaeffer, UGAR III, p. 20 P1.V = J. Nougayrol, PRU IV, pp. 153-4 (cf. p. 115-16: typology).

51. Krecher, art. cit., pp. 134-42: some 90 texts/fragments.

52. See below, Ch. 3, pp. 153-59.

53. Cf. W. Lambert, 'The section AN', in L. Cagni, Bilinguismo (cited above, Ch. 1, n. 101) pp. 393-401, esp. 394; Idem, 'The reading of the divine name Sakkan', Or. 55, 1986, pp. 152-8, esp. 158 n. 9; K. Deller, 'Studien zur neuassyrischen Orthographie', Or. 31, 1962, pp. 7-26, 186-96, esp. 194-6; C. Gordon, 'Observations on the Akkadian texts from Ugarit', RA 50, 1956, pp. 127-33, esp. 127-8; Idem, in Or. 19, 1950, pp. 91-2, and Or. 22, 1953, pp. 229-30; already F. Böhl, Die Sprache der Amarnabriefe, Leipzig, 1909 (repr. Leipzig, 1968), pp. 1-4.

54. Cf. M. O 'Connor, 'The etymology of Saracen' (cited above, Ch. 1, n. 106), pp. 613-14; Idem, 'Writing systems, native speaker analyses, and the earliest stages of Northwest Semitic orthography', in C. Meyers and M. O'Connor (edd), "Let the Word of the Lord Go Forth" (Festschrift D.N. Freedman), Winona Lake, Indiana, 1983, pp. 439-65, esp. 440-43.

55. See above, Ch. 1, nn. 86-87.

56. Cf. M. Civil, 'Bilingualism in logographically written languages: Sumerian in Ebla', in Cagni, op. cit., pp. 75-97.

57. Cf. K. Butz, 'Bilinguismus als Katalysator', ibid, pp. 99-138: visual imagery (eidos) and shorthand (Kürzelsystem) in lexical lists; see above, n. 25.

58. See below, nn. 101-102 (messenger formula).

59. A. Herdner, Corpus des tablettes en cunéiformes alphabétiques découvertes à Ras Shamra-Ugarit de 1929 à 1939, Paris, 1963: CTA nos. 162-65 = UT nos. 102-5; cf. C. Virolleaud, 'Fragments alphabétiques divers de Ras-Shamra', Syria 20, 1939, pp. 114-25; E. Dhorme, 'Textes accadiens transcrits en écriture alphabétique de Ras Shamra', RA XXXVII, 1940, pp. 83-96: RS 5.156, 5.213, 5.199, 5.303 bis.

60. J. Blau and S. Loewenstamm, 'Zur Frage der scriptio plena im Ugaritischen und Verwandtes', UF 2, 1970, pp. 19-33, 24 n. 31. I have counted 28 cases of u/i (or 'u/'i) as against 25 of w/y in the four fragments.

61. RS 20.163 = UGAR V, Paris, 1968, p. 257 (no. 153); S. Segert, A Basic Grammar of the Ugaritic Language, University of California Press, 1984, p. 19, mentions three such fragments.

62. See above, n. 53.

63. G. Driver, Semitic Writing (cited above, Ch. 1, n. 86), pp. 264-6: Fig. 107 and Pls. 47-48 = PRU II, Paris, 1956, no. 189; cf. S. Loewenstamm, Comparative Studies in Biblical and Ancient Oriental Literatures = AOAT 204, 1980, Neukirchen-Vluyn, pp. 81-90, esp. 88-90; see also UT (cited above, Ch. 1, n. 183), nos. 320, 401, 1186 and 1188.

64. Böhl, op. cit., pp. 32-3; J. Blau, On Pseudo-Corrections in some Semitic Languages, Israel Academy of Sciences and Humanities, Jerusalem, 1970, pp. 36-7; but cf. D. Sivan, Grammatical Analysis and Glossary of the Northwest Semitic Vocables in Akkadian Texts of the 15th-13th C.B.C. from Canaan and Syria = AOAT 214, 1984, Neukirchen-Vluyn, pp. 114-23.

65. W. von Soden, Grundriss der Akkadischen Grammatik, Analecta Orientalia 33/47, Rome, 1969, paras. 13b-c, 63e-g.

66. M. Liverani, 'Antecedenti del diptotismo arabo nei testi accadici di Ugarit', RSO 38, 1969, pp. 131-60.

67. J. Nougayrol, PRU VI, Paris, 1970, nos. 21, 43, 50, 59, 72, 73, 74, 102, 104, 112, 128, 138, 144, 146, 147, 148 (sample = 16 documents).

68. J. Knudtzon, Die el-Amarna Tafeln, Leipzig, 1907-15 (repr. Leipzig, 1964), nos. 206.2, 109.6, 58.6, resp.

69. J. Nougayrol, UGAR V, pp. 42-64: no.18 = RS 20.024, and RS 1. 017 (CTA 29 = UT 17); cf. J. de Moor, 'The Semitic pantheon of Ugarit', UF 2, 1970, pp. 187-228, esp. 188-9, 217-8.

70. Thus Nougayrol, op. cit., pp. 44, 57, 58, 59; Idem, art. cit. (above, n. 49), p. 31.

71. Von Soden, AHw s.v. ti'amtum; Gordon, UT, 19.2537 (s.v. thm).

72. AHw s.v. kinnārum; cf. J. Sasson, art. cit. (above, Ch. 1, n. 95), p. 170 n. 5.

73. J. Nougayrol, PRU IV, pp. 40-44 (RS 17.227), 44-6 (RS 11.772+ = CTA 64 = UT 118), 47-8 (RS 11.732); M. Dietrich and O. Loretz, 'Der Vertrag zwischen Šuppululiuma und Niqmandu', WO 3, 1966, pp. 206-45; F. Knutson, 'Literary genres in PRU IV', in Ras Shamra Parallels (cited above, Ch. 1, n. 96), II, pp. 180-84.

74. Cf. the discussion, itself complex, in Dietrich and Loretz, art. cit., pp. 227-32.

75. Similarly phy : itamarma ("acknowledged"), lines 14-16, generated SOV; cf. Böhl, op. cit., pp. 78-9.

76. Dietrich and Loretz, pp. 224-6 ad ktn, 232-9 ad ks.

77. CAD s.vv. malāku, malkūtu, malku/maliku; but also māliku ("advisor"), milku ("instruction/intelligence/spirit"), and malku ("god/demon/advice"); cf. Sivan, op. cit., pp. 179-80.

78. Böhl, pp. 4-9, 80-90; Sivan, pp. 5-6, 185-295 (glossary).

79. Nougayrol, UGAR V, pp. 230-51, 418-24 (nos. 130, 131, 137, 138); cf. S. Segert, 'Rendering of Ugaritic phonemes by cuneiform syllabic signs in the quadrilingual vocabularies from Ras Shamra', in B. Hruška and G. Komoróczy (edd), Festschrift Lubor Matouš, Budapest, 1978, II, pp. 257-68.

80. E. g. Sivan's glossary (above, n. 64) contains c. 1925 lemmata, of which 810 are actual lexical entries; of these .c. 200 are attested as common nouns/verbs.

81. Böhl, pp. 40-68, esp. 55-8; Sivan, pp. 135-82.

82. For this description of linguistic heterogeneity, see F. Corriente, A Grammatical Sketch of the Spanish Arabic Dialect Bundle, Madrid, 1977, pp. 6-9 and passim; cf. thereto J. Wansbrough, BSOAS XLI, 3, 1978, pp. 587-8.

83. See above, n. 56; Arabic script, which is not logographic, can also generate deceptive homogeneity, see below, pp. 95-6.

84. Wansbrough, 'A Judaeo-Arabic document from Sicily', BSOAS XXX, 2, 1967, pp. 305-13; N. Golb, 'A Judaeo-Arabic court document of Syracuse, A.D. 1020', JNES 32, 1973, pp. 105-23; A. Giuffrida and B. Rocco, 'Documenti giudeo-arabi nel sec. XV a Palermo', Studi Magrebini VIII, Naples, 1976, pp. 53-110; B. Rocco, 'Un documento giudeo-arabo a Trapani nel sec. XV', Sicilia Archaeologica 51, Trapani, 1983, pp. 67-69.

85. Wansbrough, art. cit., p. 307 lines 1, 6, 12, 14ff.

86. Giuffrida and Rocco, art. cit., nos. 5, 32-38; Idem, 'Una bilingue arabo-sicula', AION 24, 1974, pp. 109-22.

87. Golb, art. cit., pp. 107-8.

88. Wansbrough, 'Diplomatica Siciliana' (cited above, n. 3), pp. 19-21.

89. Exceptions were rare, e.g. amongst Karaites: cf. J. Blau, The Emergence and Linguistic Background of Judaeo-Arabic, Scripta Judaica V, Oxford University Press, 1965, pp. 38-44; Idem, Studies (cited above, Ch.1, n. 103), pp. 270-79 (vs Nemoy); H. Ben-Shammai, 'Hebrew in Arabic script - Qirqisānī's view', in S. Brunswick (ed), Studies in Judaica, Karaitica and Islamica (Presented to Leon Nemoy on his Eightieth Birthday), Bar-Ilan University Press, 1982, pp. 115-26.

90. S. Stern, Hispano-Arabic Strophic Poetry (ed L. Harvey), The Clarendon Press, Oxford, 1974, esp. pp. 33-41, 56-62, 127-60, 161-65; and thereto J. Wansbrough, BSOAS XXXVIII, 3, 1975, pp. 434-35.

91. W. Hoenerbach, 'Some notes on the legal language of Christian and Islamic deeds', JAOS 81, 1961, pp. 34-38; Idem, Spanisch-Islamische Urkunden aus der Zeit der Naṣriden und Moriscos, Orientalisches Seminar der Universität Bonn, 1965; cf. J. Wansbrough, BSOAS XXX, 1, 1967, pp. 185-87; R. Vesely, AO 38, 1970, pp. 499-502.

92. Hoenerbach, Urkunden, pp. 135-49 (no. 6), and "bilinguals" pp. 326-33 (no. 39).

93. Ibid, pp. 271-75 (no. 27), 309-17 (no. 37), esp. 316-7.

94. Alvaro, Indiculus Luminosus, ch. 35; von Grunebaum, op. cit. (Ch. 1, n. 83), pp. 57-58; Salmōn, Comment. Lamentations, ch. 1:8 (Ben-Shammai, art. cit., p. 126 n. 49).

95. Cf. Corriente, op. cit. (above, n. 82), pp. 147-50.

96. Hoenerbach, op. cit., pp. XXI-XXXV and nos. 27, 36, 28, 6, resp.

97. Cf. D. Arnaud, 'Problèmes théoriques de la transcription des textes en accadien périphérique et, en particulier, des textes provenant de Syrie', in Leclant, op. cit. (above, Ch. 1, n. 92), pp. 101-4; E. Reiner, 'How we read cuneiform texts', JCS 25, 1973, pp. 3-58, esp. 33-39; and above, pp. 13-16: final CV.

98. Cited below, Ch. 3, p. 143 n. 14.

99. Notes 99 to 245 refer predominantly to constituents of chancery format; Bresslau, Urkundenlehre, I, pp. 46-9; Wansbrough, 'Diplomatica Siciliana', p. 15; H. Ernst, Die mamlukischen Sultansurkunden des Sinai-Klosters, Wiesbaden, 1960, pp. XXIV-V.

100. Bresslau, II, pp. 193-225.

101. See above, n. 58; E. Salonen, Die Gruss- und Höflichkeitsformeln in Babylonisch-Assyrischen Briefen, Studia Orientalia Fennica XXXVIII, Helsinki, 1967, pp. 1-114, esp. 16f, 55, 57f, 62f (preterite), 71f, 79-82 (without "speak"); A. Kristensen, 'Ugaritic epistolary formulas: a comparative study of the Ugaritic epistolary formulas in the context of the contemporary Akkadian formulas in the letters from Ugarit and Amarna', UF 9, 1977, pp. 143-58, esp. 144ff; R. Pfeiffer, 'Assyrian epistolary formulae', JAOS 43, 1923, pp. 26-40; D. Pardee and R. Whiting, 'Aspects of epistolary verbal usage in Ugaritic and Akkadian', BSOAS L, 1, 1987, pp. 1-31, esp. 6 n. 13, and 15 nn. 35-36.

102. C. Westermann, Grundformen Prophetischer Rede, Munich, 1968, pp. 71-90; Knutson, art. cit. (above, n. 73), pp. 200-4, but cf. 207 (imperative); Pardee, Handbook (cited above, Ch. 1, n. 111), pp. 171-6; cf. Loewenstamm, op. cit. (above, n. 63), pp. 256-61.

103. Bresslau, II, pp. 371ff; E. Norden, Die Antike Kunstprosa, Berlin, 1909 (repr. Stuttgart, 1958), pp. 760-3, 930-60.

104. Salonen, op. cit., pp. 64-70 (Amarna), 73-6 (Ugarit): Kristensen, art. cit., pp. 147-50; Pardee and Whiting, art. cit., pp. 13-4, 28-9.

105. Bresslau, I. p. 84, II, p. 298; E. Curtius (cf. above, Ch. 1, n. 112), Europäische Literatur und Lateinisches Mittelalter, Bern, 1948, pp. 411-16: 'Devotionsformel und Demut'.

106. J. Fitzmyer, 'Some notes on Aramaic epistolography', JBL 93, 1974, pp. 201-25 (repr. Idem, A Wandering Aramean, Scholars Press, 1979, pp. 183-204: see 192-3); P. Alexander, 'Remarks on Aramaic epistolography in the Persian period', JSS 23, 1978, pp. 155-70, esp. 159, 163; P. Dion et alii, 'Les types épistolaires Hébréo-Araméens jusqu'au temps de Bar-Kokhbah', RB LXXXVI, 1979, pp. 543-79, esp. 562 n. 82, 571; Idem, 'La lettre araméenne passe-partout et ses sous-espèces', RB LXXXIX, 1982, pp. 528-75, esp. 555, 570-1 nn. 230, 233; the formula is not listed in A. Bakir, Egyptian Epistolography, from the eighteenth to the twenty-first dynasty, Cairo, 1970: see pp. 55-64 'The complimentary preamble'.

107. Pardee, Handbook, pp. 165-8, 120-2, resp.; Dion, 'Les types', pp. 574-6, 554-5, resp.

108. Bresslau, I, p. 47, II, p. 257; Dölger, Diplomatik, p. 140; Björkman, Staatskanzlei, pp. 11, 116.

109. Dölger, pp. 34, 48.

110. Bresslau, II, pp. 302-3.

111. Björkman, loc. cit.; Ménage, art. cit. (above, n. 7), p. 285.

112. Salonen, op. cit., passim; Pfeiffer, art. cit., pp. 29-34; Kristensen, art. cit., pp. 150-3; Bakir, op. cit., pp. 41-54; for an Aramaic exception, see below, n. 130.

113. Ménage, art. cit., pp. 290-9: Persian antecedents in H. Busse, Untersuchungen zum islamischen Kanzleiwesen, an Hand turkmenischer und safawidischer Urkunden, Cairo, 1959, pp. 44-45.

114. Salonen, op. cit., pp. 12-13, 16-17, 55, 57-8, 62-3, 71-2, 76, 79-82; Kristensen, art. cit., pp. 144-7.

115. Kristensen, p. 146; Veenhof, Cuneiform Archives, pp. 33-4 n. 128.

116. Salonen, pp. 58, 76, 80-1; Munn-Rankin, 'Diplomacy' (cited above, ch. 1, n. 19), pp. 76-84, 98; cf. Dölger, Diplomatik, p. 287 n. 52: 'Familie der Könige'.

117. See above, refs in nn. 106-7: Aramaic and Hebrew.

118. G. Driver, Aramaic Documents of the Fifth Century B.C., The Clarendon Press, Oxford, 1957, pp. 21-37 (texts); cf. J. Whitehead, 'Some distinctive features of the language of the Aramaic Arsames correspondence', JNES 37, 1978, pp. 119-40.

119. Driver, pp. 3-4 n. 1; J. Greenfield, 'Aspects of archives in the Achaemenid period', in Veenhof, Cuneiform Archives, pp. 289-95.

120. I. Gelb, 'Typology of Mesopotamian seal inscriptions', in M. Gibson and R. Biggs (edd), Seals and Sealing in the Ancient Near East, Bibliotheca Mesopotamica VI, Malibu, 1977, pp. 107-26.

121. J. Wansbrough, 'A Mamluk letter of 877/1473', BSOAS XXIV, 2, 1961, pp. 200-13, esp. 204-5, 210; Ménage, art. cit., pp. 288-9; an example in Skilliter, op. cit. (above, n. 1), pp. 94-6.

122. M. Larsen, 'Seal use in the Old Assyrian period', in Gibson and Biggs (edd), op. cit., pp. 89-105.

123. J. Renger, 'Legal aspects of sealing in ancient Mesopotamia', ibid, pp. 75-88.

124. C. Schaeffer, UGAR III, pp. 20-9 (Pl.V), 66-83 (Figs. 91-5, 97-9, 101-2, 104); cf. J. Nougayrol, PRU IV: Planches (seal position indicated).

125. Dölger, Diplomatik, pp. 130-51; Grohmann, Arabische Papyruskunde (cited above, Ch. 1, n. 110), pp. 114-18.

126. Gelb, art. cit., types XII-XIX and pp. 113-14.

127. Ménage, loc. cit.

128. Wansbrough (see above, n. 7), Documents = DIC, pp. 52, 62, and BSOAS 1971, pp. 22-3; cf. Ernst, op. cit. (above, n. 99), p. XXV and passim.

129. Pardee, Handbook, pp. 15-144: 48 documentary specimens.

130. Fitzmyer, art. cit., pp. 189-90; Alexander, art. cit., p. 163; Dion, art. cit. (1979), p. 561 n. 77; J. Gibson, op. cit. (above, Ch. 1, n. 118), vol. II Aramaic Inscriptions, Oxford, 1975, pp. 125-47 (Hermopolis papyri i-vii); cf. Pardee, op. cit., pp. 209-10.

131. See above, refs in nn. 115-16.

132. Salonen, op. cit., pp. 62-3 (Amarna), 71-2 (Ugarit); Fitzmyer, pp. 189-91; Pardee, pp. 147-8, 158-9; Alexander, pp. 161-2; Dion (1982), pp. 573-5 = Diagrammes I-II; Driver, pp. 12-15.

133. N. Abbott, The Kurrah Papyri from Aphrodito in the Oriental Institute, University of Chicago Press, 1938, texts I and III; M. Hamidullah, 'La lettre du Prophète à Héraclius et le sort de l'original', Arabica 2, 1955, pp. 97-110; Idem, 'Original de la lettre du Prophète à Kisrà', RSO 40, 1965, pp. 57-69, Pls. I-IV; and see Qalqashandī, VI, pp. 367ff.

134. See above, n. 121: pp. 204-5; and cf. BSOAS XXV, 3, 1962, p. 464 n. 6.

135. BSOAS XXIV,2, 1961, p. 210 n. 3; see M. Amari, 'De' titoli che usava la cancelleria de' sultani di Egitto, nel XIV secolo scrivendo a'reggitori di alcuni stati italiani', Memoria, Reale Accademia dei Lincei, CCLXXXII, Rome, 1886, pp. 3-30; C. Bosworth, 'Christian and Jewish religious dignitaries in Mamluk Egypt and Syria: Qalqashandī's information on their hierarchy, titulature, and appointment', IJMES 3, 1972, pp. 59-74, 199-216; J. Johns, 'I titoli arabi dei sovrani normanni di Sicilia', Bollettino di Numismatica, Ministero peri Beni Culturali e Ambientali, Rome, 1986, pp. 11-54.

136. Bresslau, II, pp. 225-97, esp. 229ff.

137. Ibid, II, pp. 297-325, esp. 299.

138. Ibid, I, pp. 65ff; Wansbrough, art. cit. (above, n. 84), p. 312; S. Stern, Fāṭimid Decrees: original documents from the Fāṭimid chancery, London, 1964, pp. 85-90.

139. Salonen, op. cit., pp. 57-77.

140. Ibid, pp. 14-54, esp. 17-19; Pfeiffer, art. cit., pp. 29-33.

141. Salonen, pp. 63, 103-4.

142. See above, refs in nn. 104-8.

143. Kristensen, art. cit., pp. 150-3, 157; Salonen, pp. 58-60.

144. Kristensen, pp. 153-6, 158; Salonen, pp. 15, 22-53.

145. Pardee, Handbook, pp. 148-9, 154-5; Dion (1982), pp. 531-46.

146. Qalqashandī, VI, pp. 229-30, 284-92; Abbott, Kurrah Papyri, p. 40; Wansbrough, BSOAS XXV, 3, 1962, p. 465 n. 2.

147. S. Stern, 'Petitions from the Mamlūk period (notes on the Mamlūk documents from Sinai)', BSOAS XXIX, 2, 1966, pp. 233-76, Pls. I-VII, esp. 239-42 and refs to his studies of Fāṭimid and Ayyūbid specimens; see now G. Khan, 'The historical development of the structure of medieval Arabic petitions', BSOAS LIII, 1, 1990, pp. 8-30, Pls. I-IV, esp. 24-6.

148. Qalqashandī, VI, pp. 339-40, VII, pp. 119-20.

149. E.g. Skilliter, op. cit., pp. 166 and 271: in a letter from Elizabeth I to Murad III dated 26 June 1581 "Although we are not ignorant how many good princes by the like misadventure be abused, where the doings of the Subjects are imputed to the want of good government. But such matters of importance and so well approved we may not omit: such is to us the sacred estimation of our honour, and of our Christian profession . . ."

150. Stern, Fāṭimid Decrees, pp. 107-12 and nos. 3, 4, 6, 8, 9; on the use of rhyme see above, n. 103.

151. J. Latham, 'The beginnings of Arabic prose literature: the epistolary genre', in A. Beeston et alii, Arabic Literature to the End of the Umayyad Period, Cambridge History of Arabic Literature, Cambridge University Press, 1983, pp. 154-79; cf. I. 'Abbās, Malāmīḥ yūnānīya fi l-adab al-'arabī, Beirut, 1977, esp. pp. 99-109 on the use of Greek political theory in adab treatises.

152. Qalqashandī, I, pp.85-9 and X, pp. 195-233, resp.; cf. Björkman, Staatskanzlei, pp. 4-5.

153. Qalqashandī, IX, p. 270; cf. I. Goldziher, 'Der Chaṭīb bei den alten Arabern', WZKM VI, 1892, pp. 97-102 = Gesammelte Schriften (ed. J. Desomogyi), III,

Hildesheim, 1969, pp. 27-32; Idem, Abhandlungen zur Arabischen Philologie, I, Leiden, 1896, pp. 57-67.

154. Dölger, Diplomatik, pp. 25-26 n. 94.

155. Curtius, op. cit. (above, n. 105), pp. 83-4: ars dictaminis.

156. W. Hallo, 'Sumerian historiography', in Tadmor and Weinfeld, op. cit. (above, Ch. 1, n. 37), pp. 9-20, esp. 12, 19; H. Tadmor, 'Autobiographical apology in the royal Assyrian literature', ibid, pp. 36-57, esp. 48-9; cf. D. O'Connor, 'New Kingdom and Third Intermediate Period, 1552-664 BC', in B. Trigger et alii, Ancient Egypt: a social history, Cambridge University Press, 1983, esp. pp. 185-88 for a difference between archival records and monumental inscriptions.

157. Stern, Fāṭimid Decrees, p. 35 lines 3-6 (no. 3).

158. Qalqashandī, VI, pp. 331-2; Abbott, Kurrah Papyri, pp. 40, 42.6, 47.5; Stern, pp. 47.8, 59.5, 70.11, 76.16.

159. E.g. Knutson, art. cit. (above, n. 73), pp. 208-14; Alexander, art. cit., pp. 163-4; Dion, arts. cit. (1979), pp. 559, 563, 574, (1982), pp. 532, 536, 541, and chart pp. 574-5 (P); Pardee, Handbook, pp. 149-50, 155; and S. Parker, Studies in the Grammar of Ugaritic Prose Texts, Johns Hopkins University, 1967, pp. 73-6.

160. Pardee, p. 81.

161. Bresslau, I, p. 49 n. 1.

162. PRU IV, p. 132.8 (RS 17.116), 224.11 (RS 17.422); PRU V, 1965, p. 87.9 (RS 18.147); cf. Wansbrough, 'Ugaritic in chancery practice', in Veenhof, Cuneiform Archives, pp. 205-9; UGAR VII, 1978, p. 123.5 (RS 17.435+); cf. Pardee, 'The letter of Puduhepa: the text', AfO XXIX/XXX, 1983/84, pp. 321-9.

163. Driver, Aramaic Documents, p. 24 bottom (text IV); Pardee, Handbook, p. 48. 3-4.

164. Abbott, Kurrah Papyri, pp. 47.5-6, 42-3. 6-7.

165. Wansbrough, DIC (above, n. 128), p. 52. 17; Ernst, op. cit., p. XXVII.

166. Cf. Ménage, BSOAS XLVIII, 1985, pp. 289-90; Wansbrough, BSOAS XXXIV, 1971, pp. 28-9.

167. Stern, Fāṭimid Decrees, pp. 91-102; and see above, refs in n. 147.

168. Skilliter, op. cit., pp. 86-9, 232-9: response to petition pp. 69-72.

169. PRU IV, pp. 222.10-20 (RS 17.383), 224.11-14 (RS 17.422), 226.6-10 (RS 17.391).

170. Ibid, pp. 49.9-15 (RS 17.340), 180.8-12 (RS 17.286), 218.8-10 (RS 17. 425).

171. Bresslau, I, pp. 90-1; II, pp. 301-8.

172. Ibid, I, p. 48 n. 3; II, p. 92 n. 2.

173. See above, n. 7: Wansbrough, BSOAS XXXIV, 1971, pp. 25-8 = Qalqashandī, XIII, pp. 321-51.

174. For 13th century Byzantium, cf. Dölger, Diplomatik, pp. 238-9 nn. 98 and 100: ad scripta conventio = eggraphos symphonia.

175. E.g. Wansbrough, BSOAS XXIV, 2, 1961, p. 206.11, and BSOAS XXXIV,1, 1971, p. 22.15.

176. Bresslau, I, pp. 45-85, esp. 50-4; II, pp. 76-8; cf. Grohmann, Arabische Papyruskunde, pp. 107-10; Björkman, Encyclopaedia of Islam, second edition, vol. II, pp. 301-7 s.v. Diplomatic.

177. PRU IV, p. 201 (RS 18.02); cf. Knutson, art. cit., pp. 415-17.

178. PRU IV, pp. 209-10 (RS 17.355); oath pp. 169-70 (RS 17.158).

179. Ibid, pp. 137-9 (RS 18. 06+17.365, 17. 459), 157 (RS 17.146).

180. Ibid, p. 43 (RS 17.227+), 51-2 (RS 17.340), 65 (RS 17.237).

181. Ibid, p. 87 (RS 17.338); cf. Bresslau, I, p. 48 s.v. sanctio.

182. Knutson, art. cit., pp. 155-98, esp. 155-75; D. McCarthy, Treaty and Covenant: a study in form in the ancient oriental documents and the O.T., Analecta Biblica 21, Rome, 1963; Idem, Old Testament Covenant: a survey of current opinions, Oxford, 1972.

183. Ernst, op. cit., pp. 158.19-20, 180.18-19, and cf. XXVIII-XXXI; Wansbrough, DIC, p. 61. 257-9; Idem, BSOAS XXVII, 3, 1965, p. 508. 318-9.

184. Stern, Fāṭimid Decrees, pp. 113-14; Wansbrough, BSOAS XXV, 3, 1962, p. 467 s.v. sanctio.

185. See also below, nn. 191, 246-52: R. Yaron, 'The schema of the Aramaic legal documents', JSS 2, 1957, pp. 33-61; Idem, Introduction to the Law of the Aramaic Papyri, Oxford University Press, 1961, esp. pp. 84-91; B. Porten, Archives from Elephantine: the life of an ancient Jewish military colony, University of California Press, 1968, pp. 334-43; Y. Muffs, Studies in the Aramaic Legal Papyri from Elephantine, Studia et Documenta ad Iura Orientis Antiqui Pertinentia VIII, Leiden, 1969, pp. 43, 45 n.1, 52, 184-5; B. Porten and J. Greenfield, Jews of Elephantine and Arameans of Syene (Fifth Century B.C.E.), Jerusalem, 1974, exempla pp. 4.7, 10, 13 (=Cowley no. 5), 6.14 (=Cowley no.6), 10.20 (=Cowley no.8), and passim.

186. Bresslau, I, pp. 688 n. 1, 699 n. 6, 690 n. 3, resp.; II, pp. 187, 208-11; Wansbrough, 'Mamluk ambassador' (cited above, Ch 1, n. 10), p. 519 n. 3.

187. Bresslau, I, pp. 461-2; and cf. II, pp. 163, 202-3 n.1; see below, n. 239.

188. E. g. PRU IV, pp. 201 (RS 18.02), 231 (RS 17. 123), 235 (RS 17. 135+360), 236 (RS 17. 248), 238 (RS 17. 231).

189. Ibid, Nougayrol pp. 3-4 n. 3; and p. 55 (RS 17. 334).

190. Wansbrough, DIC, p. 61, 261-2; Ernst, op. cit., pp. XXXI-XXXII.

191. See above, n. 185: dictation clause = Yaron, 'Schema', pp. 39-44, Porten, pp. 337, 340; witnesses = Yaron, pp. 44-54, Porten loc. cit.

192. Cf. Goody, op. cit. (above, n. 6), pp. 127-70, esp. 128-9, 151-2.

193. See above, nn. 120-24; D. Collon, First Impressions: cylinder seals in the Ancient Near East. British Museum, London, 1987, pp. 111-12.

194. Ibid, pp. 105-7, 123-30; H. Nissen, 'Aspects of the development of early cylinder seals', in Gibson and Biggs, op. cit., pp. 15-23.

195. Collon, op. cit., pp. 113-22.

196. Ibid, pp. 131-2, Figs. 559-61; A. George, 'Sennacherib and the tablet of destinies', IRAQ XLVIII, 1986, pp. 133-46, esp. 139-42.

197. Stern, Fāṭimid Decrees, pp. 123-42; J. Latham, 'Ibn al-Aḥmar's Kitāb Mustawda' al-'Alāma: towards a commentary on the author's introduction', in Wadād Al-Qāḍī (ed), Studia Arabica et Islamica (Festschrift for Iḥsān 'Abbās), American University of Beirut, 1981, pp. 313-32.

198. Abbott, Kurrah Papyri, pp. 27-33, texts I-III; Grohmann, Arabische Papyruskunde, pp. 128-30.

199. Qalqashandī, VI, pp. 352-7.

200. H. De Castries, 'Les signes de validation des Chérifs Saadiens', Hespéris I, 1921, pp. 232-52, Pls. I-IX, esp. 248-9, Figs. 14-16; Wansbrough, BSOAS XXV, 3, 1962, pp. 463-4.

201. Cf. Latham, art. cit., p. 325 vs Stern, op. cit., p. 134.

202. Stern, pp. 143-65: refs to Köprülü, Cahen, and Wittek.

203. Bakir, Egyptian Epistolography (cited above, n. 106), pp. 28-9; B. Williams, 'Aspects of sealing and glyptic in Egypt before the New Kingdom', in Gibson and Biggs, op. cit., pp. 135-40; J. Johnson, 'Private name seals of the Middle Kingdom', ibid, pp. 141-5.

204. Stern, pp. 138-42; Latham, art. cit., pp. 319-23, 330-31.

205. Qalqashandī, XIII, pp. 162-6, pls. on 165-166; O. Turan, Türkiye Selçuklulari hakkinda Resmi Vesikalar, Türk Tarih Kurumu 32, Ankara, 1958, pp. 22-27 and pl. facing p. 144; cf. Stern, pp. 150-2 ad P. Wittek, 'Notes sur la tughra ottomane', Byzantion XX, 1950, pp. 267-93, Pls. I-II, esp. 289 and P1. II fig. 7.

206. Qalqashandī, III, pp. 51-7, 132-8: calligraphic prescriptions illustrated.

207. Bresslau, II, pp. 163-93; Dölger, Diplomatik, pp. 41-2.

208. Bresslau, II, pp. 185, 608-10.

209. Ibid, p. 184; Dölger, pp. 16-23, Pls. I-IV; see above, n. 204.

210. E.g. F. Fales, Aramaic Epigraphs (cited above, Ch. 1, n. 94), pp. 18-24: triangular docket as sealing; Bresslau, I, pp. 679 n. 4 (Ptolemaic practice), 680 (Roman).

211. Ibid, pp. 679-92.

212. Ibid, pp. 693-716.

213. Ibid, II, pp. 548-624, esp. 596-615.

214. Ernst, op. cit., p. XXIV n. 50 and refs; Wansbrough, BSOAS XXXIV, 1971, pp. 21 n. 8, 24 and Pls. II-V; cf. variations in L. Mayer, 'Das Schriftwappen der Mamlukensultane', Jahrbuch der Asiatischen Kunst II, Leipzig, 1925, pp. 183-7, but esp. P1. 104.

215. E.g. PRU IV, pp. 183 (RS 17. 319), 190 (RS 17. 316), 201 (RS 18.02), but cf. pp. 109-10 (RS 17.28), where two of the witnesses are parties to the transaction.

216. H. Klengel, 'Zu den šībūtum in altbabylonischer Zeit', Or. 29, 1960, pp. 357-75; I. Gelb, 'Šībūt Kusurrā'im, "witnesses of the indemnity" ', JNES 43, 1984, pp. 263-76; see above, nn. 122-23: Larsen and Renger, arts. cit.

217. D. Pardee, 'YPḤ "witness" in Hebrew and Ugaritic', VT XXVIII, 1978, pp. 204-13.

218. See above, pp. 38-40.

219. Above, n. 191.

220. Ibid, and below, pp. 119-21 s.v. recognitio.

221. Wansbrough, 'Mamluk ambassador', pp. 519-21, 524-5.

222. Bresslau, II, pp. 193-225, esp. 216-22.

223. Ibid, pp. 200-02.

224. See above, nn. 84-88: Wansbrough, art. cit., pp. 307, 311, 313; Golb, art. cit., p. 108 n. 26; cf. Grohmann, Arabische Papyruskunde, pp. 111-13: Arabic shuhūd 'udūl, ahl al-'adāla; and Bresslau, II, p. 392 n. 1 on Jewish "communal witness" (Köln).

225. Bresslau, I, pp. 370-83, 482-92.

226. Above, pp. 79-80.

227. Bresslau, I, pp. 266-76, and as in n. 225 above.

228. Ibid, I, p. 187, II, pp. 184-5; Dölger, loc. cit. (n. 209); Grohmann, op. cit., pp. 122-24.

229. R. Vesely, 'Die richterlichen Beglaubigungsmittel: ein Beitrag zur Diplomatik arabischer Gerichtsurkunden', Acta Universitatis Carolinae - Philologica 4, Prague, 1971, pp. 7-23; Idem, 'Die Hauptprobleme der Diplomatik arabischer Privaturkunden aus dem spätmittelalterlichen Ägypten', AO 40, 1972, pp. 312-43, esp. 330-41.

230. Ibid, pp. 341-3; and above, p. 29.

231. E.g. PRU IV, pp. 153-4 (RS 17. 230), 154-5 (RS 17.146) = šarru/king; 196-7 (RS 17.78), 226-7 (RS 17. 393) = šākinu/vizir; 182-4 (RS 17. 319), 189 (RS 17.314), 201 (RS 18.02) = šību/witness; Wansbrough, op. cit. (Ch. 1, note 151.)

232. Bresslau, II, pp 393-6.

233. Ibid, pp. 445-78.

234. Yaron, 'Schema' (above, n. 185), pp. 33-5, 56-61; Bresslau, as in n. 232.

235. Dölger, Diplomatik, pp. 4, 36, 46-7, 293-4 s.v. menologem.

236. See above, n. 204.

237. Wansbrough, 'Diplomatica Siciliana', p. 15 n. 14; A. Noth, art. cit. (above, n. 8), p. 240 ad S. Cusa, I Diplomi Greci ed Arabi di Sicilia.

238. See above, p. 36 (bottom), and e. g. PRU II, pp. 18 (RS 16.191+272), 21 (RS 16.382); PRU IV, pp.139 (RS 17.372A+360A), 201 (RS 18.02); Yaron, 'Schema' (cited above, n. 185), pp. 33-5.

239. Wansbrough, BSOAS 1965 (cited in full above, Ch. 1, n. 236), p. 509 n. 63; Bresslau, II, pp. 476-8; and see above, n. 187: chancery blanks.

240. See above, refs in n. 106: Fitzmyer, p. 194; Alexander, pp. 166-7; Dion (1982), pp. 554-5, 560, 565; Driver, Aramaic Documents, pp. 8-10; Bakir, Egyptian Epistolography, pp. 32, 70.

241. Bresslau, II, p. 393 n. 1; Grohmann, Arabische Papyruskunde, pp. 219-32.

242. Bresslau, I, pp. 77-82; Dölger, Diplomatik, pp. 122-3.

243. Grohmann, op. cit., pp. 116-17; Stern, Fāṭimid Decrees, pp. 120-23; Ernst, op. cit., pp. XXXIII-XXXVIII.

244. Grohmann, p. 119; Björkman, Staatskanzlei, p. 117 = Qalqashandī, VI, p. 270; cf. Wansbrough, BSOAS 1962, pp. 451.22, 457.53, 468, and 1963, pp. 521, 525 = ha'; Idem, DIC, pp. 61.268, 79 n. 35, and BSOAS 1971, p. 22.36 = hr.

245. Veenhof, Cuneiform Archives, p. 15; M. Dandamayev, 'The Neo-Babylonian archives', ibid, pp. 273-7; F. Fales, Aramaic Epigraphs (cited above, Ch. 1, n. 94), pp. 1-29; Grohmann, op. cit., pp. 124-6; Stern, op. cit., pp. 166-75.

246. See above, n. 185, and for "imperial Aramaic", Ch. 1, n. 107.

247. Esp. Muffs, Studies, pp. 1-29.

248. Yaron, 'Schema', pp. 33-5, 56-61.

249. Muffs, op. cit., pp. 173-6 and esp. 150 n. 5.

250. But cf. G. Frantz-Murphy, 'A Comparison of the Arabic and earlier Egyptian contract formularies', Pt. III: 'The idiom of satisfaction', JNES 47, 1988, pp. 105-12; (Pt. I: 'The Arabic contracts from Egypt (3rd/9th - 5th/11th centuries)', JNES 40, 1981, pp. 203-25, 355-6; Pt. II: 'Terminology in the Arabic warranty and the idiom of clearing/cleaning', JNES 44, 1985, pp. 99-114; Pt. IV: 'Quittance formulas', JNES 47, 1988, pp. 269-80).

251. Idem, Pt. II; Yaron, Law of the Aramaic Papyri (cited above, n. 185), pp. 90 n. 4; Muffs, op. cit., pp. 123-8.

252. Yaron, op. cit., pp. 10-11 = 'Schema', pp. 37-8; Muffs, op. cit., pp. 173-6; but cf. Frantz-Murphy, Pt. III : objective formulation in Arabic.

253. See above, pp. 13-19, and Ch. 1, pp. 30-2, 61-2.

254. Cited above, Ch. 1, n. 183: pp. 414-22 s.v. Écritures, for specific allocation of script to language and combinations/permutations.

255. Tell Sukas: P. Riis, 'L' Activité de la mission archéologique danoise sur la côte phénicienne en 1960', AAS 11, 1961, p. 137 & fig. 6; Taanach: D. Hillers, 'An alphabetic cuneiform tablet from Taanach (TT 433)', BASOR 173, 1964, pp. 45-50; F. Cross, 'The Canaanite cuneiform tablet from Taanach', BASOR 190, 1968, pp. 41-6; Bet Shemesh: A. Herdner, 'A-t-il existé une variété palestinienne de l'écriture cunéiforme alphabétique?', Syria 25, 1946/48, pp. 166-8; W. Albright, 'The Beth-Shemesh tablet in alphabetic cuneiform', BASOR 173, 1964, pp. 51-3.

256. Kamid el-Loz: G. Wilhelm, 'Eine Krughenkelinschrift in alphabetischer Keilschrift aus Kamid el-Loz (KL 67: 428p)', UF 5, 1973, pp. 284-5; for this site, cf. also P. Bordreuil, UF 11, 1981, p. 63, and W. Röllig & G. Mansfeld, 'Zwei Ostraka from Tell Kamid-el-Loz und ein neuer Aspekt für die Entstehung des kanaanäischen Alphabets', WO 5, 1969/70, pp. 265-70; Qadesh: A. Millard, 'A text in a shorter cuneiform alphabet from Tell Nebi Mend (TNM 022)', UF 8, 1976, pp. 459-60; Sarepta: P. Bordreuil, 'L' Inscription phénicienne de Sarafand en cunéiformes alphabétiques', UF 11, 1981, pp. 63-67; E. Greenstein, 'A Phoenician inscription in Ugaritic script?' JANES 8, 1976, pp. 49-57.

257. Tabor: Herdner, art. cit., pp. 165-6; Hala Sultan Tekke: P. Aström and E. Masson, 'A silver bowl with Canaanite inscription from Hala Sultan Tekké', RDAC, 1982, pp. 72-6; P. Bordreuil, 'Cuneiformes alphabétiques non canoniques: à propos de l'épigraphe de Hala Sultan Tekké', Semitica XIII, 1983, pp. 7-15; E. Puech, 'Présence phénicienne dans les îles à la fin du IIe millénaire', RB 90, 1983, pp. 365-74.

258. C. Gordon, UT p.16 (para. 3.6): texts UT 57 = CTA 207 (RS 5.197+), UT 74 = CTA 187 (RS 6.41), UT 94 = CTA 206 (RS. 9.496), RS 22.003; cf. M. Dietrich et

alii, 'Das reduzierte Keilalphabet', UF 6, 1974, pp. 15-18; Idem, 'Entzifferung und Transkription von RS 22.03', UF 7, 1975, pp. 548-9; P. Bordreuil, 'Cunéiformes alphabétiques non canoniques: la tablette alphabétique sénestroverse RS 22.03', Syria LVIII, 1981, pp. 301-11.

259. H. Priebatsch, 'S und T in Ugarit und das Amoritische: ein Beitrag zur Geschichte des ABC', UF 7, 1975, pp. 389-94.

260. Greenstein, art. cit. (above, n. 256); Bordreuil, arts. cit. (above, nn. 256-257).

261. See above, Ch. I, n. 99: UGAR III = RS 3.389, RS 17.006, RS 19.001, RS 19.002; UGAR VI = RS 20.025; cf. also Bordreuil and Pardee, Concordance: Rs 27.237 and RS [Varia 1]; see below, Ch. 3, pp. 170-1.

262. Cf. above, n. 245; and RS 8.272 (UT 81/CTA 75), 10.045 (UT 110/CTA 65), 10.052 (UT 321/CTA 119), 11.715+ (UT 400/CTA 113), 11.716 (UT 113/CTA 71), 11.721 (UT 324/CTA 114), 11.776+ (UT 301/CTA 115), 11.797 (UT 307/CTA 121), 11.850 (UT 108/CTA 65), 11.857 (UT 119/CTA 80), 15.076 (UT 1116), 16.179 (UT 1088), 16.355 (UT 1046), 17.386 (UT 1181), 18.102 (UT 2034), 18.252 (UT 2019), 19.017 (UT 2058), 19.136 (UT 2119); also RS 19.75 (PRU IV, p. 292).

263. RS 16.291 (PRU III, p. 198), 18.116 (PRU VI, p. 118).

264. PRU II, nos. 163-75 (UT 1163-75): RS [Varia 5], 15.097, 15.080, 15.192A, 15.026, 13.004, 1-11.113, 17.361C, 17.364, 17.073, 17.361B, 17. 318B, 17. 072.

265. D. Edzard, 'Amarna und die Archive seiner Korrespondenten zwischen Ugarit und Gaza', in Biblical Archaeology Today (cited above, Ch. 1, n. 44), pp. 248-59.

266. PRU V, no. 59 (RS 18.31); cf. J. Hoftijzer, 'Une lettre du roi de Tyr', UF 11, 1979, pp. 383-88.

267. PRU V, no. 63 (RS 18.40); but cf. M. Astour, 'New evidence on the last days of Ugarit', AJA 69, 1965, pp. 253-58, esp. 256-57, for a different interpretation.

268. D. Arnaud, 'Une lettre du roi de Tyr au roi d'Ougarit: milieux d'affaires et de culture en Syrie à la fin de l'âge du Bronze Récent', Syria LIX, 1982, pp. 101-7: in Bordreuil and Pardee, Concordance = RS [Varia 25].

269. Knudtzon, op. cit. (above, n. 68), nos. 146-55.

270. Ibid, nos. 33-40 and 45-49, resp.

271. UGAR V, nos. (N) 21 (RS 20. 168) and 24 (RS 20.238) : Ugarit to Alaśiya; nos. (N) 22 (RS 20.18) and 23 (RS L.1): Alaśiya to Ugarit; cf. P. Berger, 'Die Alaśia-Briefe Ugaritica 5, Noug. Nrn. 22-24', UF 1, 1969, pp. 217-21; but also J. Strange, op. cit. (above, Ch. 1, n. 97), pp. 173-76.

272. Astour, art. cit., pp. 254-58; G. Lehmann, 'Der Untergang des Hethitischen Grossreiches und die neuen Texte aus Ugarit', UF 2, 1970, pp. 39-73, esp. 51-64, but also p. 72 for hypothesis of "natural disaster".

273. E.g. PRU IV, pp. 199-203, 205-10; PRU II, nos. 5 and 6; PRU V, no. 60.

274. M. Astour, 'Second millennium B.C. Cypriot and Cretan onomastica reconsidered', JAOS 84, 1964, pp. 240-54, esp. 246-7 (Eśuwara), but also p. 242 on the Hurrian origin of "Alasiya"; A. Knapp and A. Marchant, 'Cyprus, Cypro-Minoan and Hurrians', RDAC, 1982, pp. 15-21 (vs E. Masson).

275.   Analysis in C. Schaeffer and O. Masson, cited above, n. 261 and Ch. 1, n. 99.

276.   That is, in addition to the gentilic alṭy in UT 2, 301, 1046, 1090, 1101, 2018 and 2095, as well as the Akkadian docket al alašia to UT 119 (RS 11.857), cited above, n. 262.

277.   PRU V, no. 61 (RS 18. 147); J. Wansbrough, art. cit. (above, n. 162).

278.   C. Schaeffer, UGAR IV, pp. 31-61, Figs. 39, 41-48.

279.   PRU V, no. 8 (RS 18. 113A); E. Lipinski, 'An Ugaritic letter to Amenophis III concerning trade with Alašiya', in J. Hawkins (cited above, Ch.1, n. 3), pp. 213-17; A. Knapp, 'An Alashiyan merchant at Ugarit', Tel Aviv 10, 1983, pp. 38-45; D. Pardee, 'Epigraphic and philological notes', UF 19, 1987, pp. 204-9.

280.   See above, pp. 86-88.

281.   G. Boyer, 'La place des textes d'Ugarit dans l'histoire de l'ancien droit oriental', PRU III, pp. 283-308, esp. 305-7: RS 16.131, 16.140, 16.141, 17.084, 17.329; cf. G. Kestemont, 'Remarques sur les aspects juridiques du commerce dans le Proche-Orient du XIVe siècle avant notre ère', in J. Hawkins, op. cit., pp. 191-201.

282.   M. Liverani, 'Due documenti ugaritici con garanzia di presenza', UGAR VI, 1969, pp. 375-8: ad PRU II, no. 161 (RS 15.128) and PRU V, no. 116 (RS 19.066), and PRU V, no. 79 (RS 18.035); Akkadian are RS 15.081 and 16.287 (PRU III, pp. 37-8); B. Kienast, 'Rechtsurkunden in Ugaritischer Sprache', UF 11, 1979, pp. 431-52, esp. 432-33 n. 4 on terminology; for PRU V, no. 106 (RS 18.025) see below, n. 285.

283.   Cf. M. Cohen, 'A propos de "gage, caution" dans les langues sémitiques', GLECS VIII, 1957/60 (Séance du 26 février 1958), pp. 13-16; for Phoenician, Hebrew and Aramaic, see the standard dictionaries, and for Arabic, also Dozy, Supplément II, p. 108 ad Vocabulista (Florence 1871), pp. 141, 253 s.v. Arra; cf. J. Schacht, 'Droit byzantin et droit musulman', Convegno Volta XII: Oriente ed Occidente nel Medio Evo, Accademia Nazionale dei Lincei, Rome, 1957, pp. 210-211, 225, 228-9.

284.   Cf. N. Avigad and J. Greenfield, 'A bronze phialē with a Phoenician dedicatory inscription', IEJ 32, 1982, pp. 118-28, esp 124-5: 'rb = offer/m'rb = import; in the medieval lingua franca the term retained the significance "pledge" or "guarantee": see Wansbrough, DIC, p. 78 n. 33 "plezius vel appacator", etc.; Idem, BSOAS XXVIII, 1965, p. 511 n. 70 "caparrum sive arbon"; and below, Ch. 3, p. 155-6.

285.   For PRU V, no. 106 (RS 18.025) see the studies of J. Ziskind and D. Pardee (cited above, Ch. 1, n. 213).

286.   M. Ellis, 'Taxation in ancient Mesopotamia: the history of the term miksu', JCS 26, 1974, pp. 211-50, esp. 230 n. 79, and 244-50.

287.   Ibid, p. 249 n. 161: PRU III, pp. 69-70 (RS 16.276) and 225 ad ešretu/miksu/ širku; cf. Kestemont, art. cit., pp. 194-5 ad ma'šaru/miksu/širku; cf. Heltzer, op. cit. (above Ch. 1, n. 151), pp. 146-7, but also Idem, The Rural Community in Ancient Ugarit, Wiesbaden, 1976, pp. 35-40 s.v. tithe.

288.   J. Schacht, An Introduction to Islamic Law, The Clarendon Press, Oxford 1964, p. 76 n. 1; C. Becker, Islamstudien, Leipzig, 1924 (repr. Hildesheim, 1967), I, pp. 177, 273-5, 316; Dozy, Supplément II, pp. 106-7 s.v. maks.

289.   See above, Ch. 1, n.1; W. Heffening, Das Islamische Fremdenrecht: bis zu den islamisch-fränkischen Staatsverträgen, Hannover, 1925 (repr. Osnabrück, 1975), and thereto G. Bergsträsser, Der Islam XV, 1926, pp. 311-21; and J. Schacht, Islamics II, 1926/7, pp. 150-57, 323; Idem, Encyclopaedia of Islam, second edition, vol. I, pp. 429-30 s.v. Amān.

290.   G. Bognetti, 'Note per la storia del passaporto e del salvacondotto', cited in Wansbrough, BSOAS XXXIV,1,1971,pp. 34-5 nn. 66-73; cf. also R. Brunschvig, La Berbérie orientale sous les Hafsides, I, pp. 431-40, cited ibid, nn. 62 and 70.

291.   Wansbrough, art. cit., p. 25 n. 18 = Qalqashandī, XIII, pp. 339-42; and see above, p. 110.

292.   S. Labib, Handelsgeschichte (cited above, Ch. 1, n. 215), pp. 64-121, and thereto Wansbrough, BSOAS XXX, 1, 1967, pp. 187-8; E. Ashtor, Levant Trade, pp. 3-63.

293.   See above, Ch. 1, pp. 56-8; Heffening, op. cit., pp. 89-90.

294.   Gibson, op. cit. (above, Ch. 1, n. 118), pp. 123-31 = no. 33 Cyprus Temple Tariff A. 15, B. 10; Herdner, CTA 14.110 (Keret), 19.153 (Aqhat), 32.10, 27 (ritual).

295.   Heffening, op. cit., pp. 120-3; M. Astour, 'Les étrangers à Ugarit et le statut juridique des Ḫabiru', RA 53, 1959, pp. 70-76, esp 74-5: PRU III, p. 101 (RS 15.109). p. 140 (RS 16.132); also, M. Heltzer, op. cit. (Ch. 1, n. 151), p. 137: RS 15.138 and 16.157.

296.   Astour, art. cit., pp. 71-4; Idem, 'Ma'ḫadu' (cited above, Ch. 1, n. 150), pp. 122-5; R. Yaron, art. cit. (above, Ch. 1, n. 153); A. Rainey, 'Business agents at Ugarit', IEJ 13, 1963, pp. 313-21; Idem, 'A Canaanite at Ugarit', ibid, pp. 43-5, and 'Ugarit and the Canaanites again', IEJ 14, 1964, p. 101: on the referent of kn'ny, which I am inclined to interpret as "merchant".

297.   Munn-Rankin, art. cit. (above, Ch. 1, n. 19), pp. 93-4, 99-108; Holmes, art. cit. (above, Ch. 1, n. 29), pp. 376-81; C. Virolleaud, PRU V, p. 17 n. 1 ad no. 9 (RS 17. 139) lists the designations for "messenger" as mnd', bn ḫrn (no. 114 = RS 19.11), and most frequent: mlak (e.g. PRU II, nos. 12 (RS 16.402), 18 (RS 16.117), and 21 (RS 15.98).

298.   Ad Amarna, no. 30: Munn-Rankin, p. 100 and Holmes, p. 380; ad Arsames, no. 6: G. Driver, Aramaic Documents, pp. 27-8, 56-62.

299.   E.g. PRU IV, pp. 103-5 (RS 17.130), 153-60 (17.230, 17.146, 18.115), 169-71 (17.158), 171-2 (17.042), 179 (17.128); cf. Yaron, art. cit.

300.   PRU IV, pp. 118-19 (RS 17.133) and PRU V, no. 59 (RS 18.31); see above, n. 266, and cf. F. Fensham, 'Shipwreck in Ugarit and Ancient Near Eastern law codes', OA 6, 1967, pp. 221-4.

301.   Heffening, op. cit., pp. 95-6, 105, 109-10, 118-20.

302.   Boyer, art. cit. (above, n. 281), esp. pp. 283-8; Wansbrough, op. cit. (Ch. 1, n. 151).

303.   See above, nn. 77, 124, 231, and Ch. 1, p. 51-2; K. Kitchen, 'The king list of Ugarit', UF 9, 1977, pp. 131-42 (RS 24.257 verso); J. Nougayrol, PRU III, pp. XXXVI-XLIII; C. Schaeffer, UGAR III, pp. 66-83.

304.   Nougayrol, op. cit., p. XXXVIII (CRAI 6-2-1953); cf. the Hittite title Tabarna, ibid, p. XLIII n. 3, and Boyer, art. cit., pp. 288-89 (288 n. 3: refs Güterbock); Nougayrol, PRU IV, p. 103 (RS 17. 130).

305.   PRU IV, pp. 202-3 (RS 18.20+17.371); F. Gröndahl, Die Personennamen der Texte aus Ugarit, Rome, 1967, no. 145.

306.   PRU III, p. XLI and Pl. XVI (Nougayrol), pp. 284-5 n.3 (Boyer); UGAR III, p. 69 nn. 1-5 refs (Schaeffer).

307.   PRU II, no. 5 (RS 15.125): miśmn niqmad; no. 6 (RS 16.191+272) : kunuk niqmad; UGAR III, pp. 77-80, Figs 100-102.

308.   PRU III, pp. 41-4 (RS 16.270 ; UGAR III, pp. 79-83, Figs 103-104; also RIH 83/ 21 in P. Bordreuil and D. Pardee 'Le sceau nominal de 'Ammīyidtamrou, roi d'Ougarit', Syria 61, 1984, pp. 11-14: on the alternative spellings miśmn/ maśmn, cf. also Von Soden, 'Kleine Beiträge zum Ugaritischen und Hebräischen', Festschrift W. Baumgartner, SVT 16, 1967, pp. 291-300: 294 n. 2 s.v. miśmunnu (Hurrian?).

309.   PRU II, ños. 8 (RS 16.382) and 9 (RS 15.111).

310.   E.g. PRU II, no. 182 (RS 14.023); cf. UGAR III, pp. 81-2 and Figs. 106-108.

311.   See above, Ch. 1, pp. 6-7, 25-6, 52-5.

312.   An instructive example in the "copialettere" of Piero Zen, Venetian consul in Damascus in 1510: Wansbrough, BSOAS XXXIV,1, 1971, p. 34 n. 63.

313.   E.g. the collections of Amari and De Mas Latrie (cited above, Ch. 1, n. 164), and of G. Tafel - G. Thomas, G. Thomas - R. Predelli, G. Müller, M. Alarcón y. Santón - R. García de Linares, A. de Campany y de Montpalau: cited inter alios in W. Heyd, Histoire du Commerce, S. Labib, Handelsgeschichte, E. Ashtor, Levant Trade (see above, Ch. 1, nn. 17, 78, 215).

314.   E.g. Biblioteca Mediceo-Laurenziana, Florence: Wansbrough, DIC, p. 49; Idem, BSOAS XXVIII,3, 1965, pp. 484-5: ditto and Museo Correr, Venice.

315.   Ibid, p. 494 n. 35, and DIC, loc. cit.

316.   See above, nn. 173-175.

317.   Above, nn. 7, 171; and below, Ch. 3, nn. 43-55.

318.   Björkman, Staatskanzlei, pp. 35, 51; see above, Ch. 1, n. 167: the Venetian-Egyptian treaties of 895/1490 and 909/1504; see now D. Richards, 'A Mamluk emir's "square" decree', BSOAS LIV, 1, 1991, pp. 63-7, esp. 64 (procedure).

319.   As set out in op. cit. (Ch. 1, n. 167), pp. 12-14, 25-33.

320.   Above, n. 239: Wansbrough, loc. cit.

321.   Amari, Diplomi Arabi, pp. 115-18, 119-22 = no. XXXIII; also, the transcription in D. Barbera, Elementi....., pp. 59-63 (ref Wansbrough, 'Diplomatica Siciliana', p. 18 n. 31); and below, Ch. 3, pp. 159-61.

322.   Bresslau, I, pp.92, 618-35; see above, nn. 222, 225.

323.   Schacht, op. cit. (above, n. 288), pp. 18-19, 82-5.

324.   See above, nn. 45-47.

325.   E.g. Ashtor, Levant Trade, pp. xii-xix, 561-4.

326.   See above, pp. 80-3 and Ch. 1, pp. 30-2.

327.   See above, Ch. 1, p. 44-5.

328.   Above, pp. 87-9.

329.   W. Brice, art. cit. (above, Ch. 1, n. 200), esp. pp. 32-40; Idem, 'Some observa-
       tions on the Linear A inscriptions', Kadmos 1, 1962, pp. 42-48; and 'Towards
       an understanding of the Minoan Linear script of class A', in J. Leclant, op. cit.
       (above, Ch. 1, n. 92), pp. 51-56.

330.   H. Haarmann, Universalgeschichte der Schrift, Frankfurt, 1990, pp. 229-306,
       501-20 (Aramaic).

331.   Ibid, pp. 268-94, 410-23 (Phoenician).

332.   Ibid, pp. 282-89, 423-49 (Greek); 319-24, 493-501 (Arabic).

333.   Ibid, pp. 114-49, esp. 147-49 (typology).

334.   H. Jensen, Die Schrift (cited above, Ch. 1, n. 207), pp. 43-6 and following
       sections; Haarman, op. cit., pp. 361-4 and following sections.

335.   Ibid, pp. 69-81.

336.   Ibid, pp. 478-501: the argument seems to me defensible in terms of script
       technology (but for Arabic, cf. above, Ch. 1, pp. 35-7) rather than in terms of
       cultural transmission; both Islamic Arabic and Orthodox Cyrillic reflect
       antecedent Greek-Aramaic Christian culture.

337.   See above, Ch. 1, pp. 21-2.

338.   Above, pp. 125-8.

339.   C. Justus, 'Visible sentences in cuneiform Hittite', in M. Powell, Aspects of
       Cuneiform Writing (cited above, Ch. 1, n. 6), pp. 373-408; cf. T. Gamkrelidze,
       'The Akkado-Hittite syllabary and the problem of the origin of the Hittite
       script', AO 29, 1961, pp. 406-18: Old Akkadian origins via North Syria.

340.   J. Naveh, Early History of the Alphabet (cited above, Ch. 1, n. 93), pp. 175-86.

341.   See above, pp. 101-2 s.v. arenga; cf. Curtius, op. cit. (above, n. 105), pp. 77-8,
       186 s.v. prooemium.

342.   In D. Russell and M. Winterbottom (edd), Ancient Literary Criticism,
       Clarendon Press, Oxford, 1972, pp. 171-215, esp. 211-12: the style of letters;
       G. Grube, The Greek and Roman Critics, London, 1965, pp. 110-21, esp. 117-
       18.

343.   Curtius, op. cit., pp. 156-9: ars dictandi als Briefstil; J. Miller et alii (edd),
       Readings in Medieval Rhetoric, Indiana University Press, 1973, pp. 131-61:
       Flores Rhetorici.

344.   Curtius, pp. 354-61; Miller, op. cit., pp. 269-71: De Vulgari Eloquentia.

345.   Wansbrough, Quranic Studies (cited above, Ch. 1, n. 65), pp. 85-93; and see
       below, Ch. 3, pp. 169-70.

346.   E.g. Flores, in Miller, op. cit., pp. 138-9.

347.   Cf. Haarmann, op. cit., pp. 207-10.

348.   Ibid, pp. 66-8.

349.   See above, pp. 91-2, and below, Ch. 3, pp. 179-84 s.v. homologies.

CHAPTER 3

1. Above, Ch.2, p.78.

2. H. Schuchardt,, 'Die Lingua franca', ZRP 33, 1909, pp. 441-61; J. Holm, Pidgins and Creoles, vol.II: Reference Survey, Cambridge University Press, 1989, pp. 606-9.

3. K. Whinnom, 'Contacts de langues et emprunts lexicaux: The origin of the European-based creoles and pidgins', Orbis 14, 1965, pp. 509-27, esp. 522ff; Idem, 'Lingua franca: historical problem', in A. Valdman (ed), Pidgin and Creole Linguistics, Indiana University Press, 1977, pp. 295-310; I. Hancock, 'Recovering pidgin genesis: approaches and problems', ibid, pp. 277-94; J. Holm, op. cit., vol.I: Theory and Structure, Cambridge University Press, 1988, pp. 13-16.

4. S. Thomason and A. Elgibali, 'Before the Lingua Franca: pidginized Arabic in the eleventh century A.D.', Lingua 68, 1986, pp. 317-49, esp. 324, 342; Holm, op. cit., pp. 568-71.

5. Cf. J. Wansbrough, 'Africa and the Arab geographers', in D. Dalby (ed), Language and History in Africa, London, 1970, pp. 89-101.

6. Qalqashandī, V, p. 304.

7. E.g. D. Hymes (ed), Pidginization and Creolization of Languages, Cambridge University Press, 1971, pp. 65-90: editor's introduction to section III 'General conceptions of process'.

8. Cf. A. Grimshaw, 'Some social forces and some social functions of pidgin and creole languages', in Hymes, op. cit., pp. 427-445, esp. 428; and W. Labov, 'The notion of "system" in creole languages', ibid, pp. 447-72, esp. 465, ad Hymes, On Communicative Competence, University of Pennsylvania Press, 1971: excerpts in J. Pride and J. Holmes (edd), Sociolinguistics, Penguin Books, 1972, pp. 269-93.

9. E.g. Holm, op. cit., pp. 27-36, 61-8 (esp. ad Bickerton's LBH); cf. D. De Camp, 'Toward a generative analysis of a post-creole speech continuum', in Hymes, op. cit., pp. 349-70, esp. 352-3 ad Chomsky: competence/performance; H. Hoenigswald, 'Language history and creole studies', ibid, pp. 473-80, esp. 478 ad genealogy/typology.

10. S. Mintz, 'The socio-historical background to pidginization and creolization', ibid, pp. 481-96; R. Le Page, 'The need for a multidimensional model', in G. Gilbert (ed), Pidgin and Creole Languages, Essays in Memory of John E. Reinecke, University of Hawaii Press, 1987, pp. 113-29.

11. Wansbrough, BSOAS LIII, 1, 1990, pp. 196-9: ad Holm, Gilbert, Thomason-Kaufman (see below, n. 18).

12. F. de Saussure, Course in General Lingustics, London, 1974, p. 195.

13. D. Hymes, op. cit., p. 73.

14. M. Bakhtine, Esthétique et théorie de roman, Paris, 1978, pp. 419-20; see above, Ch.2, p. 97.

15. Above, Ch.1, pp. 44-5, 72-73, 75; Ch.2, pp.131-62, 139, 145.

16. Above, Ch.1, pp. 17-8, 29, 34-35.

17. Hymes, op. cit., pp. 69, 79 ad W. Samarin, 'Salient and substantive pidginization', ibid, pp. 117-40, esp. 133-5; C. Ferguson, 'The Arabic koine', Language 35, 1959, pp. 616-30; J. Blau, The Emergence and Linguistic Background of Judaeo-Arabic (cited above, Ch. 2, n. 89), pp. 12-17; Wansbrough, Quranic Studies (cited above, Ch.1, n. 65), pp. 87-90.

18. E.g. S. Thomason and T. Kaufman, Language Contact, Creolization, and Genetic Linguistics, University of California Press, 1988, pp. 263-342; K. Versteegh, Pidginization and Creolization: the case of Arabic, Amsterdam Studies in the Theory and History of Linguistic Science 33, Amsterdam, 1984, pp. 79-128; see below, nn. 70-75.

19. F. Southworth, 'Detecting prior creolization: an analysis of the historical origins of Marathi', in Hymes, op. cit., pp. 255-73; cf. also J. Gumperz and R. Wilson, 'Convergence and creolization: a case from the Indo-Aryan/ Dravidian border', ibid, pp. 151-67; and Versteegh, op. cit., pp. 139-42.

20. Thomason and Kaufman, op.cit., pp. 191-9.

21. C. Ferguson, 'Absence of copula and the notion of simplicity', in Hymes, op.cit., pp. 141-50.

22. Schuchardt, art. cit., pp. 443-4 (ad 444 n.1 on infinitive as imperative, add Biblical Hebrew: inf. abs. Gesenius-Kautsch, para 113 aa/bb); H. Wehr, ZDMG 102, 1952, pp.179-86, esp. 183, and A. Spitaler, BO X, 1953, pp. 144-50, esp. 147 (both reviews of J. Fück, Arabiya: Untersuchungen zur arabischen Sprach-and Stilgeschichte, Berlin, 1950; for this point, see p. 6).

23. E. Traugott, 'Pidginization, creolization, and language change', in Valdman, op. cit., pp. 70-98, esp. 78-88.

24. Thomason and Kaufman, op. cit., pp. 110-46 and 147-66.

25. K. Whinnom, 'Linguistic hybridization and the "special case" of pidgins and creoles', in Hymes, op. cit., pp. 91-115.

26. Thomason and Kaufman, op. cit., pp. 35-64, 200-13.

27. Cf. Labov, art. cit. (above, n. 8).

28. See above, Ch. 2, pp. 93-4 nn. 78-83.

29. P. Artzi, 'The glosses in the El-Amarna documents' (Hebrew), Bar Ilan 1, 1963, pp. 24-57; Böhl, op. cit. (above, Ch. 2, n. 53), pp. 80, 85-6; C. Kühne, 'Mit Glossenkeilen markierte fremde Wörter in akkadischen Ugarittexten', UF 6, 1974, pp. 157-67; UF 7, 1975, pp.253-60.

30. Böhl, pp. 42-60.

31. Kühne, art, cit., esp. UF 6, pp. 158-9.

32. W. Mackey, 'The polyglossic spectrum', in J. Fishman et alii (edd), The Fergusonian Impact: in honor of Charles A. Ferguson, Berlin, 1986, vol. 2: Sociolinguistics and the sociology of language, pp. 237-43; cf. Wansbrough, BSOAS LI, 1, 1988, pp. 123-4.

33. C. Hodge, 'The linguistic cycle', Language Sciences 13, 1970, pp. 1-7.

34. Idem, 'Egyptian and Mischsprachen', paper for Language and History in Africa Seminar, SOAS, 25 November 1971 (typescript 17pp.).

35. J. Greenberg, 'Were there Egyptian koines?', in The Fergusonian Impact, vol. 1: From Phonology to Society, pp. 271-90.

36. A. Kroeber, 'On Taxonomy of languages and cultures', Language 36, 1960, pp.1-21: excerpts in D. Hymes (ed), Language in Culture and Society, New York, 1964, pp. 654-63; cf. Thomason and Kaufman, op. cit., pp. 5-12.

37. U. Weinreich, Languages in Contact, The Hague-Paris (sixth printing), 1968, esp. pp. 1-6, 11-15.

38. Ibid, pp. 11-12, 33, 44, 64-5 (chart).

39. Ibid. pp. 83-110.

40. L. Selinker, 'Interlanguage', International Review of Applied Linguistics (Heidelberg) X, 1972, pp. 209-31; cf. Weinreich, op. cit., pp. 7-8, 71-82.

41. See above, Ch. 2, pp. 137-8 n. 321.

42. Wansbrough, 'A Mamluk Letter' (above, Ch. 2, n. 121).

43. Idem, arts. cit. (above, Ch. 2, n. 7), and Ménage, ibid, loc. cit.

44. Above, Ch. 1, pp.173-5.

45. Above, Ch. 2, nn. 187, 239: Wansbrough, BSOAS XXVIII, 3, 1965, 483-523. Page refs. in text

46. Qalqashandī, VI, pp. 182ff.

47. Above, Ch. 2, p.125-6.

48. Wansbrough, DIC, refs in p.75 n.14.

49. Idem, BSOAS XXVIII,3, 1965, refs in p. 521 n. 99; Sperber, Nautica Talmudica (cited above, Ch. 1, n. 188), pp. 147-8; Dozy, Supplément, I, pp. 278-9 II, pp. 329, 456 s.vv.

50. Above, Ch. 2, nn. 289-90; Encyclopaedia of Islam, second edition, s.vv. Consul Balyos, Imtiyazāt.

51. Wansbrough, BSOAS XXVIII,3, 1965, pp. 512 n. 72, 520 nn. 95, 97.

52. Idem, BSOAS XXV,3, 1962, p. 461 n. 2; see M. Amari, Storia dei Musulmani di Sicilia, seconda edizione a cura di C. Nallino, Catania, 1933-39, vol. III, pp. 357-72, esp. 358 nn. 1-2; L. Menager, Amiratus - Amēras: l'émirat et les origines de l'amirauté (XIe-XIIIe siècles), Paris, 1960, esp. pp. 105-9.

53. Hymes, as above, n. 8: in Pride and Holmes, pp. 269-93, esp. 290; J. Fishman, 'The relationship between micro- and macro-sociolinguistics in the study of who speaks what language to whom and when', ibid, pp. 15-32.

54. See, e.g. the studies of J. Blau cited in Ch .1, n. 103; K. Vossler, Einführung ins Vulgärlatein, Munich, 1954; E. Curtius, Gesammelte Aufsätze zur Romanischen Philologie, Bern, 1960, esp. pp. 305-49.

55. See above, Ch. 2, p. 136-7

56. J. Reinecke, 'Trade jargons and creole dialects as marginal languages', Social Forces 17, 1938, pp. 107-18: repr. in Hymes, op. cit. (above, n. 36), pp. 534-46.

57. Wansbrough, DIC, pp. 76-7 n. 25.

58. Idem, BSOAS XXVIII,3, 1965, pp. 515-6 n. 80.

59. Qalqashandī, XIV, p .61; Dozy, Supplément, I, p. 114.

60.   W. Heyd, Histoire du Commerce (cited above, Ch. 1, n. 78), II, pp. 384-5, 423, 467 n. 4, 478 n. 1.

61.   E.g. M. Van Berchem et alii, CIA, Cairo, 1894-1930, Syrie du Sud, I, pp.378-9 (no. 108) and passim, as in n. 58 above.

62.   J. Dubsky, 'The Prague conception of functional style', in V. Fried (ed), The Prague School of Linguistics and Language Teaching, Oxford University Press, 1972, pp. 112-27; J. Pytelka, 'The Prague School and studies in the language of commerce', ibid, pp. 211-23.

63.   See above, Ch. 2, nn. 249-52.

64.   Above, Ch. 1, nn. 85-6.

65.   Cf. J. Greenberg, Language Typology: a historical and analytic overview, The Hague-Paris, 1974, esp. pp. 24, 57-72.

66.   Wansbrough, Quranic Studies, pp. 89-93; cf. Blau, Emergence (above, n. 17), second edition, Jerusalem, 1981: Addenda and corrigenda pp. 216-19.

67.   S. Hopkins, Studies in the Grammar of Early Arabic: based upon papyri datable to before A.H. 300/A.D. 912, Oxford University Press, 1984, pp. xxxvii-xlvii.

68.   Grohmann, Arabische Papyruskunde, pp. 106-7 and 107-30.

69.   Above, Ch. 2, refs in n. 323.

70.   Versteegh, op. cit. (above, n. 18); cf. Wansbrough, BSOAS LI, 1, 1988, pp. 124-5.

71.   See. e.g., Hopkins, op. cit., pp. 260-4 on word order.

72.   For the pre-Islamic dispersion of Arabs, see above, Ch. 1, pp. 18-19, 40-42, 55.

73.   E.g. Versteegh's chapter IV (pp. 59-77): a markedly subjunctive (!) composition based on late and impressionistic settlement patterns.

74.   Above, Ch. 2, pp. 106-8 s.v. arenga.

75.   Cf. Wansbrough, Quranic Studies, p. 85 ad Vossler, Vulgärlatein, pp. 48-52; pace Versteegh, op. cit., pp. 133-8.

76.   De Camp, art. cit. (above, n. 9)

77.   E.g. M. Berkooz (1937: Nuzi), F. Böhl (1909: Amarna), A. Finet (1956: Mari), I. Gelb (1961: Old Akkadian), G. Giakumakis (1970: Alalah), K. Hecker (1968: Kültepe), J. Huehnergard (1989: Ugarit), R. Labat (1932: Boghazköy); and the theses of S. Ahl (1973: Ugarit), Z. Cochavi-Rainey (1988: Egypt), J. Durham (1976: Boghazköy), T. Finley (1979: Syria), S. Izre'el (1985: Amurru), W. Moran (1950: Byblos), W. van Soldt (1986: Ugarit): listed in the bibliography of S. Izre'el, cited next note; also G. Swaim (1962: Ugarit).

78.   S. Izre'el and I. Singer, The General's Letter from Ugarit: a linguistic and historical reevaluation of RS 20.33 (Ugaritica V, no. 20), Tel Aviv University, 1990.

79.   E.g. above, Ch. 2, pp. 129-131 the Ugarit-Alašiya correspondence.

80.   Izre'el and Singer, op. cit., pp. 51-81.

81. Ibid, pp. 85-109; cf. Gamkrelidze, art. cit. (above, Ch. 2, n. 339).

82. Ibid, pp. 122-3, 172-3 (Singer).

83. Ibid, p. 108.

84. E. Lipinski, 'Aḫat-Milki, reine d'Ugarit, et la guerre du Mukiš', OLP 12, 1981, pp. 79-115: RS 16.402 = pp. 99-109; cf. D. Pardee, 'Ugaritic', AfO XXXI, 1984, pp. 213-30: Rs 16.402 = pp. 215-9; M. Astour, 'Ugarit and the great powers' (cited above, Ch. 1, n. 21), pp. 22, 26.

85. Lipinski, pp. 99-100 n. 107; cf. Gordon, UT,19.116 s.v.

86. Lipinski is explicit, Pardee non-committal (p. 213 n. 3); for Puduḫepa, see A. Caquot, 'La lettre de la reine Puduḫepa', UGAR VII, pp. 122-34 (RS 17.434+) and D. Pardee, art cit. (above, Ch. 2, n. 162); either identification would yield a 13th century date.

87. See above, Ch. 1, pp. 16-7, 45-48, 72-73; Ch. 2, pp. 125-7, esp. nn. 256: Bordreuil, art. cit. and Greenstein, art. cit. (Sarepta), 257: Bordreuil, art. cit. and Puech, art. cit. (Hala Sultan Tekke).

88. Z. Harris, Development of the Canaanite Dialects, New Haven, Connecticut, 1939, pp. 1-28; but cf. A. Goetze, 'Is Ugaritic a Canaanite dialect?', Language 17, 1941, pp. 127-38; and see now G. Del Olmo Lete, 'Fenicio y Ugaritico: correlación lingüística', Aula Orientalis 4, 1986, pp. 31-49.

89. E.g. M. Dahood, Ugaritic-Hebrew Philology: marginal notes on recent publications, Biblica et Orientalia 17, Rome, 1965; but (!) cf. A. Rainey, 'Observations on Ugaritic grammar', UF 3, 1971, pp.151-72 (arranged, as is Dahood, according to the paragraphs in Gordon, UT, cited above, Ch. 1, n. 183); J. de Moor and P. Van der Lugt, 'The spectre of Pan-Ugaritism' (review of L. Fisher, Ras Shamra Parallels I, Rome, 1972), BO XXXI, 1/2, 1974, pp. 3-26.

90. Puech, 'Présence phénicienne', as in n. 87 above: pp. 374-95 (Tekke Knossos); Naveh, Alphabet, pp. 40-1, 185-6.

91. Harris, Grammar (cited above, Ch. 1, n. 118), pp.71-156; R. Tomback, A Comparative Semitic Lexicon of the Phoenician and Punic Languages, Scholars Press, Missoula, Montana, 1978.

92. E.g. J. Wansbrough, 'Metra Ugaritica: pro et contra', BSOAS XLVI, 2, 1983, pp. 221-34.

93. J. Gibson, Canaanite Myths and Legends, Edinburgh, 1978; thereto see D. Pardee, 'The new Canaanite Myths and Legends', BO XXXVII, 5/6, 1980, pp. 269-91.

94. Inventory in Gordon, UT, pp. 257-91; transcriptions in M. Dietrich, O. Loretz, and J. Sanmartín, Die keilalphabetischen Texte aus Ugarit einschliesslich der keilalphabetischen Texte ausserhalb Ugarits (KTU), Teil 1= AOAT 24, Neukirchen-Vluyn, 1976.

95. S. Segert, Basic Grammar (cited above, Ch. 2, n. 61), pp. 15, 88ff; cf. Wansbrough, BSOAS L, 3, 1987, pp. 540-1; S. Parker, Grammar of Ugaritic Prose (cited above, Ch. 2, n. 159), pp. 4, 109 = largely epistolary and juridical texts; M. Liverani, 'Elementi innovativi nell'ugaritico non letterario', Atti della Accademia Nazionale dei Lincei VIII, 19, 1964, pp. 173-91.

96.   See above, Ch. 2, p. 127-128; cf. Del Olmo Lete, art. cit., p. 36.

97.   Above, Ch. 2, esp. nn. 258-259; Harris, Canaanite Dialects (DCD), pp. 40-1, 62-4.

98.   Word-dividers: Gibson, SSI (cited in full above, Ch.1, n.118)   III, pp. 13, 28; Gordon, UT, pp. 23-4.

      GT theme: Gibson, SSI, III, p. 16; Harris, DCD, p. 62; Gordon, UT, p. 81.

      Relative pron: Gibson, p. 15; Harris, pp. 35-6, 69-70; Gordon, pp. 39-40.

      Preposition b-:   Gibson, pp. 21. 27; Gordon, pp. 92-3.

99.   Waw convers: Gibson, pp. 15-16; Harris, Grammar, pp. 39-40; Gordon, p. 69; cf. G. Young, 'The origin of the waw conversive', JNES 12, 1953, pp. 248-52; C. Gordon, 'The "waw conversive": from Eblaite to Hebrew', PAAJR L, 1983, pp. 87-90; but also W. Moran, 'The Hebrew language in its North-west Semitic background', in G. Wright (ed), The Bible and the Ancient Near East: essays in honor of William Foxwell Albright, New York, 1961, pp. 54-72, esp. 64-5.

      Def. article: Gibson, pp. 19, 24, 114, 122; Harris, Grammar, pp. 55-6; DCD, pp. 68-9; cf. Pardee, art. cit. (above, n. 84), p. 218 n. 23 ad Liverani, as in n. 95 above, pp. 181-2.

      Mimation: Harris, DCD, pp. 32-3; Gordon, UT, p. 52; Segert, Basic Grammar, pp. 51, 81; cf. J. Aistleitner, Untersuchungen zur Grammatik des Ugaritischen, Berlin, 1954, pp. 34-36.

100. Enclitic m/n: Gordon, UT, pp. 103-4, 110; Parker, Grammar, pp. 44-5; H. Hummel, 'Enclitic mem in early Northwest Semitic', JBL 76, 1957, pp. 85-107.

      Deictic t: Harris, Grammar, pp. 62-3; DCD, pp. 53-4, 70-71; Parker, Grammar, p. 46.

101. Harris, DCD, pp. 91-100; Gibson, p.32; W. Garr, Dialect Geography of Syria-Palestine, 1000-586 B.C.E., Philadelphia, 1985.

102. Gibson, pp. 135, 140-1; cf. Harris, Grammar, p. 51 (3ms suff), and Gordon, UT, p.36; but also, Del Olmo Lete, art. cit., p. 41.

103. Gibson, p. 68; Harris, Grammar, pp. 23-4, 33, 54 (based on a somehow doubled articulation of /z/); J. Fitzmyer, 'The Phoenician inscription from Pyrgi', JAOS 86, 1966, pp. 285-97, esp. 289.

104. Gibson, p. 34.14-16; Harris, Grammar, pp. 54-5 (vide Hebrew śe), but also pp. 63-4 (Punic se).

105. E.g. Tomback, op. cit. (above, n. 91); M. Amadasi Guzzo, Le Iscrizioni Fenicie e Puniche delle Colonie in Occidente, Rome, 1967; M. Sznycer, Les Passages puniques en transcription latine dans le 'Poenulus' de Plaute, Paris, 1967; cf. C. Krahmalkov, 'The Punic speech of Hanno', Or. 39, 1970, pp. 53-74.

106. Harris, Grammar, pp. 6-10, 69-70; Segert, Grammar (cited above, Ch. 1, n. 118), pp. 17-45.

107. See above, p. 158

108.   Above, Ch. 2, p. 94 n. 84: Wansbrough, art. cit., p. 312 n. 5; Dölger, Diplo-
        matik, pp. 84-86.

109.   Above, Ch. 2, p. 129, n.271: Berger, art. cit., p. 218 n. 1 (the phenomenon is
        erratic: cf. Albright, BASOR 87, 1942, p. 33 n. 7 (Amarna); Marcus, JCS 2, 1948,
        pp. 223-4 (Amarna); Goetze, JCS 2, 1938, p. 224 (Hittite Akkadian)).

110.   Above, Ch. 2, p. 102 n. 127.

111.   E.g. above, pp. 147, 151-52 and Ch. 2, pp. 138-45.

112.   R. Whitaker, A Concordance of the Ugaritic Literature, Harvard University
        Press, 1972, pp. 615-16 s.v. thm.

113.   Harris, Grammar, pp. 9, 18, 21, 23-4, 29-30, 33, 47, 54, 60, 65, 69; Gibson, pp.
        28-30, 66-8, 123-41.

114.   See above, refs in Ch. 2, n. 261; E. Masson, Cyprominoica, répertoires,
        documents de Ras Shamra, essais d'interprétation, SIMA XXXI, 2, Göteborg,
        1974.

115.   Above, Ch. 1, p. 60-1, Ch. 2, p. 121-1; J. Daniel, 'Prolegomena to the Cypro-
        Minoan script', AJA 45, 1941, pp. 249-82; J. Faucounau, 'Etudes Chypro-
        Minoennes' I-III, Syria LIV, 1977, pp. 209-49; IV-V, Syria LVII, 1980, pp.
        375-410; cf. J. Best and F. Woudhuizen, Ancient Scripts from Crete and
        Cyprus, Leiden-New York, 1988.

116.   See, e.g. the studies of Astour in Ch. 1, n. 31, Ch. 2, n. 274; and of Holmes,
        Hellbing, and Strange in Ch. 1, nn. 24 and 97 above.

117.   O. Masson, Les inscriptions chypriotes syllabiques, Paris, 1961; H. Buchholz,
        'Zur Herkunft der kyprischen Silbenschrift', Minos 3, 1955, pp. 133-51.

118.   Above, Ch. 2, pp. 89-91; e.g. CIS i no. 89 (Idalion) Resef = Appollon, cf.
        Buchholz, art. cit.

119.   Above, Ch. 1, pp. 35-38.

120.   Above, as in n. 111.

121.   Gibson, op. cit., pp. 30-41, 41-64, 78-92, resp; cf. above, n. 104.

122.   Above, Ch. 1, nn. 92-93., esp. Naveh, Alphabet, pp. 175-86.

123.   J. Chadwick, The Decipherment of Linear B, Cambridge University Press,
        1967, pp. 22-3, 74-6, Fig. 17 (chart).

124.   Above, Ch. 2, pp. 91-92, 145

125.   Above, pp. 91-92, 145; C. Becker, Islamstudien (cited above, Ch. 2, n. 288), I,
        pp. 150, 185f.

126.   A. Bach, Geschichte der Deutschen Sprache, Heidelberg, 1949, p. 100.

127.   Above, Ch. 2, pp. 97-98: Kristensen, art. cit. in nn. 101, 104.

128.   Above, Ch. 2, pp. 112-14, 119-21, 122-23, resp.

129.   See G. Steiner, After Babel: aspects of language and translation, Oxford
        University Press, 1975, esp. chs. 4-6.

130.   Above, n. 14.

131.   Above, Ch.2, nn. 177, 204, 238.

132.   Ibid, nn.101-103, 107.

133. Steiner, op. cit., pp. 414-70, esp. 425-6.

134. Above, n. 12.

135. Above, n. 13; cf. Steiner, p. 472 n.1 (ref Hymes).

136. Above, nn. 25, 39; see also H. Blanc, Communal Dialects in Baghdad, Harvard University Press, 1964, pp. 12-16.

137. Above, n. 63 = Ch.2, nn. 249-252.

138. F. Fales, op. cit. (above, Ch. 1, n. 94), pp. 1-29; see also above, Ch. 2, pp. 114-18, 122-3, 127-8.

139. Fales, pp. 29-105, esp. 43-7; cf. A. Millard, 'Assyrians and Arameans', IRAQ XLV, 1983, pp. 101-8; J. Greenfield and A. Shaffer, 'Notes on the Akkadian-Aramaic bilingual statue from Tell Fekherye', ibid, pp. 109-16; Idem, 'Notes on the curse formulae of the Tell Fekherye inscription', RB XCII, 1985, pp. 47-59.

140. Fales, pp. 88-90 (syntax), 91-102 (lexical), 253-7 = no. 58.5 obv; ṭḥm is something of a problem: see refs in nn. 109, 112 above.

141. See, e.g. R. Cooper, 'A framework for the study of language spread', in R. Cooper (ed), Language Spread: studies in diffusion and social change, Indiana University Press, 1982, pp. 5-36; L.Brosnahan, 'Some historical cases of language imposition', in J. Spencer (ed), Language in Africa, Cambridge University Press, 1963, pp. 7-24; Grimshaw, art. cit. (above, n. 8); Mintz, art. cit. (above, n. 10).

142. L. Calvet, Les langues véhiculaires, Paris, 1981 (PUF: Que sais-je? no. 1916); Idem, Les Langues du marché, Paris, 1985; Idem, 'Trade functions and lingua francas', in J. Fishman et alii (edd), The Fergusonian Impact (cited above, n. 32), vol. 2, pp. 295-302.

143. See above, Ch. 1, pp. 35-8 (refs. n. 107), 57-8; Ch.2, pp. 124, 140-1.

144. Above, Ch. 2, pp. 128-131.

145. Above, Ch. 1, pp. 58-67, 72.

146. Cf. e.g. V. Monteil, L'Arabe moderne, Paris, 1960, esp. pp. 162-81, 291-5.

147. Above, Ch.1, pp. 15-6, 43-8, 50, 68-73.

148. Above, Ch. 1, pp. 54-68; Ch.2, pp. 135-44.

149. Above, n. 2 s.v. Sabir.

150. H. & R. Kahane and A. Tietze, The Lingua Franca in the Levant: Turkish nautical terms of Italian and Greek origin, University of Illinois Press, Urbana, 1958.

151. Ibid, pp. 40-41: e.g. Ital. vela di straglio = Turk. velaistralya ("staysail", no. 705); Ital. patta d'oca = Turk. kaz ayagi ("bowline bridle"): goosefoot, no. 482).

152. Cf. the studies of Ménage, Skilliter and Wittek, cited above, Ch. 2, nn. 1, 3, 7.

153. Kahane and Tietze, op. cit., pp. 41-5 and passim.

154. See above, Ch. 2, pp. 110-11, 144-5.

155. Cf. F. Rossi-Landi, Linguistics and Economics. The Hague-Paris, 1975, pp. 137-58.

156. Ibid, pp. 70-120.

157. Ibid, pp. 121-37.

158. Above, Ch. 1, pp. 3-5.

159. Cf. Grimshaw, art. cit. (above, n. 8), esp. pp. 440-1; and Greenberg, op.cit. (above, n. 65).

160. Above, Ch. 1, pp. 24-6; Ch. 2, pp. 136-7.

161. Above, Ch. 1, pp. 44-5; Ch.2, pp. 138-9.

162. Above, Ch. 1, p. 54-5.

163. Above, Ch. 1, pp. 27-28, 33.

164. Above, Ch. 1, p. 5-6.

165. Wansbrough, 'Moroccan amir' (cited above, Ch. 1, n. 164), esp. pp. 468ff.

Index